232

D0952132

THUNDER ALONG
THE MISSISSIPPI

THUNDER ALONG THE MISSISSIPPI

The River Battles that Split the Confederacy

WITHDRAWN

By

JACK D. COOMBE

This edition published in 2005 by
Castle Books, ®
A division of Book Sales, Inc.
114 Northfield Avenue
Edison, NJ 08837

Published by arrangement with
De Capo Press,
a subsidiary of Perseus Books L.L.C.
387 Park Avenue South
New York, NY 10016

Originally published by
SARPEDON
166 Fifth Avenue
New York, NY 10010

Library of Congress Cataloging-in-Publication Data

Coombe, Jack D.
    Thunder Along the Mississippi : the river battles that split the Confederacy / by Jack D. Coombe.
    p. cm.
  Includes bibliographical references (p.) and index.
        1.   United   States—History—Civil   War,   1861-1865—Riverine operations. 2. Mississippi River Valley—History—Civil War, 1861-1865. I. Title.
E470.8.C66   1996
973.7'5—dc20   96-18422
                                                                    CIP

ISBN-13: 978- 0-7858-1677-5
ISBN-10: 0-7858-1677-1

Printed in the United States of America

To the late F. Van Wyck Mason,
whose phenomenal work first fired my interest in the
Civil War with its many individual dramas.

Contents

PHOTO ACKNOWLEDGMENTS

The publishers are grateful to the following institutions for their courtesy in making available the illustrations reprinted in this book.

(First Section) 1. Missouri Historical Society. 2. Book Sales. 3. The U.S. Navy. 4, 5. The U.S. Naval Institute Archives. 6, 7. The U.S. Navy. 8, 9, 11, 12. The U.S. Naval Institute Archives. 10. Book Sales. 13. The Mississippi Department of Archives and History. 14–19. Book Sales. 20. The U.S. Naval Institute Archives. 21–28. Book Sales. 29. The U.S. Naval Institute Archives. (Second Section) 30. The U.S. Navy. 31. Author photo. 32. The U.S. Naval Institute Archives. 33–35. Book Sales. 36. From Crandell's "History of the Ram Fleet and Marine Brigade," Society of Survivors. 37. The U.S. Navy. 38–42. Book Sales. 43. The Mississippi Department of Archives and History. 44, 45. Book Sales. 46–48. The U.S. Naval Institute Archives. 49. Author photo. 50. "The Union Fleet Passing Vicksburg" by Tom Lovell, © 1989, The Greenwich Workshop, Inc. Courtesy of the Greenwich Workshop, Inc., Shelton, CT. For information on limited edition fine art prints and books by Tom Lovell call 1-800-243-4246. 51–53. Author photos.

Preface

The shots fired by a Southern artillery battery on a commercial steamer bent on bringing supplies and reinforcements to beleaguered Fort Sumter were the first fired in anger in the Civil War. Those shots heralded the beginning of the conflict and, at the same time, opened a new phase of naval warfare—one involving fighting on rivers instead of vast stretches of oceans. More importantly, they heralded the coming of age for the fledgling United States Navy.

I have always been of the opinion that there should be an up-to-date, intimate look at the young navy, especially in the sometimes savage gunwale-to-gunwale slugfests on the waters of the Mississippi River during 1862. These gunboat fleets, though incorporating the latest innovations in steam engines, weaponry and armor, were specifically designed to operate in the shallow channels and narrow confines of a river. The ungainly riverine ironclads were the object of derision for saltwater sailors and others accustomed to the sleek, aesthetic lines of the frigates of the line in the navy at that time, but they earned their stripes, so to speak, in actual combat.

The lessons learned in the building and employment of these ironclads helped shape the future of our navy. The wooden ships eventually became outmoded, then virtually archaic, and their place was taken by great fleets of iron vessels that would plow the oceans and seas of the world.

To this work I have intended to bring, in addition to sound research, a realistic picture of naval warfare, having experienced it myself in the Pacific during WWII. I have attempted to share with the reader both the realistic horrors of close-encounter fighting and the strange fascination with mortal combat that participants often seem to be reluctant to discuss openly. The physical and mental processes of men in battle, be it on land or water, hasn't changed drastically through the centuries, even if the technology of war has.

In addition, I will argue that the battles on the Mississippi River constituted a pivotal factor in turning the tide against the Confederacy by forcing it into an intolerable strategic position. The struggle for control of the Mississippi opened the floodgates for Union gunboats to steam down the mighty Father of Waters, thus forcing the Confederacy out of its Kentucky-Tennessee-Mississippi axis and isolating it from the important western states with their vast resources of manpower, food, and materiel.

I have taken some liberties in respect to naval terms, with full knowledge that they have changed throughout the years. However, I am mindful that this was primarily a river war, and that riverboat nomenclatures were different from that of the regular navy. For example, in the regular navy, the term normally used for the smokestacks is "funnels," or just plain "stacks." In riverboat parlance, they were called "chimneys," because they were exceptionally tall in order to increase draft in the boilers to which they were directly connected; there were no forced-draft systems then.

In today's navy, the area containing the steering wheel is called the "bridge," or "deckhouse." In river gunboats it was referred to as the "Texas," a term in use for as long as steamboats plied the rivers. Today's "main deck" was called the "hurricane deck" in riverine craft. In this work, I have preferred the term "vessel" in respect to river craft, rather than "ship."

Many people contribute to the writing of a book of history. To name every single one would be impossible because of space limitations. But some of those who have contributed substantially and vitally to this work are to be thanked publicly. The author is most obliged to the staff of the Vicksburg Military Park, including Terry Winschel and Leonard Curtis of the military archives.

Special thanks are due to Elizabeth Joyner, supervisor of the U.S.S. *Cairo* site, who allowed me a close-up view of the secrets of this venerable, resurrected ironclad, and who cheerfully opened her specialized naval archives. Warm thanks are due Gordon A. Cotton, the director of the Old Court House Museum in Vicksburg, for his generous hospitality. Thanks also to Victor Bailey, librarian at the Jackson, Mississippi, Historical Archives, who went out of his way to see to my needs and those of my research assistant. Appreciation is due John E. Ellzey, the librarian at Ricks Memorial Library in Yazoo City, Mississippi, and to the Yazoo Historical Society for invaluable material about the city itself and the site of the old Yazoo River Shipyard and its famous product, C.S.S. *Arkansas*. The staff of the Missouri Historical Society Archives in St. Louis were excellent hosts for this research duo, as were Cheryl Snerring and Kathleen Harris of the Illinois Historical Society Archives. A grateful nod goes to friend and neighbor Jim Buer for the loan of a valuable book.

I would be remiss not to mention the staff of Northwestern University's Government Documents Department for opening their collection and for their invaluable assistance. I am also deeply indebted to the Northbrook Library Reference Department, in my Illinois hometown, for untiring efforts in obtaining rare volumes.

My agent, Gerry Wallerstein, was always available with her expertise and her invaluable support, during my periods of doubt and tension. Lastly, to Peg, my research assistant and my dear wife, go my most sincere thanks for her unflagging work in editing my drafts, and for taking on the "author's widow" mantle, during the many months of my hermit-like existence.

Introduction

On the misty morning of January 9, 1861, a lone vessel plowed its way into the spacious mouth of Charleston Harbor and headed upstream. Her Captain, John McGowan, and his crew were keeping a wary eye on the mercifully silent parapets of Fort Moultrie on Sullivan's Island to port and especially on Cumming's Point to starboard, where it was reported that the South Carolinians had established a battery of artillery.[1]

Large, burnished plates beneath the bridge windows attested to the fact that this vessel was the merchant steamer *Star of the West.* All sounds on board were kept to a minimum, except for the usual rhythmic thrussing of the walking beams, powered by two vertical beam engines and, of course, the sibilant slappings of the huge paddle wheels. Ahead lay her destination: Fort Sumter.

The *Star of the West* was a 1,172-ton, brigantine-rigged, side-wheeled merchant steamer commandeered by the Federal Government as a transport/supply vessel.[2] It had sailed from New York's Governors Island four days earlier, loaded with supplies and 200 troops under the command of First Lieutenant Charles R. Woods of the 9th Infantry. Its mission was to reinforce the beleaguered Union garrison of Sumter, which had suddenly found itself an intolerable symbol of Federal sovereignty in the South.

Something *had* to be done. Soon after the hastily convened South Carolina Secession Convention issued an ordinance, on December 20, 1860, to the effect that the Union was dissolved and that the state had seceded, Major Robert Anderson, commander of the Federal troops at Fort Moultrie on Sullivan's Island on the northern border of Charleston Harbor's entrance, swiftly spiked the guns, burned the carriages and rendered the fort useless. Using a fleet of small boats, he transferred his men to the then-unfinished Fort Sumter, under cover of darkness on December 26, because it appeared there was nowhere else to go.[3]

Fort Sumter was one of a series of coastal defense sites authorized by the U.S. Government after the War of 1812. Built on a shoal in Charleston Harbor, it was a pentagonal structure with walls 50 feet high and 50 feet thick. The plan was originally to arm the structure with 140 guns, but slow government bureaucracy, as well as the lack of a sense of urgency due to a dirth of foreign enemies, kept the fort from receiving its full complement. At the time of the *Star of the West* incident, it was armed with only 48 guns and manned by 78 personnel.

When President Buchanan became aware that Fort Sumter was in danger of assault by Southerners, he ordered his cabinet to draw up a plan for sending reinforcements of supplies and troops. At first the warship *Brooklyn* was chosen, but she was soon replaced for the mission by the *Star of the West*. One reason was that the *Brooklyn*'s 16-foot draft was considered too deep for the main channel in Charleston Harbor. A more likely rationale was the fear of provoking the South Carolinians with a warship.

Nature and armies, however, abhor vacuums. As expected, the South Carolinians quickly moved into the abandoned Fort Moultrie and began to install heavy ordnance. Unknown to Captain McGowan, who arrived off the mouth of the harbor after dark on the 8th, the Southerners had learned of the ship's coming through a sympathizer in the U.S. Senate, Louis T. Wigfall. Soon after the *Star of the West* left New York, Wigfall sent a telegram to Governor Pickens of South Carolina, informing him of her likely destination.[4]

Daylight found the ship a courageous trespasser steaming into the harbor, following an unknown steamer, and under intense scrutiny by friend and foe alike. No doubt, Captain McGowan and Lieutenant Woods nervously shifted from wing to wing on the bridge, in order to study the embrasures of the forts on either side of the harbor entrance.

There was no fire from Moultrie, the bastion that had become famous for devastating elements of the British fleet in 1776. That meant the Southerners had not yet gotten their guns operational; perhaps it would be a safe passage after all.

But adding to the skipper's worries was the lack of intelligence about Fort Johnson, at the tip of James Island, south of

Charleston, concerning a battery that was rumored to have been established there. Major Anderson at the fort had earlier reported an additional battery on Morris Island in the harbor. It did seem that no matter what course and position his ship took, she would be in danger. In spite of it all, he kept the 228-foot-long vessel plowing on toward her destination.

So far so good. It would appear to all on the ship that those who were manning the guns guarding the harbor entrance were still asleep.

Suddenly, a puff of smoke arose from Morris Island and a shot arched high and plunged into the water ahead of the steamer. This was followed by another that landed close to the bow. Apparently the Southerners were aware of the *Star of the West's* mission after all, and had decided to either halt or sink her.

There were more shots—one hit near the rudder and another landed off the starboard bow and skidded across the forechains; a desperate, long-range shot of over 2,000 yards, it came uncomfortably near. By now, all hopes that the vessel could slip through to Sumter unnoticed had evaporated. For the men aboard the steamer, the only remaining question was how many Southern guns in and around Charleston Harbor would soon join in the attack.

McGowan conferred with Woods and his staff about the situation, and unanimously decided to exit the harbor. The situation had gotten out of hand and it was not worth the risk of losing the defenseless ship, its crew and the 200-man troop contingent. It was obvious the fort was surrounded by hostile forces, and would eventually be bombarded and surrendered. Indeed, it looked like a doomed mission for the *Star of the West*.[5]

In Fort Sumter, groans of frustration must have been heard when the personnel saw the steamer head about and sail out of the harbor. Clearly, more than one man threw his hat down and stomped on it, in an act of frustration, when their commanding officer, Major Anderson, decided against firing back in retaliation, because of his fear of starting a war.[6]

Brigadier General Clement A. Evans wrote: "The whole affair was a trivial play that might be classed as comic were it not part of an awful national tragedy . . . if fired on [*Star of the West*] the cry would be raised that South Carolina had begun war with the United States by firing on an unarmed vessel carrying provisions to a starving garrison."[7] In effect, though the war would surely come, it would need a greater spark to ignite than the tentative mission of a relief vessel.

Nevertheless it is on record that the first shots fired in anger in the war between the states were fired at a ship and not at Fort Sumter. It was a harbinger of things to come, except that the warships that would soon be built bore little resemblance to the harmless coastal paddle steamer.

In March 1863, a Union gunboat flotilla about to attack Fort Pemberton on the Tallahatchie River encountered a Rebel steamboat that had been sunk in front of the fort to block their way. This vessel had fled north up the Mississippi from New Orleans in the face of Admiral Farragut's ferocious onslaught. On approaching the obstacle, still partly visible as it rested in the mud of the river bottom, the Federal men realized this steamer had once been the most famous vessel afloat. It was none other than the *Star of the West*, which had been captured by Texans in 1861 and incorporated into the Confederate Navy as the *St. Philip*. The Union gunboats it was meant to block were scarcely imaginable at the time the steamer had sailed onto center stage in history. The Federal sailors now traversed the South's waterways in squat, ironclad batteries, bristling with thirteen or more heavy guns, and they were in the practice of taking on any Confederate fort on shore that would dare offer them resistance. In two short years, these powerful new vessels of the Union gunboat flotillas had become war-winning weapons.

After the *Star of the West* incident in 1861, the wheels of military bureaucracies on both sides of the Mason-Dixon Line began to stir. When the first shots were fired on Fort Sumter, they began to spin, and the navies on both sides—more so than the armies— would exercise creativity and originality in their inventions. On land, armies would march and employ horse-drawn transport exactly as they had done for thousands of years; afloat, both sides were about to enter the modern age with armored, mobile firepower platforms. In Charleston Harbor, the Union steamer was fearful of aggression from the shore. In a few short years it would be the other way around.

The course of the Civil War was determined largely by the fact that the opposing capital cities—Washington and Richmond—lay little more than a hundred miles from one another. It was in a relatively small geographic area that the largest armies, and at times the most brilliant commanders, maneuvered and fought, each side seeking the elusive "decisive" victory that would settle the conflict in their own favor. But the Confederacy was a huge country, as was the (remaining) United States of America. Strategically, the battles that doomed the Southern seccession were those fought in the west—fundamentally the seizure of the Mississippi River by the Union. Sherman's march across the Deep South, including the elimination of any resources a Virginia field army could call upon, was made possible first by the combined-arms efforts of the Federal armies in the battle for the Mississippi and its tributaries.

The "what if's" of the Civil War are various and complex, and it would not be proper to attribute the outcome—conclusively—to any one of the multitudinous campaigns. Suffice it to say, however, that when final victory was won by the Union, it was the "western" general, Grant, who accepted the surrender in Virginia at Appomattox. The Rebel armies in the east had achieved an astonishing record of success, against great odds. However even as they were demonstrating command brilliance and battlefield skill, their country was being seized out from under them by the efforts of Union forces along the river "highways" in Kentucky, Tennessee, Mississippi, Arkansas and Louisiana.

By 1865 the South's effort to field large armies had become untenable due to Federal invasions and occupation of their commercial centers and ports. The cutting-edge of the Union advances was, from the beginning, its inland navy, which fought together with the land forces and provided an attacking advantage that the South could never quite match.

This is not to say that the war, after July 4, 1863, was a foregone conclusion. Many of the locations described in this book as falling to Union forces in their march toward Vicksburg—Paducah, Fort Donelson, Fort Pillow, Nashville—would in fact be contested again, generally by Confederate cavalry that proved to be as far-ranging on land as the gunboats were on the rivers. However, once the Confederacy had been split, the Rebels were doomed to wage a war with diminishing returns. In the first year of the war, planners in Washington determined on an essential, two-step strategy: blockade the Southern coast, and seize the Mississippi River—these steps would assure that the Confederacy would not survive. Chickamauga, the Wilderness, the great cavalry raids and scores of other battles would only be sequels of bloodshed, because the naval strategy enacted in 1861, reaching fruition in mid-1863, guaranteed that the South could only grow weaker and weaker with time.

What follows is the story of how the two sides fought the river war, feeling their way as new technology and tactics were tried. There were visionary thinkers, such as Eads and Mallory; dauntless captains like Farragut and Brown; dithering generals on both sides, as well as dynamic leaders like Grant and Johnston. And there were thousands of ordinary sailors, soldiers and rivermen who found themselves swept into the maelstrom on the Mississippi. It is the story of an untried weapon (the ironclad) and how it came to dominate naval warfare, in so doing changing the course of history. The river war of 1861–63 was marked by frantic building, long pauses and brisk, decisive actions where the vessels often stood gunport-to-gunport, and heroes were created by the score.

Today the quiet Mississippi still meanders its way down to the Gulf, and many of the old forts have disappeared beneath the shifting path of its current. But in the mind's eye the impact of cannonballs against armor can still be seen, and the drifting smoke of gunpowder still lingers near the shore. It was largely on the river that the ultimate outcome of the Civil War was decided.

THUNDER ALONG
THE MISSISSIPPI

CHAPTER ONE

Unprepared on the Water

When the Republican Abraham Lincoln was elected president of the United States, the question of whether the Southern states would try to leave the Union became essentially answered. Fort Sumter, off Charleston, South Carolina was attacked and its Federal garrison surrendered on April 13, 1861. As both North and South hastened to field large armies for their imminent first battlefield confrontation, however, the chances of a naval battle between the two antagonists was remote. The Confederates simply had no navy and the Union's flotilla of ships, having had little to do for 20 years, was small and ill-prepared.

Out of a total of 90 U.S. Navy vessels, only 42 were in active service and most of these were scattered around the world: in the Mediterranean, off Africa, in the Pacific and off South America. In addition, twenty-one ships were listed as "unserviceable."[1] The navy had a pre-war personnel complement of some 1,200 officers and 6,400 men, although after seccession 259 officers resigned or were dismissed.

Of the ships in service, all were wooden and of either sail or paddlewheel propulsion, only a few being screw-propelled. The idea of ironclad vessels had not yet caught on in the Navy Department or in other high echelons of government, although these were already being developed in Europe. The French, in fact, had employed ironclad floating batteries with success against Russian fortifications in the Crimean War (fought 1854–

56), and both the French and British navies maintained an iron-clad vessel in their respective fleets. By the 1860s, most European navies were already thinking in terms of both steam replacing sail and iron replacing wood, at least for coastal fighting. On the high seas meanwhile, where a nation's naval power had heretofore always been measured, the wooden, sailed warship continued to reign supreme.

After Fort Sumter, it was presciently argued in the U.S. Congress that a million and a half dollars be appropriated for the construction of armored ships or ironclad batteries, but the only result of the ensuing debate was a vote to construct one metal gunboat, to be named the *Monitor*. It would in fact fall to the naval combat officers themselves to be prime movers for the new generation of warships that would soon appear.

Strategically, the North enjoyed immense advantages over the South in terms of both population and industrial resources. The Union still consisted of 23 states with a total population of 22,700,000; the Confederacy had 11 states populated by 9,000,000, 3,500,000 of whom were slaves. Economically, figures before the war indicated exports from the Union at $331,000,000 as opposed to the South's $31,000,000, most of which was cotton.[2] The greater advantage in machine facilities lay with the Union, while the Confederacy was more of an agrarian society with minimal heavy manufacturing resources at its command.[3]

On the other hand, strategically speaking, the Union required greater resources, because in order to successfully prosecute the war its plans needed to be more ambitious. The Confederacy, after all, did not need to occupy the territory of the United States or eradicate it as a nation. The South simply needed to be able to exist as an independent country and didn't need to conquer anybody; it simply needed to defend itself. The shortest path to discouraging Yankee war aims was for the South to achieve military victories. However, the Southern cause would also be helped by simply avoiding defeats. It was the North that absolutely had to win the victories or else the war would be considered impractical.

The two nations were comparable in geographic size, though the Confederacy possessed far more coastline (not including

California and Oregon): some 3,500 miles of coast with 189 harbors and navigable rivers. In naval terms, this presented an immense challenge to the Union, particularly when they determined on the strategy of a blockade. The South, in turn, would not need such a gigantic fleet as the North, but it did need warships that could hold key areas and prevent Union fleets not only from strangling the young nation in deep water, but from invading Southern territory through inland rivers. And these warships needed to be state-of-the-art.

A week after Fort Sumter, the Confederates received a boost at the expense of the Union when they occupied the Norfolk Navy Yard. When Virginians, immediately upon their state's secession, walked into the 90-acre yard they found the U.S. Navy ships *Pennsylvania, Germantown, Raritan, Columbia* and *Dolphin* burned to the water's edge, and *Delaware, Columbus* and *Plymouth* scuttled and sunk. Also burned was a formerly beautiful ship of the fleet called the *Merrimac.* Two ship's houses, a drydock, rigging loft, sail loft and a gun carriage depot were burned to the ground. On the other hand, some 4,000 shells, hastily tossed into the harbor by the withdrawing Union troops, were easily recovered, along with a large number of guns and carriages that were left in haste. A magazine with 2,000 barrels of powder, plus vast amounts of projectiles and fixed ammunition were recovered and later put to use in the Confederate cause.

Had they chosen to, the Union forces could have easily defended the navy yard by using the warships there, plus an added flotilla and a sizeable contingent of troops that could have been brought up, without serious interference from the Southerners.[4] As it was, the inept abandonment of the navy yard constituted an embarrassment for the Union and a delight for the South—a classic case of haste based on fear.

In Washington there was no end to debate in government and civilian circles over the affair. One great advantage of the Union at the outset of the war was its superiority in ordnance and military infrastructure. Now they had handed the Rebels tons of ordnance, ammunition and the beginnings of a fleet and a navy yard in which to service it, something they did not previously have. Norfolk was the only major navy yard the Confederacy was to have throughout the war.

President Lincoln, as aware as any man that the war was liable to become a long, grueling affair, recognized the need for an exceptional secretary of the navy, and fortunately found him in the person of Gideon Welles. History would confirm the choice of this crusty, energetic individual destined to become, along with Edward Stanton, one of the most loyal and efficient members of the president's cabinet.

Born in Glastonbury, Connecticut, in 1802, Welles was a graduate of Norwich University in 1826, and later distinguished himself as editor of the *Hartford Times*. President Polk appointed him Chief, Bureau of Provisions and Clothing of the U.S. Navy, from 1845 to 1849, no navy department as such having yet been created. At the time Welles was a Democrat, but later switched to the Republican Party and remained so for the rest of his life.[5]

After Lincoln appointed him Secretary of the Navy, in March 1861, Welles put into effect the "Anaconda Plan" blueprinted by General Winfield Scott, General Chief of the Army.

This plan, formulated by the elderly general, was to strangle the Confederacy much like the notorious prey-crushing snake after which the plan was named. To prevent the South from acquiring resources and materiel, a massive blockade of the southern Atlantic Coast, extending around Florida and all the way along the Gulf of Mexico to Texas, would be put in place. This would coincide with a chain of fortified positions erected or seized down the Ohio and Mississippi rivers, from Louisville to Paducah, Kentucky on the Ohio, and the Mississippi River points of Memphis, Vicksburg and New Orleans. This second phase of "Anaconda" would not only block resources and commerce, but actually split the Confederacy in two. Lincoln readily agreed with the plan and, as its first provision, declared the blockade.

Because the existing U.S. Navy was in no condition for a major war, Welles sprung into action; he called for the chartering or buying of 89 merchant marine vessels for service. Seven big sloops of war were contracted to be built (though only four were actually completed), and vessels ranging from 1,500 to 2,000 tons were rapidly constructed. Within months of Fort Sumter, the Union fleet was already in action against fortifications on the

Carolina coast. For the first time in this crisis, the industrial might of the North was beginning to make itself felt.

The technology of naval ordnance had advanced considerably in preceding years, even if the ironclad concept had not. At the outbreak of war the U.S. Navy, as with most world navies, still clung to the old battle-line concept, used most successfully by the British, and employing massive smooth-bore salvos. Gun calibers, as a result, had remained the same for many years.

Until this time naval ordnance consisted of smooth-bore cannons designated in the weight of the ball, i.e., 8-pounders, 12-pounders, 24-pounders, etc. But one John Dahlgren, a naval ordnance man and commandant of the Washington Navy Yard, developed a new gun that featured a fat breech tapering toward the muzzle—the famous "soda bottle" guns of Civil War fame. He designated their bores in inches, instead of pounds; i.e., 8-inch, 10-inch and even 15-inch. These guns were superior to the old ones, much more powerful and with a longer range; obvious advantages in power and distance made them desirable for mounting on vessels, for field pieces and for land fortifications. One massive 20-inch Dahlgren was built, but was never used in battle, apparently because the technical ability to get such a large shot into the muzzle did not yet exist.

Also significant was the development of the rifled Parrott gun, named after its inventor, R.P. Parrott, who, because of the great pressures produced in a rifled gun, conceived the idea of heat-shrinking a wrought-iron band around the breech where the pressures from gases were the greatest. The projectile contained a grooved brass ring around its base that allowed it to be forced into the rifling by the gases produced in burning powder, thereby giving it greater range and accuracy. The Parrott gun was used successfully by both sides and it came in 3-pounder, 20-pounder and 30-pounder sizes.

In the realm of ammunition, armor-piercing shells had of course not yet been considered necessary. However a new innovation was the shell that exploded on a target rather than simply being a solid ball that smashed its way into ships, troops or fortifications. The shell was detonated by a fuse that was ignited by the powder flash in the breech.[6]

All these technological advances were coming into play at the beginning of the Civil War, and the North with its enormous industrial capacity was able to manufacture these weapons in great volume. The Confederates, on the other hand, had only two major manufacturing facilities: the Tredegar Iron Works in Richmond and Leeds & Company in New Orleans. This industrial shortage was to haunt the Confederacy throughout the war and would eventually contribute to its defeat.

Like Lincoln, the newly elected president of the Confederacy, Jefferson Davis, also realized the importance of having a strong secretary of the navy, and in his case this meant a man who could build one from scratch. Davis launched a search to find the right man for the post and settled on Stephen Russell Mallory, a lawyer and politician from Florida.

Born in 1813, in the West Indies, Mallory was an ambitious man with a quick mind and seemingly limitless energy. He was appointed Inspector of Customs in Key West in 1833, where he spent his spare time studying law. After his admission to the bar, President Polk appointed him Collector of Customs in Key West. His political career began in 1850 when he was elected to the U.S. Senate, where he served his state honorably and efficiently. He resigned from the Senate in 1861, after Florida seceded from the Union. Though Mallory would be subject to bitter criticism in the years ahead, as "Anaconda" tightened its grip, the fact is that Davis made a good decision in choosing him as Secretary of the Navy to the Confederacy.

Unlike his Union counterpart, Welles, Mallory foresaw the importance of ironclad warships, as well as the underwater mines (then called torpedoes) that would affect many naval actions in the months to come.[7] Mallory put in place an ambitious program, but he was hampered by a lack of funds and a shortage of shipbuilding facilities, skilled workers and necessary materiel. Although small yards existed for building light, shallow-draft vessels, none of these could be converted to the building of larger craft.

However, Mallory did have some vessels on hand: one naval vessel, the *Fulton* (a 1,000-ton side-wheel sloop that never got into action), four revenue cutters, three slavers and two privately owned steamers. These vessels, pitifully few, at least provided a start.[8] Aside from limited materiel and few shipyards, the Confederacy also suffered from a shortage of ship's crews, American expertise having always been centered in New England. As it appeared, "the U.S. Navy was woefully unprepared, but the Confederacy had no navy at all."[9]

The fact that, by war's end, the South produced a number of vessels that passed into naval legend as fierce and gallant warships is a remarkable achievement. Nevertheless, the Confederate Navy, when one was finally formulated, never operated as a unit or fleet; vessels nearly always acted independently. This was especially evident during the Mississippi River actions and was in part due to flaws in the command structure when navy and army fought combined-arms actions. Throughout the Mississippi River campaigns, and to their detriment, Confederate naval command would largely remain subordinate to the army.

The Mississippi and its adjoining states, especially south of Illinois and Missouri, were fated to be a pivotal region in the struggle to come. The region's strategic value had already been recognized in the Anaconda Plan, but military eyes in Washington were at first fastened upon the Atlantic Coast and the proposed blockade. However, Southern strategists had early on seen the importance of the western "spine" of their Confederacy and had moved to place both troops and fortifications at strategic points to protect it.

The military importance of the Mississippi River Valley is best understood in light of the South's secessionist movement, which had affected some but not all of that river's border states. After the fall of Fort Sumter in April 1861, and the secession of the states of Arkansas, Mississippi, Florida, Alabama, Georgia, Louisiana, Texas and Virginia, the Confederate military looked west to where the border states of Kentucky and Missouri were waffling in their loyalties to either side; Southern commanders decided to move swiftly in that region. However, Missouri and Kentucky stayed with the Union, partly by Lincoln's handling of the issue of slavery, and partly by the quick work of a few military leaders in disarming Rebel militias.

Kentucky was the swing state in this melee of secession because it not only bordered the Ohio and Mississippi rivers, but it promised to be the western anchor of the defense perimeter in Confederate strategic thinking.

That promise was almost fulfilled when Kentucky Governor Beriah Magoffin issued a response to President Lincoln's call for 75,000 troops on April 15, stating that he would "furnish no troops for the wicked purpose of subduing her sister southern troops." However, the governor stood firmly alone, because powerful pro-Union sentiment was present in the legislature and that body elected to stay with the Union. It was, in fact, due to the threat of Union troops being sent in that overwhelming public sentiment kept Kentucky in a state of neutrality.

Missouri, on the other hand, was at first strongly in favor of the Confederacy. A plan to seize a Federal arsenal near St. Louis by a small detachment of the regular army failed. A few skirmishes between Confederate and Union troops occurred, including an abortive attempt to invade the state capitol at Jefferson City. But Missouri remained in the Union camp and it was a fortunate thing indeed, because a Missouri in Confederate hands would have meant control of the Mississippi River much farther to the north, and would have outflanked Cairo, Illinois.

When Missouri failed to turn, Cairo, situated at the tip of Illinois where the Ohio River meets the Mississippi, remained a veritable dagger pointed into Southern territory. Both antagonists had seen the importance of this river "port," and while the Union poured in troops and established their great inland naval base there, the Confederates, led by Albert Sidney Johnston, moved swiftly to establish fortifications along its approaches.

An imposing figure, both in physical stature and military expertise, Johnston had been appointed General Commanding the Western Department of the Army of the Confederate States of America, by Jefferson Davis. His command stretched from the Alleghenies in the east to Missouri in the west. He moved decisively in his department by establishing military positions along the Mississippi River into Kentucky, defying that state's supposed neutrality, and in Tennessee and Mississippi. Strong forts were built at Belmont, New Madrid, Columbus, Memphis, Fort Pillow and Vicksburg.

Union generals in the west, hastily recruiting and training their armies, knew that this ring of strongholds had to be destroyed or captured in order to split the Confederacy down the Mississippi to the Gulf. In the meantime they had to outbuild and outrecruit the Rebels in order to forestall a possible Confederate offensive. There was no Union navy yet established on the Mississippi River, and the Confederates were rumored to be bringing up gunboats on the great Father of Waters.

On August 26, 1861, a tall, bearded naval officer boarded a train in Washington, D.C., and headed west. His orders were to take command of the Federal Naval Forces on Western Waters, and his assignment to this post was to prove momentous for the future course of the war. His destination was the new naval station at Cairo, Illinois, where a new fleet of gunboats was under construction, some already launched and others still on the ways.

He was to replace Commander John Rodgers, U.S.N., who had not been inefficient at his job, but rather had fallen victim to a clash of personalities between the Commander of the Western Department, Major General John Charles Frémont, and shipbuilder James Eads. The feeling in Washington was simply that a more senior navy man than Rodgers was required.

When the officer arrived in St. Louis and reported to General Frémont, he found Eads' shipyards at Carondelet, south of St. Louis, and at Mound City, a few miles upriver on the Ohio, bustling with activity. The ways were filled with craft being built from the keels up, after designs of Samuel Pook.

Commissioned river craft were being converted into gunboats, and others were busily engaged in military transport. In addition, General Frémont had ordered 38 mortar boats to be built. That flamboyant, controversial army officer had the foresight to see the possibilities of fighting on inland waters: gun-bearing craft were not enough; floating artillery bases would also be needed.

This then was the core of the Federal navy on the rivers of the west, when Captain Andrew Hull Foote, U.S.N., came upon the scene to take charge.[10]

CHAPTER TWO

Birth Pangs
of Ironclads

General John Frémont, whom Captain Andrew Foote consulted upon his arrival in St. Louis, was a controversial and flamboyant figure. A Georgia native, he had taught mathemetics in the navy before joining the U.S. Army Topographical Engineers Corps. Later he earned the name "Pathfinder," because of his explorations of the Rockies, and went on to play a prominent role in the battles against the Mexicans in California. In 1849 he became wealthy when gold was discovered on his property and in 1856 he was the Republican nominee for president (losing to Buchanan). At the outbreak of war, he was appointed Major General and put in command of the Western Department, which included the shipyards where Foote would conduct his first inspections.

Those shipyards were located in Carondelet, some ten miles to the south. Foote traveled to his destination on the St. Louis & Iron Mountain Railroad, which ran from Plum Street in St. Louis to Carondelet and hence to Belmont, with a spur leading to Iron Knob.

The bustling village, with a population of over 11,000 people, lay about an hour's ride from St. Louis. It was vastly overcrowded because it was host to the massive James B. Eads yards located on a low slope leading to the River des Peres, a tributary of the Mississippi River. An influx of artisans and laborers had swollen the boundaries of the hamlet far beyond that which the founders had ever dreamed, and makeshift dwellings had mushroomed across the landscape, in addition to the frame houses already there. Furthermore, the residents were dismayed over the growing plethora of saloons and sporting houses to serve the workers and military personnel.[1]

Captain Foote would have been impressed by the sprawling shipyard, at the foot of Marceau Street, that contained six long sheds, a dozen ways, a forest of cranes and hoists and a marine railway—a new innovation by one Primus Emerson, in the 1850's, consisting of a series of rails that extended from a boat shed and upon which was a car or cradle that could either run boats out of the water to the shed, or launch a vessel from the shed into the water. The shipyard, originally built by Emerson, then known as the Carondelet Marine Railway Company, was leased to Eads for the construction of the gunboats.

Later in those sheds would be built five gunboats: *Carondelet, St.Louis, Louisville, Pittsburgh* and later the giant *Benton,* which was destined to become the most powerful ironclad afloat. Across the turgid, coffee-colored Ohio River, three more gunboats were to be built: *Mound City, Cincinnati* and *Cairo,* at the smaller shipyard at Mound City, Illinois. In addition, Eads had five sawmills and a rolling mill available in St. Louis, plus two foundries that built engines for him on the spot.

On the day of Foote's arrival, September 6, 1861, he was ushered through a maze of construction materials and sheet iron: wood from Minnesota, armor plate from Pittsburgh and machinery from Cincinnati, Pittsburgh and St. Louis. This was a crash building program and, upon receiving the contract, Eads had promised Washington he would build the gunboats within forty-six days.

The crusty and energetic Eads, who was now in his forty-first year, and who presented an imposing figure with his luxuriant sideburns and heavy chin whiskers, had enjoyed a distinguished career even before being called out of semi-retirement by President Lincoln in 1861. He had been a partner in a highly successful firm called "James B. Eads Salvage and Construction Company," and had invented a diving bell used in the salvage of marine wrecks. He was considered an authority on navigating the

Mississippi and had become a wealthy man at an early age. Small wonder that Lincoln recognized his worth and called upon him to serve his country.[2]

The redoubtable Eads had wasted no time in converting the leased Carondelet property into a thriving shipyard, with 800 workmen, and a program to build gunboats according to the designs of Samuel Pook. Pook, an enigmatic man about whose life little is known, designed a series of river warcraft that were to become known as "Pook's Turtles," because their most prominent feature was, to all intents and purposes, a shell.[3]

By this time, the fledgling Union Navy's Mississippi River fleet already boasted three timberclad gunboats, all converted river steamers which at this moment were moored to floating docks at Cairo, Illinois, about 145 miles downriver. They had already participated in the capture and occupation of the cities of Paducah and Headland at the mouths of the Tennessee and Cumberland Rivers, respectively, and had even reconnoitered down the rivers to inspect the brand-new Confederate forts: Henry on the Tennessee and Donelson on the Cumberland. This then was Foote's existing river flotilla, a harbinger of a greater fleet yet to come.

Andrew Hull Foote was no stranger to ships of all kinds. The deeply religious fifty-five-year-old Connecticut-native was the son of a prominent merchant shipper and public official in New Haven. Young Andrew had grown up near the ocean and had developed a deep love of sailing.

Foote entered West Point in 1822, but resigned after six months to accept an appointment as a midshipman in the U.S. Navy. For the next two decades he served in the Caribbean, Mediterranean and Pacific theaters. His religious nature rebelled against the tradition of issuing rum rations—a tradition borrowed from the British Navy—and he organized a sort of naval temperance society that later saw the rum tradition abolished in 1862. He was commanding the Brooklyn Navy Yard when called to take charge of naval forces in the Upper Mississippi River theater of action.[4]

Those who saw Captain Foote after his arrival in St. Louis would have taken note of a stocky man with a head of frizzled hair, penetrating eyes, a razor-straight nose and a gray beard. But it was his boundless energy that would have impressed them most, and that energy was immediately put to work on his burgeoning "Turtle Fleet." Once finished, these unlovely ironclads would be launched into the River des Peres, floated down to the Mississippi and thence downriver to the naval base at Cairo to be fitted out with ordnance and manned with crews. The same would apply to those built in Mound City, neither shipyard being equipped to install ordnance; Cairo would be the great fountainhead of ammunition, materiel, weapons and personnel for the coming Mississippi campaigns. The "Turtles" would be complemented by General Frémont's construction of 38 mortar boats which were nothing more than 8-inch siege mortars mounted on armored rafts. The latter would provide considerable firepower in the battles to come.

It is curious to note that no evidence exists that the Carondelet shipyards were ever again used for the repair of river craft. As the war progressed, battle repairs and materiel attrition were handled either on the spot or brought to Cairo or Mound City for repairs.

After his inspection of the shipyard and his introduction to the hulls of the new gunboats, Foote took a copy of Pook's specifications along with him to Cairo, on board a steamer. One can imagine him studying those specs and anticipating the imminent challenge of river fighting, consciously suspending his ocean-going-vessel knowledge and absorbing Pook's strange but ingenious designs.

According to Pook, each 500-ton displacement vessel was to be 175-feet long, with a 50-foot beam and a 7-foot hold. These vessels were designed from the keel up for fighting on rivers, and their shallow drafts, usually six feet, would become major factors in the fighting to come. In addition to the cramped engine and fireroom, the hold would contain magazines, shot lockers, shell room, coal bunkers and the crew's quarters and mess. It was a lot of materiel to cram into a hull 175- by 50-feet.

Being an officer, Foote would have noticed with interest the space devoted to officers' quarters. These consisted of a large section aft, with a cabin for the captain, eight staterooms for junior officers and two messrooms. Each stateroom would be fitted with a berth, bureau and washstand. A table would be placed in the captain's quarters and in each messroom. It would be crowded back there, especially with the big paddlewheel aft. As for the latter, it would be a centerline, stern paddlewheel, 20 feet in diameter, in an opening 18 feet wide and running 60 feet forward. There would be plenty of motive power; the Merritt engines, mounted at a 15-degree angle, would have cast-iron cylinders with a bore of 22 inches and a piston stroke of 6 feet.

For the boilers, the designs called for five units, 36 inches in diameter and 28 feet long. Beneath each would be a firebox and in front of them would be two "chimneys" (as river sailors call smokestacks), 44 inches in diameter and 28 feet high. As rivermen knew, those tall chimneys would be necessary for proper draft.

Looking at the specs, a navy man might have wondered whether the power plants would be enough to propel a craft of 500-ton displacement, and how the armor would affect the speed. Specifications prescribed five miles per hour up stream and nine miles per hour downstream. He would then have to check the specs on the rectangular casemates: 55-degree angles, sloping sides leading to the flat deck. Forward, the sides would slope 45 degrees; this was necessary to deflect cannon balls.

The armor itself would be made from 75-ton, charcoal/iron plating, 13 inches wide, 11 feet long and $2^{1}/_{2}$ inches thick. A navy man would have to wonder if the plating would deflect cannon balls with a regular trajectory, but it was questionable whether or not it could withstand plunging shot like that from mortars or artillery on a high bluff.

The power plant unit would be protected by boiler iron and would be vulnerable to cannon balls, as would the steering house, or "Texas," as river sailors call it, because of the thinner iron plating. Well-trained Confederate gunners would turn the Texas into a virtual slaughterhouse for its occupants.

All of this did not apply to the *Benton*, which would be constructed later from a twin-hulled catamaran snagboat. This huge vessel would have a 202-foot length and a 72-foot beam. She would be armed with 16 guns and protected by $3^{1}/_{2}$-inch plating and, as flagship for the Union flotillas, become the most formidable river gunboat afloat.

The two hulls of the catamaran were 20 feet apart and would be planked over, extending from side to side; then the hulls would be joined 50 feet from the stern. In this space would go a big paddlewheel powered by two inclined engines with a 20-inch bore and a 7-foot stroke.[5] It has been recorded that when the *Benton* returned from her trials up the Ohio River, Captain William D. Porter, of the timberclad *Essex*, remarked to Captain Foote that the gunboat was too slow; whereupon Eads replied, "Yes, but plenty fast to fight with."[6]

Also part of the riverine fleet, when Foote took command, were the the "timberclads" *Lexington, Tyler* and *Conestoga*. These ponderous vessels had briefly been the backbone of the river fleet before the construction of the ironclads. They were former freight/passenger steamers with conventional side paddlewheels, of 500 tons displacement. Roughly, they were 180 feet long with a beam of 42 feet, a draft of 6 feet and a 7-foot hold. They were powered by a single 2-horsepower engine with a 24-inch bore with a 7-foot stroke, and produced a speed of from 7–10 knots, which was fairly swift for such bulky, heavy vessels. Protective plating consisted of 5-inch oak bulwarks, hence the term "timberclads." They were fitted with four 32-pounders and four 8-inch Dahlgrens, and would primarily be used to give fire support to land and amphibious operations.

One curious aspect of the riverine fleet concerns the crews, which at first were a mixture of rivermen, soldiers and civilian volunteers. The fleet was under the jurisdiction of the army, but with naval officers in command. It was only later that the fleet would become, officially, a part of the U.S. Navy.

Life aboard the "turtles" was not easy for the officers and men; cramped and confined quarters made for harsh living conditions. Aside from the 251 men aboard a vessel 175 feet long and 51 feet wide, with a 6-foot draft, much of the space was occupied by a large paddle wheel and attending machinery of boilers and engines, plus coal bunkers, ammunition and shot lockers, not to mention 13–14 guns. With an overhead of only a few feet, one can gain an idea of what cramped quarters were like on a Civil War gunboat.[7]

By way of comparisons, the 3,200-ton *Merrimac,* which we will hear more about later, was 263 feet long with a comparable beam of 51 feet and 22-foot draft with a much larger compartment overhead, for a complement of 320 men. The 987-ton *Monitor,* on the other hand, was 179 feet long with a 41-foot beam and a 10-foot draft and had a ship's complement of 49. Warships in those days were crowded.

Still, in spite of the fact that the riverine vessels were designed to fight on rivers and not on deep seas, many traditional naval routines were observed, some of which must have caused consternation to the non-navy personnel aboard. As an example: Reveille was piped-to around 5:00 A.M., followed by routine scrubbing and/or holystoning the decks. The latter, vital to upkeep of wooden decks, consisted of a group of crew members dragging heavy stones across a heavily sanded and wetted deck; following would be men with water and brushes and brooms. Crew members generally hated this routine in navy life, but those decks *had* to be sparkling clean, according to navy tradition.

Breakfast would be piped at around 8:00 A.M. The typical regulation ration for sailors consisted of the following: a pound of dried or salted beef or pork, a half pint of beans or peas, a quarter pound of dried fruit, two ounces of butter, two ounces of cheese, 14 ounces of biscuit and a quarter ounce of coffee or tea. Officers' rations were considerably more palatable and were usually cooked and served from their own galley.

In 1964, when the sunken gunboat *Cairo* was raised from the Yazoo River, many new things about life on board were discovered. For instance, meals for the crews were cooked in a wood-burning stove, called "The Southern Belle." The men ate in messes of about 15 and each mess possessed a chest containing tin plates and cups, knives, spoons and forks and a jug of molasses. Each crewman had his initials etched on his own utensils. The galley also contained a large chopping block, with a two-handled cleaver. Fresh meat was cut on this block, whenever it was available, usually by foraging parties that roamed the countryside.

Although their diet seems austere, consisting of mostly dried foods, the crews of both navies, whenever possible, would obtain rations by foraging the countryside and by catching fish in rivers and streams.

The crew stood watches on one of the typical regulation watch schedules, revolving around the 24-hour clock, from midnight to midnight, and maintained while afloat or at anchorage, except in combat situations. Many of these same regulations are observed in the U.S. Navy today.

During leisure times, the crews busied themselves with a variety of activities, such as playing cards, smoking, wood carving or, for those who were literate, writing and/or reading letters for themselves or others. Some crews contained musicians who regaled the men with banjoes, guitars, harmonicas and an occasional fiddle. Singalongs were always popular with the men. Now and then vessels would have "mascots," generally dogs, and a lot of time was spent tending to and playing with the animals.

Part of the "turn-to" time was no doubt spent painting topside, which was the bane of all navy men. There being no drydocks for painting the hulls, most of the work was relegated to bulkheads and decks. Saturdays were generally spent mending or washing clothing, called "make or mend day." Sundays were marked by captains' inspections and religious services, held either by a chaplain or by the captain himself, although chaplains were more likely to be found only on larger vessels. The remainder of the day was devoted to such activities as games, rowing regattas and fishing over the sides of the vessels.

Civil War naval uniforms reflected those worn in today's navy. Officers wore the traditional peaked cap, a frock coat with shoulder bars, and gold lace bands on the sleeve that announced the rank of the wearer: for example, a captain would wear shoulder bars similar to those of the army, with a blue cloth ground, silver rank badges with an eagle and anchor in the center of three 3/4-inch gold lace bands on the sleeves. Confederate navy officers wore much the same design as that of their army—in steel gray, with gold lace bars on sleeves, except that the top bar was looped.

Enlisted men in both navies wore the traditional "sailor" uniforms, with collars, neckerchiefs and "pancake," or flat hats. Petty officers wore fouled anchor rank badges on the right or left sleeve, depending on the rank. Seamen of both navies wore cotton whites in the summer and wool blues in colder weather, much like today's navy. There was always the possibility that upon special occasions, a mixture of both colors would, when ordered, be worn by enlisted personnel.

Meanwhile, in the Confederacy, Steven Mallory was laying the groundwork for a navy, most ominously with the conversion of the captured *Merrimac*, at Norfolk Navy Yard, into the ironclad *Virginia*. However, no gunboats were yet available to match the growing ironclad fleet of the Union in the Trans-Mississippi sector. As a step in that direction, the 500-ton steamer *Eastport* had been purchased and would be converted at a Tennessee River site. In addition, Mallory had ordered the construction of two ironclads to be built at the shipyards in Memphis and New Orleans. However these would be too little and too late.

The case of the *Eastport* and the two planned gunboats was an example of the bureaucratic bumbling that would weaken the Confederacy in combined-arms actions. There was no policy concerning who was to command what, and, exacerbating the situation was the fact that naval officers were generally below the rank of army commanders, who exercised control over all naval matters.

Similar bureaucratic difficulties ran rampant in the new Confederate government. In March 1862, the *Daily Missourian Republican* wrote that the Rebel Congress had failed to remove the "injunction of secrecy from department head reports" and that the Navy Department estimates had been increased under the "secret acts of the Provisional Congress which had authorized the enlistment of two thousand additional seamen and large additions of officers."[8]

In addition, there was concern over the lack of supplies and manpower as well as lack of materiel—especially iron plating—for construction and outfitting the boats. And, though Confederate inventors were coming up with new devices like mines and torpedoes—ideal weapons to offset the North's advantages in weight and numbers—the Southern high command was not quick to take advantage of these initiatives.

But at the moment, Mallory was concerned about countering the Union blockade. For this reason, fast ships called "blockade runners" were pressed into service. Privately owned, for the most part, many were built in Britain for just this purpose. Other British-built vessels were obtained by the Confederacy and used effectively as commerce raiders. In order to avoid violating the high-seas neutrality laws, these vessels would sail out as merchantmen, then be commissioned at sea and armed as vessels of war.

The Southern blockade runners were fairly successful at their job, considering they supplied the Confederacy with goods estimated at $200,000,000, including 600,000 small arms and rifles among other items. In fact, these vessels supplied 60 percent of Southern guns and ammunition, quantities of food, shoes, lead, clothing and medicine, using the valuable "King Cotton" as payment for many of these supplies. Inevitably, as the North's blockade tightened and more Union ships were pressed into service—up to 600 by 1864—these vital Confederate operations became increasingly difficult.

However, concentration on the Atlantic theater of action was to tie the hands of the Confederate Navy, in respect to new construction, for months to come, and was largely responsible for the failure of that navy to block Grant's assaults on their forts on the Cumberland, Tennessee and the Mississippi.[9] The stark, cold fact of the matter was that the Confederacy would be unable to stem the tide of blue rolling into Kentucky and Tennessee in the months to come.

CHAPTER THREE

The Blossoming of Little Egypt

Fall 1861 saw the Missouri/Kentucky/Tennessee sector of the Midwest in a state of flux. The Confederates had shattered Kentucky's fragile neutrality by sending in troops and supplies with the intention of bolstering their western line of defense.[1] Confederate General Albert Sidney Johnston, based in Bowling Green, had built his line beginning at Columbus, Missouri, some 35 miles south of Cairo, and had fortified Belmont, across the river on the Kentucky side as well. New Madrid, Missouri, and Island No. 10, off Tennessee, were further strongpoints, the latter situated in a loop of the Mississippi where it could block any traffic downriver. This was a military arm aimed directly at Cairo and was painfully obvious to Union leaders; it soon jolted them into taking counter-measures.

To the east, near the Kentucky border, Johnston built two forts: Henry on the Tennessee River and Donelson on the Cumberland, the two being 12 miles apart at a point where the rivers flow almost parallel. A glance at a map will reveal the wisdom of his strategy: the Tennessee comes up from the south, from Alabama, and flows into the Ohio River at Paducah, Kentucky; the Cumberland, on the other hand, flows from Kentucky's eastern mountains, past Nashville, Tennessee, and empties into the Ohio at Smithland, Kentucky. After the outbreak of hostilities, the Union Army, in a swift and decisive move, occupied these strategic towns, thereby controlling the mouths of both rivers. Forts

Henry and Donelson, however, would block any Union advances along either river. From the Confederate standpoint, it was obvious that if the two rivers were to fall into Union hands, gunboats could thunder up and down, destroying vital bridges, capturing any river craft and transporting troops at leisure. The territories penetrated by the rivers would essentially be lost.

The center, or hub, of Confederate strength in this theater was Bowling Green, Kentucky. From there, Johnston was to direct any and all movements against Missouri, Kentucky and Illinois, and defend his carefully built line of defense from Union assault. As would be the case so often in this theater, he was strapped for troops, so he was content to hold the line and wait for these to be recruited.[2]

In 1861, it should be remembered, the nature of the border states was not yet clear to either side. Kentucky and Missouri hadn't seceded from the Union, but on the other hand, neither had they rallied to Lincoln's banner. Through Union eyes this Confederate defensive line could possibly have been turned into an offensive staging ground at a moment's notice, a gray storm rolling northward against Cairo, Illinois. Fortunately, Illinois Governor Yates, soon after hostilities began, strengthened defenses there with troops and artillery, two forts and the genesis of a powerful naval base for the coming fleet of river-fighting craft. At the core of all this activity was the fact that both antagonists had eyes on Kentucky. As events would prove, that state was "to be the starting point of the series of campaigns which brought the rebellion to an end."[3]

The State of Missouri had also become a vital link in the secessionist drama. In St. Louis, a significant event occurred on May 10, 1861, when some 670 state militia men, under command of George Frost, held their annual encampment, called "Camp Jackson," in Lindell Grove in the First District. It had been the custom for each Missouri district militia to assemble at an encampment for a week in April. It appeared that Frost, the commander of the First District, had chosen an encampment within marching distance to the St. Louis Arsenal. A Southern sympathizer, he desired to swing Missouri into the Rebel camp and, with the backing of Governor Jackson, plotted to seize the arsenal, gain the arms therein and thus accomplish their goal. But a flaw in the plan sowed seeds of destruction for the occupants, when they opened the gates of the camp to visitors.

Among the "fairest of Missouri daughters" visiting was a familiar figure in a Jenny Lind carriage, veiled and blind Mrs. Alexander. Later, as "she" ascended the stairs of her home, some visitors on the porch spotted cavalry boots under the black bombazine gown. It was revealed, some hours later, that "Mrs. Alexander" was none other than Captain Nathaniel Lyon, of the Second U.S. Infantry, who had been on a reconnaissance of Camp Jackson.[4]

Soon after, a contingent of Federal troops, led by Colonel Thomas Tasker Gantt, surrounded the camp and forced a surrender, after placing artillery within range. The prisoners were marched up Olive Street, where a large crowd of sympathizers had gathered. There was physical resistance, shots were fired, and 31 spectators were left dead, with many more injured. Among those watching the parade down Olive Street "was an Illinois store keeper named Ulysses S. Grant. Another bystander was the manager of a St. Louis street car company, an executive named William T. Sherman."[5]

After Southern-sympathizer troops had been neutralized in Missouri, General Frémont, as did his successor, General Halleck, realized that the next moves would be downriver, in order to break the Confederate line—especially at the Mississippi "elbow." A powerful river fleet would be needed and needed soon.

That fleet had its beginnings during October 1861, when on the cold, bitter day of the 12th a large crowd gathered at a launching way in the Eads shipyard at which the gunboat *St. Louis* was about to hit the water. As was the custom, many dignitaries, both civilian and military, plus yard workers, were in attendance.

From the river and at the docks, all vessels present would have tied down their whistles and, amid a great deal of cheering and clapping, the gunboat hull would receive her new name. Then as if on cue, an army of workers would swing mauls at chocks, knocking them out from under the hull, and the marine railway would carry it broadside into the narrow river. After a few minutes of rocking back and forth, in the hull's attempt to find its equilibrium, a few workers aboard would toss lines to eager hands on a dock and, shortly, the new hull would have been secured, ready for fitting out.

It was a propitious event for all concerned, and the military men did not waste time taking possession of the craft. It appeared that Eads had delivered on his promise—a little late, perhaps, but close enough for the Union cause. Ironically, Eads was not paid for his efforts for a long time. He had invested much of his own money to keep the project going.[6]

The fitting-out process included the installation of post-construction woodwork, furniture in the wardrooms and captain's cabin, equipping the vessel with necessary gear such as anchor and chains, miles of hemp lines, finishing touches on the boilers and engines, plus any necessary repair work. After that, the installation of main ordnance would be done at Cairo.

Few words in our language conjure up visions of faraway, exotic places like the name Cairo, in faraway Egypt. However, *our* Cairo, in Illinois, is far removed from the exotic and mysterious. In the first place, it is pronounced "Kay-row"; secondly, it is a peninsula flanked by two rivers and was full of water and mud in 1861. It was not "faraway" but, rather, located at the southernmost tip of Illinois.

This important peninsula was first visited by French explorers, missionaries, and by George Rogers Clark. Cairo was established in 1855, and by the beginning of the Civil War had a population of 2,200. Of that number, 55 were negroes. Cairo was one of the most important pieces of real estate in the country, during the fall and winter of 1861–62, both the Union and Confederacy realized its strategic importance.

Records show that many people never expected an invasion of Cairo. In fact, Illinois State Senator Lyman Trumbull wrote to a friend, stating he never believed Cairo would be attacked, but that Governor Yates was "omitting no preparation to be ready in case an attempt was to be made." He specified that there were plenty of men and materiel at Cairo, and more nearby ready to be moved at a moment's notice. He reported that on May 10, 1861 Yates had shipped 2,700 men with 15 pieces of field artillery, plus six-pounders and one twelve-pounder to Cairo from Springfield.[7]

Much to his credit, Governor Yates had already ordered a contingent of soldiers and artillery to Cairo, soon after Fort Sumter surrendered. By June of 1861, 12,000 Union soldiers were in and around Cairo, Villa Ridge and Bird's Point, across the Mississippi River. The latter piece of real estate, named after Adam Bird, a founder of Cairo, was important because any artillery placed there would command the Cairo waterfront. Trumbull also pointed out that another 38,000 men were within a 24-hour ride.

In order to further strengthen Cairo as a military camp and as a naval base, the energetic Governor Yates managed to round up 7,000 new guns, 6,000 rifled muskets, 500 rifles and 14 batteries of artillery, in the autumn of 1861, which were shipped to the city and installed in record time. These additions made Cairo a formidable installation indeed.[8] Cairo became an enormous military camp with a huge parade ground and clusters of barracks on all sides. Countless dress parades were witnessed by hordes of reporters from the roof of the St. Charles Hotel. Military protocol became the order of the day for the entire city; it was to become the fabric of its citizens' lives for the next couple of years.

Located at the tip of a peninsula, Cairo was surrounded by water on two sides; therefore a levee, some 15 feet high, was built around the city. Because the land was flat and low, it became extremely muddy during heavy rains or swollen-river stages, in spite of the levee, which made it a virtual mud pond. It must be remembered that during that time, paved roads were a rarity in Illinois, as they were throughout the Midwest.

The only year-around access to Cairo was by the Illinois Central Railroad, which entered over a causeway across a morass of swamp to the north of the city. Once within city limits, the road split and ran in a loop along the levee, around Camp Defiance and up the western shore to rejoin the junction again. Over this railroad came many divisions of soldiers and equipment that were destined to go downriver to split the Confederacy by capturing the fortifications in Missouri, Kentucky, Tennessee,

Mississippi and finally clear down to the Gulf of Mexico. Also, over these tracks came such luminaries as generals Grant, McLernand, Buell, Halleck, McMillan and, from time to time, top members of Lincoln's cabinet.

General Frémont also established a naval base on the Ohio River side of Cairo. It consisted mainly of the floating wharfboats of Graham & Halliday Company and Given, Haynes & Company. The wharfboats were simply flatboat hulls covered with shed-like structures. (The Western Navy Headquarters was located in the Graham & Halliday craft, within which held forth Captain A.M. Pennock, U.S.N., who was appointed commandant of the station.) It was here the gunboats from Carondelet and Mound City were fitted out with crews and ordnance.

The street parallel to the levee, under which were moored the wharfboats, was called Ohio Street, and along it were the Quartermaster's office and warehouse, Post and District Headquarters and the Ohio Building, in which General Grant had his quarters while in Cairo. Also on Ohio Street was the famed, magnificent, five-storied St. Charles Hotel, the focus for not only reporters and visiting dignitaries, but for many important social functions for Cairo's elite citizenry.

West of Ohio Street, along Halliday Street, a throng of saloons and bawdy houses served the military personnel until they were closed down by General John A. McLernand on October 11, 1861.[9] Further west was Commercial Avenue which contained such old and established firms as Koehler's Gunshop, a drug store, the city's post office, the popular Atheneum Theater, plus a blacksmith and a harness shop. A block south of this site was the huge parade grounds.

Cairo quickly gained the attention of the entire country, drawing many reporters to observe the military build-up. *The New York Times* referred to Cairo as "the Gibraltar of the West, along with a heavy chain of torpedoes stretched across the Mississippi."[10] However, there is no evidence that such a chain existed and, if it did, it would have been a menace to all navigation and not only to the military.

England's famous novelist Anthony Trollope visited wartime Cairo in 1862, and wrote a dismal report on the city. He complained that "the inhabitants seemed to revel in dirt." He also crabbed about the hotel accommodations there, especially the bathroom facilities.[11]

Scattered around Cairo were a variety of installations for the citizenry, as well as the military, including stables, a hospital and a wheelwright shop. A fort was constructed at the apex of the heart-shaped city that consisted of a flat-topped mound upon which were placed three 24-pound cannons and an 8-inch mortar. Contemporary drawings also reveal a command house and a ship's mast for the colors. This facility was first named "Fort Prentiss," after the Union officer Benjamin Mayberry Prentiss, who had served honorably in the Mexican War. The name was later changed to "Fort Defiance" until the fort was dismantled after the war was over. Today the site is named Fort Defiance State Park.

Life at Camp Defiance was rigid but not intolerable. A regulation poster informed the troops that, after 8:00 P.M., there would be no "loud singing, no cheering or firing arms." Soldiers were urged to attend Sabbath services "in an orderly and Christian-like manner."[12]

Apparently food was no problem. There were plenty of "G.I." provisions, and locally grown fruit was plentiful. One soldier wrote to his wife that peaches were for sale every day in camp and that he had spent most of his money buying the fruit. He also wisely predicted a big battle soon to come in Kentucky.[13]

The powerful installations at Cairo appeared to be more than enough to repel any marauding Confederate force from downriver. As an extra precaution against a force coming down the Ohio, two more batteries were placed along the levee to the north. Even more batteries were placed to the north on the Mississippi side, lest any threat come from that direction. With Cairo in strong Union hands, the Mississippi was made secure from its confluence with the Ohio to the north.

In 1861, among Kentucky, Tennessee and Missouri, only Kentucky was a declared "neutral" and the truth of its neutrality seemed a variable. When President Lincoln called upon the governors of these states for troops, on April 15, all refused to mobilize men for the Union. It was as if they were sitting on a political fence, marking time and waiting to see what direction events were taking. Meantime, Kentucky's Governor Magoffin, who later grudgingly declared his state neutral due to popular demand, declined to object when General Johnston established Rebel fortifications on Kentucky soil. These forts would soon be challenged not only by the thousands of troops assembling in Cairo, but by the flotilla of Yankee ironclad gunboats.

On October 22, 1861, the *Carondelet* slid down the ways; she was rapidly followed by sisters *Cincinnati, Louisville, Mound City, Cairo* and later the *Benton*. Within 100 days, including *Pittsburgh* and *St. Louis*, a flotilla of eight powerful ironclads were built and launched, from both Carondelet and Mound City shipyards. This flotilla had an aggregate of 5,000 tons, heavy armor, an average speed of nine knots (with the exception of *Carondelet*, which had trouble maintaining five knots, even at forced draft) and a total of 107 guns.

In respect to the *Benton*, there is an interesting story, related by Eads himself, concerning her maiden voyage. It seems that now-Flag Officer Foote invited Eads to come on board and make the trip to Cairo for armament. Eads was an old hand at navigating the fickle waters of the Mississippi and his expertise would be invaluable should the water level drop, ice floes appear and there be some danger of grounding. Eads accepted, packed his bags and came on board, happy to be on the river again.

Then on a cold October morning, the *Benton* cast loose, slipped down the River des Peres and out into the floe-dotted Mississippi River. All went well until she ran aground on a sandbar, 30 miles downriver, fulfilling Foote's worst fears. Anchors were put out and, using the boat's winches, attempts were made to move her off the bar. In navy parlance this is called "kedging." However, it was to be of no avail. Oddly, during the hours spent in trying to kedge her off the bar, Eads was not consulted, despite his being aboard for that very purpose.

The struggle went on overnight, but the heavy craft of 633 tons held fast, and to make matters worse the river began to drop. It was obvious that Captain John Winslow and his crew were unable to make any progress. Finally, unable to restrain himself any longer, Eads approached the skipper and offered his considerable experience in these matters. The fatigued skipper looked at Eads and said, "At last. Yes, Mr. Eads, if you will undertake to get her off, I'll place the entire crew under your direction."[14]

The shipbuilder then issued orders for breaking out some heavy hawsers intended for fleet use at Cairo. He suggested they run out three, secure them to the largest trees on shore, and then connect them to three steam capstans on the bow. In this manner, the boat would easily be dragged off the bar. If three lines failed to do the job, Eads maintained, then more would be used with the winches.

Eads' plan was swiftly put into action, and the next day the *Benton* was refloated. During the action, a snatch block chain broke and severely injured Captain Winslow, who was released from duty and sent home for recuperation. Though Winslow was indeed unfortunate to miss the great river battles to come, his consolation was supplied on June 19, 1864, when his new command, the U.S.S. *Kearsarge*, sank the notorious Confederate man-of-war *Alabama* off Cherbourg, France.

With Eads and Flag Officer Foote aboard, the *Benton's* arrival at Cairo was greeted with enthusiasm by naval personnel, many of whom requested permission to visit her. The *Benton* was sent on trial runs downriver. After returning, she was moored for the fitting out of her ordnance: 16 guns—seven 32-pounders, two 9-inch guns and seven army 42-pounders.

At any given time during this period, the scene at Cairo's floating naval base would have been similar: one or two gunboats moored to the wharfboats while others were anchored out in the stream. Nested around the wharfboats, with their noses aground, dozens of steamers waiting to take on supplies and/or troops; others would be landing goods. Scattered around would be steam tugs and other assorted river craft. On the river bank, wooden sheds bustled with activity day and night, with piles of materiel stacked nearby.[15]

While the Union river fleet was being assembled, plans of action were being formulated by the army and navy commanders. Their ultimate goal was to control the Mississippi River and its tributaries, from Cairo to the Gulf. But the first obstacles, and the closest, were the facing Rebel strongholds at Columbus, Kentucky and Belmont, Missouri, at which General Leonidas Polk, C.S.A., had heavily fortified the Columbus bluffs.

Polk was somewhat of an anomaly in the world of army leaders. In 1831, he resigned a commission at West Point to study theology, and was later ordained as an Episcopal priest. In 1838, he became a bishop, and at the time he was tapped by Jefferson Davis to join the Confederate cause as a major-general he had become the Bishop of Lousiana.[16]

The former bishop was not a military man in any sense, having been commissioned on the whim of Davis. However, when charged with defending the western shores of the Mississippi, he saw the importance of Cairo early in the game, and set his eye upon that important piece of real estate. His first step was to establish fortifications to command both sides of the river immediately downstream. He cast an astute eye on the Kentucky shore, at a slight bend in the Mississippi where high bluffs rise vertically from the river.

Polk chose the town of Columbus for his heaviest concentration of guns. From those heights he could command the approaches of the river from the north. He set about constructing massive earthworks behind which he planted 142 pieces of artillery, mostly 32- and 64-pounders, plus a total of 10,000 men.

Across the river, which was 800 yards wide at this point on the Missouri shore, was a small hamlet called Belmont, surrounded by forests and a few corn fields. There he established a works containing a battery of artillery, a regiment of infantry and a squadron of cavalry, all under the command of Brigadier-General Gideon Johnson.

Polk had originally planned to occupy Paducah and Eastland, but the Union Brigadier General Ulysses S. Grant had beaten him to it; so he contented himself with strengthening his positions on the Mississippi in order to prevent Union excursions into Tennessee and Alabama.

Grant, in turn, saw these fortifications as thorns in his side. Upon orders from General Frémont, he assembled transports at Cairo, loaded them with 2,000 troops and, in the company of the timberclads *Tyler* and *Lexington*, shoved off on November 7 to push downriver on what was planned to be an occupation of the Rebel positions on the Missouri side.

The formidable timberclads sat at the bend of the river, about a half mile above Belmont and around a mile from the Columbus bastion, ready to use their 14 guns to support Grant's troops and to engage the Columbus batteries, which they did, moving in a circle to confuse the Confederate gunners. The *Tyler* received one hit in return.

Grant meanwhile landed three miles above Belmont and marched his army down in two columns. Meeting a Confederate force of equal strength, Grant's men were driving them from the field until Rebel reinforcements arrived. Then the Union men retreated, making haste back to the transports. Grant was the last man to board (and in a much-remarked show of equanimity went up the plank while riding his horse). The transports retreated upriver under covering fire from the gunboats. One Federal unit did not make it to the boats in time, however it eventually was able to walk back to Union territory.

The battle at Belmont was a tactical defeat for the Union, costing 120 killed, 383 wounded and 104 captured or missing. Still it was a satisfactory first battle for the green Union troops in what was, after all, their own initiative. Polk, like Grant, gained nothing of strategic importance and, in essence, what was to have been a battle turned out to be a big raid. The action did provide Grant and his colleagues an important lesson in the value of gunboats in supporting military movements and engagements on land, as well as ferrying troops over water.

Soon after this engagement, the Union War Department made some command changes, one of which was to profoundly affect future events in the Mississippi campaign. The overall command structure was now called the Department of Missouri and, after a long and bitter contretemps, Frémont was finally removed from command and replaced by Major General Henry Wager Halleck, a soldier-scholar whose orders were to clean up the administrative mess left by Frémont who, because of his arrogance, had alienated Grant and even President Lincoln.

Halleck, on the other hand, was a respected leader with a

high intellect. Having written three books—one on military science, the other two on mining law—he had been labeled "Old Brains" by his contemporaries. He came to his new post vowing to clean up the department itself and to vigorously pursue the coming campaigns in the Mississippi theater of action.[17] Halleck was an able administrator and organizer, although weak in actual field leadership, having served only in various departmental posts during the Mexican War. Since Halleck exercised rather extreme prudence and caution on questions of the battlefield, the Union might well have been ill-served by his command; that is, if men like Grant had not been present to act as his sword arm.

The military picture in November 1861 revealed the Confederates still in control of their river fortresses. To make matters worse, Albert Sidney Johnston was strengthening the powerful forts Henry and Donelson on the Tennessee and Cumberland rivers, respectively; thus the situation for the Union was not good. A lot of pressure was on Halleck and Grant to do something about it, with all possible haste. The Confederate grip on Kentucky had to be broken.

CHAPTER FOUR

Preliminary Clash at Fort Henry

For Albert Sidney Johnston, the Tennessee and Cumberland Rivers were key elements in keeping his Columbus/Henry/Donelson/Bowling Green line of defense intact. Both rivers flowed into the Ohio, the Tennessee after swinging through northern Alabama and the Cumberland after passing Nashville. Both streams were arteries into the heart of the Confederacy and their possession determined which side would control Kentucky and western Tennessee.

The tall, powerfully built Johnston had had a long and distinguished career that included service in the Black Hawk War in 1834 and the Mexican War in 1849. He was a Kentuckian, appointed to West Point in 1822, and was a regimental adjutant in the campaign against Black Hawk. He also briefly served as Secretary of War for the Republic of Texas. He was appointed to the rank of General in the Confederate Army in August 1861.

Among his admirers was Jefferson Davis, who appointed him the second-ranking general in the army (after Joseph Johnston, no relation). In 1861, Davis placed him in command of the Western Department, calling him "the greatest soldier, the ablest man, civil or military, Confederate or Federal, then living."[1] Davis believed that the South's best chance for survival would lie in adopting a posture of strategic defense, a view that would put him at odds with generals like Robert E. Lee, who thought they could beat Union armies in the field, and that the South's best interests would be served by actively seeking to do so. Davis' preference for holding key points, conserving strength and wearing the Union down, would be tested by Johnston's strategy in the west.

The Confederate citadels on the Tennessee and Cumberland were built where the rivers flow parallel only twelve miles apart near the Kentucky border, and were put under the overall command of Brigadier-General Floyd Tilghman. One of these forts, however, turned out to be a paper tiger, as the Federals were to prove. Fort Henry was constructed on lowland and was always in danger of being flooded—especially in February, during which it could be under two feet of water. In fact, Captain Jesse Taylor, C.S.A., who was sent to Fort Henry as an experienced "artillerist," was convinced that the location was "made with extraordinary bad judgment."[2] In recognition of Henry's vulnerability, the Confederates were also in the process of building Fort Heiman on higher ground across the river, but their plan would soon be overtaken by events.

In addition, Fort Henry had only one road in the rear, leading to Fort Donelson, and this road could have been easily cut off by an invading army. Then there was also a shortage of manpower because, in spite of pleas for reinforcements, General Johnston refused to spare any from his army at Bowling Green. Thus, Tilghman had only 5,000 men to man both sides of the Tennessee, plus a lack of heavy ordnance. Captain Taylor reported the strength of Henry to consist of six smoothbore 32-pounders, two forty-two pounders, one 128-pounder Columbiad, five 18-pound siege guns and one 6-inch rifle.[3] The fort consisted of five bastions for artillery facing the river and five bearing on the land. An abatis of fallen timbers surrounded the fort to the east, while rifle pits flanked the road to Donelson.[4]

During late January 1862, the stage was set for an assault on the forts and both combatants were steeling themselves for the first real military action of any significance in the Mississippi theater. And the Federals were building a fountainhead of power at Cairo, Illinois.

In Cairo, in late January 1862, there was a flurry of activity: dozens of steamers, nose to the shore, their tall stacks resembling a forest of barren trees, belching smoke; paddlewheels churning slowly to keep the vessels from swinging in the strong currents; receiving lines of blue-clad troops while a gunboat may have been moored to one of the wharfboats, being provisioned.

Out in the turgid Ohio, would have been the rest of the fleet, perhaps the *Carondelet* and some of her sisters *St. Louis, Cincinnati* or the huge *Benton*, Foote's flagship.

The vessels out in the stream would have been tugging at their anchors in the powerful currents, while occasional puffs of black smoke would exit their tall stacks to be whipped away by the strong winds. Around them, like so many waterbugs, would have been a smattering of small craft, coal and ammunition barges and a swarm of steam tugs. Also visible might have been the ungainly timberclads *Tyler, Lexington* and *Saratoga*. Beyond these, dim shapes would mark the presence of more auxiliary craft.

In fact, Anthony Trollope described some gunboats he had seen "close under the terminus of the railway with their flat, ugly noses against the muddy bank." He posited them to be very formidable and that they had been "got up quite irrespective of expense." The British writer went on to describe some troops he had seen as "having long hair, unkempt and many of them were drunk and mud-clogged up to their shoulders."[5]

In the town, on cluttered Ohio Street, would have been a stream of people going in and out of the brick Ohio Building, where General Grant had his headquarters. The street itself would have contained a hodgepodge of traffic: drays, military vehicles, people on horseback or on foot. If an observer was diligent, he might have caught a glimpse of the general himself dressed in fatigues and smoking the ever-present cigar. It was to be some time before Grant would order a full-dress uniform.[6] There was a war to be fought, and the general put appearance on the back burner, for the time being.

As early as January 6, Grant had petitioned General Halleck for permission to move on Forts Henry and Donelson, pointing out that they blocked the gateways into the west wing of the Confederacy. Therefore, Grant argued, if they were in Union hands, Johnston would be forced to move east and evacuate

Kentucky. Halleck refused and Grant was reported as being "very crestfallen."[7]

Finally, Grant enlisted the help of Flag Officer Foote in his petitions to Halleck. The navy commander informed the Major General that both Grant and himself were of the opinion that "Fort Henry, on the Tennessee River, can be carried with four ironclad gunboats and troops, and be permanently occupied." He also stated that it was he who first made the proposition to Grant to move on Fort Henry.[8]

Halleck reversed his position and granted permission for the assault mission, recommending "swift action." He wrote General McClellan in Washington about his decision, and informed the commanding general that a feasible plan would be to move up the two rivers, making Nashville the major objective. By so doing, Columbus would be turned, thus also forcing the abandonment of Bowling Green. He added that the attempt should not be made with less than 60,000 men.[9] In the meantime, Halleck also informed Flag Officer Foote that additional men for crews would be sent to Cairo as soon as possible.

Grant fired off a message to Halleck informing him that the assault force "will be off up the Tennessee at 6:00 P.M. Command 23 regiments in all."[10] In Paducah, troops were filing aboard hastily assembled steamers to join the force coming up from Cairo. Grant didn't have time to wait for the recommended force of 60,000.

At dawn, on February 2, 1862, Flag Officer Foote's gunboat flotilla got underway in the middle of a driving rainstorm, followed by General Grant, his officers and 15,000 troops in transports. The gunboats chosen for this expedition were *Essex*, (Foote's flagship), Commander W.D. Porter; *Carondelet*, Commander H. Walke; *St. Louis*, Lieutenant Commander L. Spaulding; *Cincinnati*, Commander R.N. Stemble; plus the timberclads *Tyler*, Lieutenant Commander William Gwin; *Lexington*, Lieutenant Commander J.W. Shirk; and *Conestoga*, Lieutenant Commander S.L. Phelps. It was a lethal package of floating firepower.[11]

The armada rendezvoused with the Paducah force and then the entire flotilla of gunboats and transports proceeded up the Tennessee River, gunboats in the van and transports following.

But preparing to attack a Rebel army is one matter; preparing for nature quite another. The unusually brutal February rainfall had raised the river to flood stage, causing a variety of troubles for the flotilla. Against them came all manner of flotsam: uprooted trees, branches, stumps, old boats, outhouses and snags of all sizes and shapes.

These encumbrances rose up on the bows and foredecks of the vessels, much to the consternation of the crews—who toiled feverishly to dislodge them—thus slowing the progress of the flotilla to the extent it had to anchor on the lee side of the river for the night.

On the following day, the fleet steamed in single column, amid even more debris and wreckage in the swollen river, until it reached its assigned anchorage at Panther Island, six miles below Fort Henry and the partially constructed Fort Heiman on the west bank.

After a hurried conference on board the *Essex* between Grant, Foote and Captain Porter, it was decided that a reconnaissance mission was needed to ascertain the enemy's artillery strength. So the bulky timberclad churned upstream to fire a few rounds and received a couple of shots in return, one of which plowed through the vessel's pantry and officer's quarters and then lodged in the steerage. The gunboat beat a hasty retreat.[12]

The incident had a profound effect upon Grant and his commanders. The shots had come from a rifled gun (the six-inch rifle), and they were extremely accurate. As a result, Grant put his troops ashore near Panther Island to march on the fort from the north; the gunboats would steam up to the fort and bombard it in an effort to provide cover for the infantry assault. Another column would move on Fort Heiman.

It was during their approach that the members of the flotilla got their first glimpse of a Confederate torpedo, later to be known as a mine, which the flooded river had torn loose from its moorings. The cylindrical device, about five feet long, featured a hinged, iron arm to which were attached two sharp prongs designed to catch in the wooden bottom of a boat and activate a firing mechanism that would detonate 70 pounds of powder—enough to sink a gunboat. Luckily for the fleet, the flood stage had swept away a good many of the devices, thus diminishing the danger.

When one of the torpedos was brought aboard the *Essex* for examination, General Grant came on board to inspect it, along with Flag Officer Foote. As a crew member took it apart, some wet powder escaped, emitting a whistling sound. All present assumed they had bought the farm, and they scattered in every direction. General Grant beat Foote up the forward ladder leading to the main deck of the gunboat. When Foote asked, "Why the haste, General?" Grant replied, "That the navy may not get ahead of us."[13]

Grant's battle plan was finalized: his army would land at a spot called "Bailey's Ferry," eight miles from the fort. General McLernand's troops would then advance to the fort, cut off any retreat eastward and then invest it. Meanwhile, General C.F. Smith would lead a force to take partially completed Fort Heiman, occupy it and plant guns to support the gunboats' bombardment.

Meanwhile, unknown to Grant, General Tilghman had read the handwriting on the wall and decided to send all but 90 of his men overland to Fort Donelson, keeping the artillery Captain Taylor and a Major Gilman to command the guns. As the gunboats advanced, the former wrote, ". . . far as the eye could see, the course of the river could be traced by the dense volumes of smoke issuing from the flotilla—indicating that the long-threatened attempt to break our lines was to be made in earnest."[14]

The gunboats were advancing on the fort in two divisions: Division One with the four ironclads, followed by the Second Division, comprising the timberclads. Because of the narrowness of the river at this point, the *Carondelet* and *St. Louis* were lashed together. This proved to be an advantage, because it allowed six bow guns to salvo in unison while presenting the boats' thickest armor toward the enemy.

As they steamed around the bend and the fort came into view, the *Cincinnati* had the honor of firing the first shot, followed by salvos from the rest of the flotilla. As Captain Taylor described it, "They [the gunboats] showed one broad sheet of flame." He then gave the order to respond with "as pretty and as simultaneous a broadside as I ever saw flash from a frigate."[15]

Relentlessly, the gunboats blazed away at the fort. The river resounded from the heavy gunfire. Shots arched into the fort, throwing debris high in the air. The small Confederate garrison, knee-deep in water as they were, fought back and shells plunged around the gunboats, some of them hitting home.

It is not difficult to reconstruct what must have gone on within the casemates of the gunboats during action. With three or more guns to the side, and the nine-foot overhead with sloping sides, it must have been cramped. The iron plating would no doubt cause heat to rise into the high 90's and, on very hot days, to over 100°. The routine would be automatic for a seasoned, well-trained crew. With six to eight men on a gun, two at the muzzle would swing into action: one man would drop a powder bag into the muzzle, and the second would ram it home with a long rammer equipped with a strip of rawhide with which to mark the depth of the rammer thrust. The first muzzle man would drop a round shot into the bore, and the second would ram it home. The chief gunner would pierce the bag through a hole in the top on the breech, using a vent pick, and insert a primer. The gun would be run out of the port, by a system of ropes and pulleys. The gunner would hook a lanyard to a flintlock-type hammer over the vent. On command to fire, he would yank the lanyard and the hammer would fall and strike the primer.

The flash would illuminate the casemate; the noise would be deafening. The gun would recoil savagely against the ropes and pulleys; billows of burnt powder smoke would boil in through the open gunports, setting eyes to watering and throats to coughing. Quickly, the gun would be run in and a crewman would swab out the bore, with a water-soaked sponge on a rammer, lest a lingering spark would ignite the next powder bag prematurely, causing much damage to those around the gun. Added to this would be hits on the armor plate from enemy shots. The resounding, heavy clanging would deafen ears, and in many cases would cause bleeding from them to add to the misery.

It would be a mechanical, numbing process, the crews in a trance-like state, automatically loading, running out, firing, running in, swabbing out and reloading. After cease-fire, sanity would return and the zombie-like gun crews would resort to some kind of normalcy; but there would be sore eyes, ringing ears and a general state of numbness—called battle shock—for some time.

The fight was fairly short, barely under two hours long. When their rifled gun was hit and two 32-pounders disabled, the Confederates struck their colors and surrendered. The power of the floating guns was too much for them.

A cutter with officers was lowered from the flagship and sent in to receive surrender terms and, because of the high water, was able to float in through the sally port. The Confederates later maintained that if the action had been delayed for forty-eight hours, the fort would have been abandoned anyway due to flooding, thus saving the Federals the effort. As for the land assault, the heavy rains had made the roads impassable, causing Grant and McLernand to come up late.

Casualties for the beleaguered Confederates were 5 killed, 11 wounded and 5 missing. But the fleet suffered, too. During the battle, the *Essex* received a hit in her boilers, killing and wounding 40 men, and Captain Porter was badly scalded by escaping steam, being blown overboard and later rescued by a seaman. The *Cincinnati* was heavily damaged with over 30 hits, as was the *Carondelet*, which also suffered 30.

The victory was a balm to a worried Lincoln administration and there must have been a huge, collective sigh of relief when word was received in Washington. Gideon Welles sent off a congratulatory letter to Flag Officer Foote, announcing that Foote's telegraphic dispatch, announcing the victory, "gave the highest satisfaction to the country."

The Secretary added that he "cordially and sincerely congratulated Foote and the officers and men under his command on these heros' achievements accomplished under extraordinary circumstances and after surmounting great and almost insuperable difficulties." The Secretary went on to say that the labor Foote and his men had performed, and the services they had rendered in creating the armed flotilla of gunboats on the western waters, and "in bringing together for effective operation the force which has already earned such renown, can never be overestimated."[16]

As soon as the battle ended, Foote ordered Lieutenant Commander Phelps to sortie up the Tennessee with the timberclads *Tyler, Conestoga* and *Lexington*, to destroy the railroad bridge of the Memphis & Ohio Railroad that crossed the bridge and terminated in Memphis. Then he was to "proceed up the river as far as the stage of water will admit and capture the enemy's gunboats and other vessels which might prove available to the enemy."[17]

Phelps did in fact come upon three Rebel steamers that were in the process of being burned by the Confederates. One of these craft, the *Samuel Orr*, was loaded with mines and cannon balls. Phelps brought his vessel to a standstill, 1,000 yards away. As he had feared, the mines exploded; not only was the gunboat damaged, but the river area for a mile around was "completely beaten up by falling fragments and a shower of shot, grape, balls, etc."[18] Phelps' cautious instinct saved him and his whole command. It was unfortunate for the Confederates to have lost so much ammunition and shells, to say nothing of precious steamers. All of this would have been welcome at Fort Donelson.

In retrospect, the most astounding fact of the Fort Henry engagement was the surrendering of a land fortification to a naval flotilla unassisted by land forces—something new in the annals of warfare. This feat would not be repeated in the Civil War, and, meantime, any doubts about the value of the crash Federal program to build a gunboat fleet in the west had been put to rest.

Three years later, in January 1865, the spectacular naval bombardment of Fort Fisher at Wilmington, North Carolina, by Admiral David Dixon Porter's 60 warships smashed open the pallisades of what was thought to be an impregnable fortress. Landing craft brought in 1,600 marines, while an army moved in from the land side. The fort was taken after it had been softened up by naval bombardment. It became a military certitude from then on that enemy forts could only be taken by ground troops supported by naval gunfire.

The elation over Fort Henry was short-lived. All Union forces, whether civilians, officers or enlisted men, came to the sobering realization that Fort Donelson, the much stronger of the two forts, on the nearby Cumberland River, was next and that it promised to be a tougher nut than Henry. With his army now in enemy territory, however, Grant was anxious to assault the fort before Rebel reinforcements came from the eastern part of the state.

Grant knew that General Halleck would disapprove until every element of the plan was in place. He sent off a wire to the effect that he was moving on the fort immediately; he then marched overland and didn't wait for an answer.[19] Halleck finally wired his approval, and promised to send reinforcements. The wire arrived at about the time Grant's army was poised in front of Fort Donelson.

CHAPTER FIVE

Striking Back at Anaconda

After the fall of Fort Henry, General Johnston wrote that the capture of that fort gave the Federals "control of the navigation on the Tennessee River, and their gunboats are now ascending . . ." He went on to predict that if Fort Donelson were to be taken, "it will open the route to the enemy to Nashville, giving them the means of breaking bridges and destroying the ferry boats on the river as far as navigable."[1]

The general's astute comments graphically illustrate the predicament the Confederacy was in at this time, not only for lack of ships to combat the Union blockade, but for river gunboats to maintain control of its own internal waterways. The rivers of the South now threatened to become highways for Federal penetration, and, rather than conduits for commerce, they would become barriers held by Union arms to prevent economic intercourse.

As usual, a lack of personnel, in addition to a lack of industrial plant and resources, was a problem for the new Confederate Navy. Most eligible personnel were already bearing arms, and army officers willing to let go of fit men in the ranks were hard to come by. In the early days of the war, what ships the Confederacy had were undermanned.

Jefferson Davis wrote that his navy was organized into two classes of vessels: first, those intended for river and harbor defense, such as as ironclads, rams, floating batteries, or river steamboats converted to gunboats; second, a group of ocean-going steamers of moderate size, including some with great speed.[2] The latter group contained the famous cruisers and blockade runners.

The manpower problem grew to such an extent that, in December 1861, Stephen Mallory wrote to General Polk at Columbus, Kentucky, requesting the furlough of troops to "assist in the construction of gunboats at Memphis." With a bit of rancor, referring to Grant's escape after the action at Belmont, he added, "One of them at Columbus would have enabled you to complete the annihilation of the enemy."[3]

At the outbreak of war the only vessels immediately available to Mallory were on the east coast. The successful building and commissioning of the *Virginia*, from the captured Union ship *Merrimac*, earned the South a spectactular ironclad gunboat, however short-lived its career. Although the Southerners had been efficient in creating strongholds at key points along their rivers, during the Civil War such citadels would no longer suffice. The stark threat of Union gunboats on western waters, plus the assaults on Belmont and Fort Henry drove home the fact that the South needed gunboats and needed them fast. Stephen Mallory commenced drawing up plans for the construction of iron vessels that would be able to fight the Union flotillas on even terms.

After discovering that the existing facilities at New Orleans were inadequate for the construction of ironclads, he established yards at nearby Jefferson City. Before long, at that facility, keels for the ironclads *Louisiana* and *Mississippi* were laid. Plans were made for a fleet of 44 vessels; however, shortages of materiel and manpower, in addition to Union encroachment of territory, would intervene.

President Davis lamented that "there was a lack of skilled labor, of ship yards, and of material for constructing ironclads, which could not be readily obtained or prepared in a beset and blockaded country . . ."[4] He complained that there was not enough iron plating, or even railroad iron, with which to plate the vessels; therefore, the Confederacy would need to rely on land batteries, torpedoes and marching forces to match the Union strength.

As he predicted, those materiel and manpower shortages

greatly hampered the Confederate cause, and the problem was exacerbated by the lack of manufacturing facilities. Except for the established Tredegar Iron Works at Richmond, there was a paucity of such plants. However, by rolling up their proverbial sleeves, the Confederates did manage to establish foundries and rolling mills in Alabama, Georgia, North Carolina, South Carolina and Florida. These ad hoc installations managed to keep the naval effort afloat for some time.[5]

Although materiel managed to find its way into the Confederate naval program, the shipyard problem was still more difficult to solve. The facilities at Algiers, across the river from New Orleans, while sufficient for building seagoing ships and fine river craft, were wholly inadequate for the construction of ironclads.

But things brightened somewhat when the industrialist brothers Asa and Nelson Tift entered the picture. The Tifts had patriotically heeded the call from Richmond and announced they would build ironclads for the budding, hard-pressed Confederate Navy. After receiving permission, they set about establishing the shipyard at Jefferson City, near New Orleans. They managed to procure lumber and arrange for the New Orleans ironworks and rolling mills to supply building materials. In order to obtain more manpower, the Tifts even dispatched a steamboat upriver to "borrow" slaves from surrounding plantations.[6]

The keels for two ironclads, *Louisiana* and *Mississippi*, were laid in October 1861, though their construction was dogged by continued shortages. Much of the inefficiency in management was caused by the Confederate military commander at New Orleans, General Mansfield Lovell, who, along with General Johnson Kelly Duncan, was unable to provide efficient leadership. The absence of clear-cut naval authority, which could have coordinated the construction, manpower and military command aspects of the effort, was a serious handicap to the South.

Later, Davis was to rue the fact that the *Mississippi*, which held such promise for the Confederate fleet was "in such unfinished condition as to be wholly unavailable when the enemy arrived."[7] This powerful gunboat—at least on paper—deserves a closer look, if only for what could have been.

The *Mississippi*, as planned, would have been 260 feet long, with a 58 foot beam and a draft of 12 feet. Her armor plate would have been 3.75 inches and her armament would have boasted 20 guns, two of them 7-inch rifles. (The rest of the guns were not specified.) She would have carried three heavy engines, with 16 boilers. Had she been completed, the *Mississippi* would have been a worthy adversary, along with her sister *Louisiana*, which was to have been a trifle larger—264 feet long with a 62-foot beam—with an armament of two 7-inch rifles and seven 32-pounders. The brothers Tift were counting on these two leviathans to enhance their reputation as shipbuilders. As fate would have it, however, numerous gaffes, shortages and confused management sank the whole project before it was completed. The gunboats would never be ready in time for the coming Union naval onslaught.

In addition to a collection of converted steamers with little or no armament, the Confederates did manage to build two vessels that would be capable of taking on the Union's upper Mississippi fleet of gunboats: the *Manassas* and the *Arkansas*. The former was a converted river towboat, *Enoch Train*, with an exceptionally strong bow. This man-of-war was constructed at Memphis and, after her bow was extended, she was fitted with a cast-iron prow. With her main deck covered with iron plate, she resembled a huge floating cigar. This ugly and ungainly vessel was destined to give the Federals a lot of headaches before her relatively short career was finished.

Other "gunboats" finally available to the Confederate river fleet included *McRae, General Beauregard, General Lovell, Little Rebel* and *General Sumter*, among others with which we will become acquainted later. None of these vessels was a match for the Union gunboats. Unfortunately, the Confederacy's river craft were simply not of the same quality as its sea-going vessels, although they did manage to hold their own for a time and to slow Union advances.

It appeared that Confederate sea vessels were not much different from their Union counterparts. For the most part they were standard side-wheel steamers altered in various ways to become fighting crafts. Unlike the river ships, the deep-sea vessels used for privateering or blockade busting, for example, were of deeper draft and had considerably more speed.

The Confederates did go far in improvising in order to make up for their lack of strength, including their invention of a workable submarine. These subs were intended to sneak up on a Union ship and stick a "torpedo" on it. The poignant history of the C.S.S. *Hunley*, in fact, ended with its destruction of the Union warship *Housatonic* on February 17, 1864, the first case of a successful submarine attack. (The *Hunley* was also destroyed in the explosion, after having previously sunk twice in training, once with its inventor on board.) Thirty feet long, five feet high and four feet wide, this vessel carried an eight-man crew and was propelled by a man-powered crankshaft running its entire length. Using ballast tanks and horizontal fins, she was able to submerge completely.

The torpedo, or what was actually a mine, as used by the Southern naval craft, was a crude but effective device. Even Davis himself commented on its effectiveness when he wrote that the system of torpedoes was more effective than any other means of naval defense. Even though the destructiveness of these devices had been known for a long time, no successful method had been found to adapt them to ironclads. He said, "It remained for the skill and ingenuity of our officers to bring the use of this terrible weapon to perfection."[8] His comments were soon to prove prophetic.

Another innovation of the Confederate States Navy was a wooden torpedo boat, 30 to 40 feet long with a six- to eight-foot beam, which also featured a torpedo spar. Although, as with their submarine, this concept would reach fruition in future conflicts, during the Civil War it was no more effective than its underwater brother.[9]

Although a shortage of manpower plagued Mallory's navy, he did manage to obtain qualified officers. In fact, 243 line officers had left the U.S. Navy to join the Southern cause and, in addition, an academy of sorts was established on board the brigantine *Patrick Henry*, based at Drewry's Bluff on the James River. This establishment turned out an impressive line of junior officers. However, in the realm of seamen, it was a different story. They were less than 4,000 strong in the Confederate fleet; the commerce raiders and blockade runners, for the most part, were manned by foreign sailors.[10] As the struggle for control of the Mississippi River continued, the Confederates worked feverishly to commission and man vessels to counter the Union threat.

The Union gunboat fleet, meanwhile, had already been tested under fire and was now eyeing a bigger prize. Fort Donelson, the vaunted Confederate bastion on the Cumberland, was being reinforced with troops and remained a key to the Rebel defense line in Tennessee. And, together, Ulysses S. Grant of the Army and Andrew H. Foote of the Navy were planning an all-out river and land assault.

CHAPTER SIX

General Buckner's Bitter Legacy

Flag Officer Foote, in his battle plan for the gunboat assault on Fort Donelson, emphasized the need for precision in their gunnery and coolness under fire to his crews. He admonished them against random firing, which would not only be a waste of ammunition, but would actually encourage the enemy when he saw "shot and shell falling harmlessly around him."[1] He then ordered the fleet of gunboats and auxiliary vessels to make preparations for a February 11 departure from Cairo.

Meanwhile Grant, camped at Fort Henry, was anxious to attack Donelson. Curiously, since his troops had not even been needed for the reduction of Henry, he reported to Halleck that he was contemplating the use of infantry and cavalry alone for the attack on Donelson. This may, however, have been a bit of bravado designed to ensure that Halleck gave him his head; at the time, he and his troops were struggling with a rapidly rising river at the captured fort.[2]

As the wheels of the military campaign began to turn slowly, Foote wired Secretary Welles that he was taking the gunboats *Louisville, Pittsburgh* and his flagship *St. Louis*, plus the timberclads *Tyler* and *Conestoga*, along with supporting craft, up the Cumberland River to cooperate with General Grant's army in the attack on Donelson. But first, the *Carondelet* was to proceed upstream to reconnoiter the enemy bastion.[3]

Enter Commander Henry Walke, U.S.N. Recently given command of the U.S.S. *Carondelet,* after captaining the gunboats *Tyler* and *Lexington,* Walke was about to take his gunboat and steer it into history as the first naval vessel up the Cumberland, and the initiator of the attack on the Confederate fortress.

Walke was a Virginian by birth, but grew up in Ohio. In 1827, he entered the navy and was promoted to lieutenant in 1839. From 1840 to 1843 he sailed around the world on the *Boston.* Then, during the Mexican War, he served on the brig *Vesuvius* and took part in naval operations under Commodore Perry. Later, in 1855, he was appointed commander, and was the skipper of the storeship *Supply* from 1858 to 1861. After Fort Sumter, he was called to the Mississippi theater of action and given command of the timberclads. Ramrod-straight, he resembled a New England farmer with his high forehead, bushy chin whiskers and aquiline nose. A talented sketcher, some of his drawings, famous for their meticulous detail, have been reproduced in many books through the years.

At 5:30 A.M., on February 10, 1862, bells clanged, bosuns pipes shrilled and the U.S.S. *Carondelet* came to life for its mission to the Southern stronghold. Having anchored off Paducah for the night, Captain Walke rose early and was in the pilothouse, ready for morning reports from his division officers. The transport steamer *Alps* was to tow the gunboat partway to Donelson, to save the warship's fuel and wear on its engines. By daybreak, *Alps* had already secured lines to the vessel's bows, and was standing by to await further orders, paddlewheels churning against the strong river current.

The crew's usual morning routines were suspended. Instead, they were kept busy removing the encumbrances of snags, twigs and assorted flotsam that had piled up on the foredeck during the night, because of the flood stage of the Cumberland. The rattle of wheels and the creaking of chocks below attested to the fact that Gunnery Officer Richard Adams was putting his crews through their paces, in preparation for the fighting ahead.[4] Also busy, but unobserved by the captain, Assistant Surgeon James McNeely was preparing his hutch for the expected casualties.

Deep in the bowels of the boat, Chief Engineer Faulkner and his two assistants, Charles H. Cavin and Augustus Crowell, were busy checking the boilers and engines in preparation for the moment when the gunboat sallied forth on her own. The stoker crews were busy feeding the boilers. In the stores compartment, located in the stern, Chief Carpenter Oliver Donelson and his crew checked the boat's supply of lumber, tools and iron plates for repairs to the hull, should these be required. Not a soul on the gunboat was idle.[5]

The orders from General Grant to Flag Officer Foote were clear: all preparations were to begin immediately. The *Alps* would tow the gunboat to within two miles of the fort, at which point *Carondelet* would anchor and await orders to coordinate its bombardment with Grant's investment of the works from the west. Upon a signal, Walke would steam his vessel a mile from the fort and open fire.[6] *Carondelet* would be alone on this mission, because the *Cincinnati* was at Cairo receiving repairs and *Mound City* and *Cairo* were reconnoitering elsewhere. That would leave *St.Louis*, *Pittsburgh* and *Louisville*, and the ungainly timberclads *Tyler* and *Conestoga* for the flag officer to bring down to join the *Carondelet* in the all-out river fight with the powerful Confederate batteries of the fort.

Commander Walke's officers were busy checking and re-checking every aspect of their divisions—particularly Gunnery Officer Adams and his ordnance crews. For getting underway bulky anchors were pulled up and then hosed down and secured in their hawsepipes. Then, as cable slack from *Alps* was taken up, the gunboat shuddered moderately while gradually moving out into midstream. The vessel throbbed as the great paddlewheels got into synchronization with those of the *Alps*.

At this time of year the river was cloaked by winter. Noisy flocks of birds fluttered up from the heavy forests rising away to the west, beyond the river's snow-clad banks. It would have been a familiar and peaceful scene were it not for the presence of the ugly gunboat on its deadly mission.

But the crew were doubtless too busy to appreciate the beauties of the area. There were endless duties to sharpen their combat readiness—even underway—as have taken place on every war vessel of the world dating back to ancient Greek triremes. Constant drilling on a vessel of war was, and is, the very essence of combat readiness, similar to field exercises in the army.

The *Carondelet* was a powerful instrument of war—cumbersome and slow, but packed with formidable firepower. Her punch lay in the armament of her three divisions. Division One, the bow battery, consisted of two 42-pound rifled guns and a 64-pounder. The Second Division, or the two broadside batteries, consisted each of two rifled 42-pounders, two 64-pounders and four 32-pounders. The Third Division, or stern battery, consisted of two 32-pound smoothbores.[7] Of all her guns, at least six could hurl shot over two miles. This impressive firepower would be sorely needed in the hours to come.

Finally, on the 12th, *Carondelet* was towed toward an eastern bank at which it anchored and tied up, awaiting orders from General Grant, whose troops were then investing Fort Donelson from the land side. At noon a yawl, containing an artillery officer, rowed out to the gunboat and delivered an order from the general for Walke to take the *Carondelet* upstream close to the fort and to commence a bombardment to cover the army's movements.[8] Shortly after that, the gunboat moved out in midstream and, with paddles thrashing and the irregular hissing and popping of the escape valves, her red bands on each funnel gleaming in the morning sun, she moved slowly toward her objective.

Below, the gun crews were moving around various color-coded racks and chests that held such needed artillery items as shot tongs, priming wires, fuse wrenches and gunlocks. The black guns, with white stripes painted down the middle of the barrels for better sighting in smoke-filled or dark compartments, were being prepared for their deadly missions. Meanwhile, those in the pilothouse would have gotten their first clear view of Donelson.

Unlike Fort Henry, situated close to the water, Donelson occupied a bluff 120 feet high on the east bank of the Cumberland. It featured artillery batteries in three layers: the lower being 25 feet above water; the second, 50 feet above and the third on the summit. The embrasures contained 15 guns in all, including a 10-inch Columbiad and ten 32-pounders.[9] Also unlike Henry, which was stripped of men just prior to its demise, Donelson had the benefit of an army of approximately 17,000 to occupy the bluff in and around the bastion. Three brigadiers, Floyd, Pillow, and Buckner commanded the Rebel forces (Tilghman had surrendered at Fort Henry), with Pillow the senior officer.

The place was an ideal fortress by location. To the north, Hickman's Creek flowed into the river, forming a natural barrier; to the south, Indian Creek did the same as it flowed a little way above the town of Dover. By now, both streams were rain-swollen and they, combined with the river, formed a natural moat around the position on three sides. Though the fort itself simply protected the artillery that commanded the river, the geographic situation on the bluff determined that the large Confederate army assigned there was part of the "fortress position"—potentially unassailable, but also fixed to that location.

Surrounding Donelson to the west and to the south around Dover, the Confederates established a line of rifle pits and a series of abatis. On first consideration, the place looked impregnable—a Southern bastion that could not be removed.

In the meantime, Grant was digging in to the west of the fort, with 15,000 men and eight batteries. He was, however, expecting 5,000 fresh reinforcements due soon on transports from downriver. On his right, he placed General McLernand's powerful division to cover the roads running south and southwest of Dover, the most likely route of an enemy break-out attempt. On his left, Grant placed C.F. Smith's division, whose left flank bordered Hickman's Creek. His center was occupied by Lew Wallace's division, he of *Ben Hur* fame. With the gunboats commanding the river, the fort was surrounded on all sides. The fight to come promised to be a bloody affair, with strength pitted against strength.

His army in place and his artillery batteries on station, General Grant took up headquarters in the Crisp house to the northwest. The next move would be up to the gunboat fleet that would cover his investment and take some of the pressure off his forces. The U.S.S. *Carondelet* was about to take center stage in this grim drama.

On February 14, Captain Henry Walke stood in the Texas (deckhouse), a spyglass planted in one eye, studying his target. He did not like what he saw. The enemy had dug holes and planted guns on the bluffs. Those gun emplacements reminded him of those "dismal-looking sepulchers cut into the rocky cliffs near Jerusalem." But they were far more "repulsive."[10]

Of course, the captain knew that those guns emplacements atop the bluff could subject his vessel to a withering, plunging fire to the foredeck and Texas, where the *Carondelet* was most vulnerable. But, danger or not, Captain Walke had his orders. After the *Carondelet* reached a wooded point, a mile downstream from the fort, Walke ordered the forward and stern anchors dropped.

His orders informed him that his boat was to deliver a demonstration, using his three bow guns. The demonstration was to have a dual purpose: determining the enemy's artillery strength, as with Fort Henry, and covering Grant's investment.

Moments later, he gave the order to up anchor, approach the fort and fire. Inside the casemate, lanyards were pulled and brilliant yellow flashes flooded the casemate, followed by billows of acrid, choking smoke. The successive concussions beat the inside of the boat, like a gigantic barrel being pummeled in anger. All who could watched as the shots arched high and plunged downward into the enemy's earthworks, sending dirt and debris skyward.[11]

At first there was no response from the fort. The *Carondelet* kept firing round after round; still no response. In all, the gunboat delivered 139 shells to the fort.[12] She crept closer and closer, as the Confederate gunners held their fire. Then the Southerners opened up, boring in on this audacious intruder with all they had. Many missed, but a 100-lb. roundshot hit her casemate, penetrated the engine room and burst a steam heater. The shell bounced around inside the ship, chasing personnel like "a wild beast pursuing its prey."[13] Several men were wounded. Later, Walke retrieved the ball and kept it as a souvenir.

Walke then ordered a withdrawal to the anchorage to unload the wounded to the *Alps,* which was now acting as a hospital ship. That accomplished, he returned and continued the bombardment throughout the afternoon. The *Carondelet* finally broke off its duel with the fort as dusk approached and returned to the anchorage with lookouts posted astern for signs of the flotilla.

Map showing the extensive Confederate positions around Fort Donelson.

Shortly after dark, a lookout reported huge clusters of lights downstream. At last Foote was arriving with the gunboats, plus transports and supply vessels. The transports nosed into the riverbanks and disgorged columns of troops and their supplies, while the gunboats paddled upstream to join the *Carondelet* at the anchorage. The big assault would shortly begin.

General Grant had ordered Foote and his flotilla to close with the fort on February 14, as near as possible and to bombard it relentlessly, in timed coordination with his land movements. Unfortunately, the width of the river did not allow the gunboats to heave to and deliver broadsides; instead, they were to steam line abreast and use their bow guns. The timberclads would follow close behind.

The General himself found a spot on the riverside for a vantage point from which to watch the bombardment.[14] Behind the fort could be heard the sullen thudding of field guns, announcing the land investment of the Confederates.

The gunboats churned forward, stacks belching huge columns of ebony smoke, relief valves popping and paddlewheels slapping hard. They moved to within one mile, then down to a matter of yards, but again the fort remained ominously silent.

At about 200 yards—pointblank range—the flagship *St. Louis* opened fire, followed by *Pittsburgh, Carondelet, Louisville* and the timberclads. The river resounded with the thunderous crashing of heavy guns, while immense cloud after cloud of gunsmoke was whisked away by the wind.[15] Heavy explosions within the fort were an indication that the works were receiving a fearful battering. Inside Donelson, a Confederate officer took similar note of the gunboat bombardment: ". . . about noon on February 14, the enemy's gunboats came up and attacked the fort and for more than an hour, the thunder of artillery deadened the air."[16]

The Confederate gunners coolly let the flotilla approach to right underneath the muzzles of their guns, and then a tumultuous barrage of cannon fire came from the fort. Shot and shell shrieked down with jarring splashes amidst the ironclads. At first, Union personnel thought the Confederates were not up to the effort. What the gunboat officers and men failed to realize was that the fort's gunners wanted the vessels in close, and were meanwhile calmly getting the range of their targets. When they finally got that range, the flotilla would pay dearly for its apparent hubris.

Hit after hit was made on the thin topside armor of the Union gunboats, and soon confidence began to give way to apprehension in the fleet. It is strange that the *Carondelet*'s previous experience had not been driven home: Not only were the boats too close to the fort, but some of their own shots were arching over the fort and landing amid Grant's men to the west.

Those in the pilothouses anxiously peered through the slits in the forward bulkhead (the slits were cut at a 45-degree angle to better deflect musket shot), intently studying the hits on the fort and in their own midst. When a shot was spotted coming toward the vessel, the crew, as previously taught, would bend from the waist down, to avoid decapitation. Unfortunately, some crewmen aboard the gunboats failed to heed the warnings and were lost.

Seeing the gunboats reeling, the Rebel gunners poured it on. The whole arena was a kaleidoscope of blinding flashes, the ear-splitting thunder of bursting shells, the thuds of heavy shot slamming into the water, the sharp clang of cannon balls hitting armor and the eerie whistle of the rifled conical shells from the enemy. Billowing clouds of blue-gray smoke hung over the fleet, temporarily blotting out sight before the wind whisked them away.

Damage to the fleet was extensive. The *St. Louis* took a hit in her Texas that killed the helmsman and wounded Flag Officer Foote. *Louisville* was next, her tiller ropes shot away, dropping her out of the fight. *Pittsburgh* got her share too: two hits in the bow, one of which thudded through coal bags piled around her vitals, scattering coal, fracturing pipes, crashing through bulkheads and wounding crewmen. Her tiller ropes shot away, her steering gone, her wheelhouse shattered, and with her hull badly damaged, *Pittsburgh* dropped downstream, out of control, toward *Carondelet*, which was nursing her own wounds from two 128-pound shots and some from the timberclads whose shells fell short, spraying the ironclads ahead.

Adding to the *Carondelet's* problem was the explosion of a gun in its First Division. The nervous loader must have failed to tamp a charge deep within the thicker breech of the gun, where exploding charges would be safely contained. The barrel burst in three pieces and wounded a dozen men. About the same time, an enemy shell struck the anchor, shattered it to pieces, ripped off the flagstaff on the bow and part of one stack. The same ball slammed into a boat davit, which splintered and dropped its lifeboat into the water. Still another ball sheared off pieces of the starboard casing, as if it were bark on a tree, laying open a huge gash in the side. Captain Walke, nevertheless, stuck to his guns and continued firing at the fort, creating a bank of smoke behind which the flotilla retreated. Meanwhile, the *St. Louis* took hits that shattered her boats and sliced off one stack.

Just then a ball hit *Carondelet's* pilothouse, mortally wounding helmsman Billy Hinton and knocking Walke to the deck, momentarily unconscious. When the commander got to his feet it was only in time to face a new danger: the *Pittsburgh* was bearing down, straight for them. The out-of-control gunboat struck the *Carondelet* hard, knocking off the rudder and spinning the vessel around. Then the *Pittsburgh* dropped astern, leaving *Carondelet* alone in the arena.

The Confederate gunners had spotted the red-striped stacks of their nemesis from the day before and, noting she was in real trouble, now poured out a torrent of fire on Walke's hapless gunboat. Her remaining stack was riddled, more plating stripped away and the bow struck repeatedly, as the Rebels tried to "skipshot" balls into her exposed waterline.[17] Now alone, the *Carondelet* was taking a fearsome beating at the hands of the fort's gunners. Covering the retreating fleet, however, she kept up a determined fire even as she finally retired downstream.

The Confederates were elated to see the once formidable flotilla—including the hated *Carondelet*—battered, seemingly out of control and in full retreat. Foote later estimated that the enemy must have brought up 20 heavy guns to bear upon his fleet.[18]

If the Union fleet had become slightly cocksure after its triumph at Fort Henry, it had by now gained a healthy respect for the enemy's resolve and his gunnery. But instead of skulking and licking his wounds, Foote sent *St. Louis*, minus one funnel, and *Louisville*, with her tiller repaired, back to the arena the next day to demonstrate to the Confederates that, in spite of the punishment they took, the Union gunboats were still ready to fight.

The toll for the flotilla: *Carondelet*, 36 hits from 32- to 128-pounders, including an eight-inch shell from the timberclad *Tyler*, plus four killed and 30 wounded; *Pittsburgh*, 32 hits and two wounded; *St. Louis*, 59 shots and two wounded, including Commander Foote; *Louisville* had her rudder shot off, with four killed and five wounded.[19] The timberclads sustained no damage. Meanwhile, the wounded flag officer was transferred to the *Conestoga* for medical treatment.

General Pillow sent a message to President Jefferson Davis to the effect that the fort had won a major victory over the Federals. The

feared Union ironclad fleet had been beaten off, and the defenders had suffered little in the process. In fact, a spate of bad luck
had hit them early in the fight. A six-inch rifle burst, killing three
Confederate crewmen and wounding seven. Then a priming wire
jammed in the vent of one of the Columbiads, putting that piece
out of the fight. Finally, the explosion of a 42-pounder during
reloading killed three men. In any case, though it had become
apparent Fort Donelson would not fall to the gunboat flotilla,
Grant's steadily growing army had now sealed in the works on
land.

The ground action heated up, as skirmishers and batteries on
both sides exchanged a more or less continuous fire. A fierce
attack by three Illinois regiments on the Confederate right was
beaten back with heavy losses. A Major Spencer wrote that his
Rebel troops slept on their guns in the snow and sleet and that the
enemy's artillery was well handled. In fact, one Union shell "tore
up the ground around us and cut off saplings and limbs around
and above us, killing some of our horses and knocking the end of
a caisson off."[20]

The obvious determination of the Union forces, plus the fact
that they, unlike the Rebels, were gaining strength, prompted generals Pillow, Buckner and Floyd to decide that the fort would have
to be abandoned. There was no escape by the river, because of
the gunboats. The road to Charlotte, however, running east of the
town of Dover, would be a good route through which to evacuate.
The only problem was that General McLernand's division stood
in the way. The Confederates decided to launch a major attack
against this Union right flank and roll it back, opening a route for
withdrawal.

On the 15th, Grant received a note from Flag Officer Foote
asking for a conference on board the *St. Louis* about the disposi-
tion of the gunboats. When the general arrived at the river, a boat
was waiting to take him midstream to the anchored flagship.
There, Foote requested permission to take the damaged gunboats
to Mound City.

Foote also inquired whether the general would be willing to
lay siege meanwhile. Grant's aim had been to attack Fort Donelson and defeat the Confederate forces there, not necessarily to

camp his army in midwinter in an investment of the works. Grant saw the necessity of such a move by the gunboats, but was not sure about the siege.[21]

The Confederates, in any case, furnished their own answer. No sooner had Grant landed back on shore when an officer rode up to inform him of a heavy attack on the right by Pillow and 8,000 men who had broken through the Union line. Confederate cavalry, under Colonel Nathan B. Forrest, had ridden through the gap and were threatening to get behind the Yankee front. McLernand's division had been pushed aside, many of his men having run out of ammunition and some fleeing in disorder. For Grant, the battle was both a crisis and an opportunity.

The Federal troops had been badly bloodied, but the enemy was not yet pouring out of Donelson to escape. General Floyd suddenly became indecisive and, besides, the Rebel troops were exhausted.[22] Pillow on the other hand sensed that he had won a great victory and enlisted Buckner's brigade to help exploit his success. At this point, Grant could well have concentrated on reconstructing his shattered right flank and reorganizing his line. Instead, however, he ordered immediate counterattacks. Lew Wallace's division would attempt to retake the Federal right. Meanwhile, on the left, General C.F. Smith had been demonstrating against Confederates on his front while husbanding his force in anticipation of orders. Now Grant ordered him to attack the Rebel right.

Charles Ferguson Smith was one of the most capable officers under Grant's command. He had distinguished himself in the Mexican War and had won three brevets. The commanding general, Grant, was himself junior in rank to Smith and in fact had been a student of his at West Point. But Smith accepted his position and, as far as is known, never complained about his lot.

The old general (albeit after perhaps one of the least inspirational exhortations to attacking troops on record: "You are only damned volunteers . . . you came to be killed and now you can be.") led the charge into the Confederate right flank and straight into the face of withering fire, his white mustache flowing over his shoulders, serving as a sort of rallying point for his men. The Confederate right was protected by thick abatis; however, it had been denuded of troops for Pillow's thrust, and the Union attack succeeded.

When Smith stopped he was strategically ensconced on the fort's right, and the hard-fought escape route for the Confederates had meanwhile been closed by fresh Union troops. The Rebels' best shot had been fought back and the situation for them was now more critical than before. That night a strange conference took place at a two-storied tavern in Dover, between generals Floyd, Buckner and Pillow. That the fort should be surrendered, there was no doubt. They had already received word that General Hardee had evacuated his troops from Bowling Green to Nashville; there would be no relief from that sector.

But who would do the surrendering? Pillow, the senior officer, demurred, citing that he was wanted for embezzling in Washington; Floyd, also with skeletons in his closet, refused; so the lot fell on the unfortunate Buckner. Nathan Forrest would have none of it and announced he would take his command out that night. Pillow, commandeering all the river transport available at Dover, embarked with 1,500 men. According to Major Selden Spencer, who was present at the conference, Pillow "sneaked up the river, and his insufferable conceit has probably not allowed him to comprehend that he is totally incapable to command a brigade. . . ."[23]

General Buckner sat down and penned the document of surrender terms, asking for a commission to be appointed by Grant to agree on the terms. Then he called for a courier to take the document through the lines to General Grant, who at this point was at a farmhouse to the north of the battle zone.

The next morning, General Smith brought Buckner's dispatch to Grant, saying, "Here's something for you to read, General." After reading it, Grant handed it back to Smith. "What answer shall I give, General?" He waited until the imposing Smith obtained a drink from a flask in order to shake out the chill of the morning. Smith then barked his reply: "No terms to the damned Rebels."

Grant chuckled, grabbed pen and paper and wrote out a message which he read to the crusty old warrior: "Yours of this date, proposing armistice and appointment of commissioners to settle terms of capitulation, is just received. No terms except an unconditional surrender can be accepted. I propose to move immediately on your works. I am, Sir, very respectfully your obedient servant, U.S. Grant, Brigadier General." Smith grunted, then remarked, "It's the same thing in smoother words."[24] Thus was penned what was to become one of the most famous dispatches in U.S. military history.

Fort Donelson was surrendered on February 16, 1862. The magnitude of the "bag" seemed overwhelming to some. Among the first Union troops to enter the fort was a private, Jonathan Blair, who wrote his wife that after the surrender he and his men took 25,000 prisoners, a stand of arms, "a great many cannons with 30 cavalry horses and wagons and estimated contraband [that] was worth $300,000 of property." According to his (high) estimate, over 2,000 enemy troops had been killed.[25]

After the surrender, Grant paid a visit to Flag Officer Foote on the *Alps*, and found the wounded commander in bed, nursing his leg. He informed Foote about the unconditional surrender and how General Buckner accused him of being ungenerous and unchivalrous. Foote informed him that the *Carondelet* and *Pittsburgh* would be sent to Cairo for repairs and the rest of the flotilla would steam up to Dover to await further orders. Grant then sent gunboats up the river to destroy the bridge of the Memphis and Ohio Railroad at Clarksville, where the Confederates had a garrison. Soon after, Foote and one of Grant's staff boarded the gunboat *Tyler* and, along with the *Cairo*, proceeded up the Cumberland, where they found the Confederate works abandoned and a populace eager to please the victorious Yankees.[26] The *Carondelet* had lobbed more shells into Fort Donelson than any of her sisters, and had been struck 54 times. Now she was to go home for badly needed repairs and for further excursions into history.

Slowly, painfully, *Carondelet* slipped into the turgid waters of the Ohio and made her way to Cairo, reaching the town on the 17th in a pea-soup fog so thick it caused her to steam past the city unnoticed. There was a moment of panic when she turned back and blew her whistle to call the attention of the naval base. The populace, after hearing rumors that a Confederate army was approaching Cairo, thought the *Carondelet* to be an enemy gunboat, and took alarm. When she finally docked, there was relief and jubilation over the great victory at Fort Donelson.[27]

Meanwhile, Grant penned a note to General Halleck in St. Louis: "We have taken Fort Donelson and from 12,000 to 15,000 prisoners, including generals Buckner and Bushrod Jackson; also 20,000 stands of arms, 48 pieces of artillery, 17 heavy guns, from 2,000 to 4,000 horses and large quantities of commissary stores."[28] (These figures might be given precedent over Private Blair's, quoted above.)

Grant's army had suffered over 2,800 casualties in the battle for the fort, the Confederates somewhat fewer not counting the huge prisoner windfall. Some 4,000 Confederates had gotten out prior to the surrender. Aside from the 1,500 men who left with Floyd and Pillow, over 1,100 sick and wounded had been evacuated just prior to the investment. Forrest's cavalrymen, some 700 strong, found an icy backwater near the river and were able to wade through, followed by hundreds of other Rebels, singly and in small groups, who were not yet ready to give up the fight.

The fall of Fort Donelson rolled like a thunderclap across the Union. President Lincoln wired his congratulations to Halleck, although he expressed concern that General Grant would be overwhelmed from outside and that "fear would require all vigilance, energy and skill of yourself and Buell acting in full coordination."[29]

An Illinois farmer wrote in his journal that news of the victory was "flying with lightning speed over the land." He related how the citizens of Springfield procured a battery of 10 guns from the arsenal and offered "the grandest salute ever fired in the state."[30]

In the South there was gloom. The carefully planned Columbus/Donelson/Bowling Green line was broken and Confederate forces had fallen back on Nashville where they argued the merits of making a stand against the hordes of Yankees, plus the accursed gunboats that were rumored to be closing in on the city. Rumors were rampant that the city would soon be shelled into submission. Therefore, the troops of General Hardee and Colonel Forrest (who had turned up in that city) looted all civilian and military stores, some under protection of the bayonets of troops to keep angry citizens at bay. The goods were shipped south, and the Rebel army moved to take up positions at Murfreesboro. On February 25, Union General Don Carlos Buell's troops entered and occupied the abandoned city of Nashville. The chain reaction thus begun would eventually result in the withdrawal of all Confederate forces from western Tennessee.

This was the first major Union victory of the war and it was unique in that it "swallowed a Confederate army entirely."[31] The victory also put Kentucky firmly in the Union camp and it gave Grant a foothold in Tennessee, allowing his armies to go forward 200 miles into enemy territory.[32] President Lincoln was so elated over the victory that he promoted Grant to the rank of Major General of Volunteers.[33]

In a sense, the victories of Forts Henry and Donelson were a coming-out party for Foote's gunboats. Although they did not shatter the myth that a ship is no match for shore-based batteries with big guns, and even though the flotilla took a thorough beating at Donelson, they did, nevertheless, soften the defenses considerably. General Johnston told his superiors in Richmond that "the best open earthworks are not reliable to meet successfully a vigorous attack by gunboats."[34]

The victories were to make Grant a national hero overnight. The term "unconditional surrender" was forever attached to his two initials, "U.S." Not being one to rest on his laurels, he wired Halleck about his success at Fort Donelson and suggested that, inasmuch as the way to Clarksville and Nashville was open, he should move at once on these objectives.[35] Soon after, Clarksville was evacuated and Union troops occupied Nashville, forcing the Confederates further south.

The consternation felt in Richmond was graphically expressed by President Davis, who wrote that the loss of Forts Henry and Donelson "had opened the river routes to Nashville and North Alabama" and thus "turned the military positions at Bowling Green and Columbus and had subjected General Johnston to severe criticism." In the South, he declared, the public press was "loaded with abuse and the government was denounced for entrusting the public safety to hands so feeble."[36] Secretary Mallory, who had been working tirelessly to create some sort of navy from scratch, came under fire because "the Confederacy was wretchedly helpless in the water."[37]

Though it is impossible to put a good face on the Fort Donelson debacle from the Confederate point of view, the disaster may have seemed larger during that first year of the war than it does in retrospect. After all, in battles to come the Confederates would lose more men in some of their victories than they lost on the Cumberland. And the attempt to invest so heavily in a line near the Kentucky border might have been ill-advised from the start. Strategically, moreover, the battle held grave implications for the path the Confederacy would follow: the concept of defending fixed points to wear down Yankee attackers had been called into question, and the better method now seemed the alternative idea of a flexible defense that included offensive operations. This was a strategy that in fact would play to two of the Confederacy's major strengths: men named Lee and Jackson. To leave the initiative with the Union, particularly with the mobile firepower they could call upon from their gunboats, seemed a recipe for further disasters.

In any case, although Fort Donelson was a bitter pill to swallow for the Confederacy in February 1862, it would be less than two months before the tables would be turned. Then, it would be Grant's army with its back to a river, and in between two streams. And it would be the Confederate army bearing down, around a small church called Shiloh.

Meanwhile, back on the Mississippi, the stronghold of Columbus had been evacuated and its troops pulled down to Fort Pillow, some 80 miles downriver. By this time, the Confederates had given up all hope of cementing Kentucky or even holding most of Tennessee west of its eastern mountains, and their hopes were pinned to maintaining their second defensive line, extending from Memphis, Corinth and Huntsville to Chattanooga.

It was to be a last-ditch stand for the Confederates' Tennessee/Missouri/Arkansas sector of the river. However, General Johnston did order reinforcements to beef up defenses on Island No.10, upstream from New Madrid. This island fortress stood firmly in the way of Federal river traffic to points south. It was heavily fortified with guns, men and materiel, plus a floating battery had been brought upriver and anchored at the island's southern end.

The island had sealed off all approaches to New Madrid and henceforth to Memphis and southward down the Mississippi. The island was unapproachable by land, because of swamps and a large lake to the east and a line of heavy batteries to the north. Somehow the island had to be bypassed. That could only be done via the river and, as expected, the task was to fall to the lot of Flag Officer Foote and his gunboats.

CHAPTER SEVEN

Calm Before the Storm

The day after the fall of Fort Donelson, Foote's gunboats churned up the Cumberland and destroyed the Tennessee Iron Works above Dover, thereby denying the Southerners the use of one of their few sources of iron products. On February 19th, the vessels discovered a deserted fort at Clarksville, on the Cumberland, which the Confederates had used as a stronghold and supply base. For the rest of the month gunboat movements consisted mainly of reconnaissance forays on the Mississippi, Cumberland and Tennessee rivers while the Rebel armies retreated to the east and south.

The Rebels had first fallen back on Nashville, however Union General Don Carlos Buell was headed there from his base at Louisville so Nashville was abandoned. The Southerners shifted to Murfreesboro, taking with them tons of ammunition, stores and materiel; other units fell back on Corinth.

General Grant was later to write that the Union made a mistake, soon after Donelson, by not taking the huge army at hand and marching on Chattanooga, Corinth, Memphis and Vicksburg. Because of the great influx of volunteers in the North, plenty of reserves would be available.[1] However, much of the blame lay at Halleck's doorstep for not realizing the strategic possibilities that lay before him. He was turning out to be an extremely cautious general and prone to wait until every piece of the puzzle was in place before moving. A Napoleon would have seized upon the strategic initiative granted him by the huge victory, but, as the English General Marshall-Cornwall wrote: "Halleck was no Napoleon."[2] At the same time it should be noted, and despite his self-image, neither was Halleck's counterpart in the east, George McClellan, who was still in the midst of his grandiose preparations for an assault on the peninsula near Richmond.

On February 23, Foote brought his ironclads and two mortar boats down the Mississippi to reconnoiter the Confederate stronghold at Columbus, which Halleck thought was still heavily fortified. In fact, the Confederates were pulling out, although, to the river observers, the works looked "formidable as ever."[3] For their part, the Confederates still present hurled a few shots at the flotilla, to inform the Yanks that they were alive and well and to give the impression that their works would not be surrendered without terrible cost.

Then, in a clever ploy, the Confederates sent a white-flagged steamer out to the flotilla under the pretext of asking for a conference on an exchange of prisoners. Meanwhile, they finished loading steamers, rafts and barges with materiel and sailed down the river to the safety of Island No.10 and New Madrid. The flotilla was deceived, and repercussions came fast in the Union ranks; remonstrations were made for complying with the enemy's false flag of truce.[4]

However, river actions continued. On February 25, troops were loaded on seven transports and, under escort of the *Cairo*, plowed their way up the Cumberland, landed and occupied Nashville. The effective use of gunboats was by now fully recognized in both Washington and Richmond. Plans were drawn in both capitals for more of these highly effective fighting machines. Their usefulness was vividly portrayed in a Nashville newspaper that had declared, "We have nothing to fear from a land attack, but the gunboats are the devil."[5]

A dawning March 1 found the gunboats *Tyler* and *Lexington* up the Tennessee River, supporting a landing party of sailors and sharpshooting troopers on a mission to reconnoiter Confederate strength in that area. This mission cost the lives of several men, and it was the first instance in this war in which sailors lost their lives fighting on land.

As a result, Flag Officer Foote promptly issued an order forbidding any excursions on land by navy personnel, stating that it was the job of the army to do land fighting and that sailors were needed to man the guns on their floating "forts."[6] Foote telegraphed Washington for funds to fit up the uncompleted gunboat *Eastport*, captured on February 7, because she was a fast ship. He maintained—and events would prove him correct—that the 280-foot, 510-ton vessel would be a real asset to the Union

The majority of the gunboat fleet was still on the Mississippi, where the Confederate strongholds of Island No. 10 and New Madrid were virtual bones in the throats of Union commanders. These strongholds were under the command of General Pierre Gustave Beauregard, a veteran of the Mexican War, a former superintendent of West Point (for one week in January 1861), and a hero at the first Battle of Bull Run. Despite Northern incursions into Tennessee, it was Beauregard's intent to continue to block the Mississippi River as far north as possible against Federal incursion. His commands, fortified by troops from Columbus, were entrenched, heavily armed and ready for a fight. He sent for some river craft and on March 5 dispatched a gunboat upriver to reconnoiter. This craft, the *Grampus*, a 252-foot sternwheeler which Union Commander Walke later described as the "sauciest little vessel on the river,"[7] suddenly confronted Foote's gunboats in mid-stream. At first she struck her colors and hove to, as if to surrender. The commanders of the Union flotilla, however, seemed paralyzed, not knowing what to make of the encounter.

When the captain of the *Grampus* saw the sluggish reaction of the fleet before him, and presumably after having assessed its strength, he ordered a reversal of course; the gunboat dashed off, blowing her whistle, alarming the Confederates of the Union fleet's approach.

The Federals discovered, much to their chagrin, that the enemy had constructed a chain of forts on the bluffs above Island No. 10, and had heavily fortified the island itself so that its guns commanded the river from every direction. Foote hurried back to Cairo and related his findings. However, the flag officer insisted that his gunboat charges were unable to assault Island No. 10 and New Madrid because they had been seriously damaged in the struggle for Fort Donelson and needed immediate repairs. He therefore ordered around-the-clock repair work on pilot houses, hulls and machinery. He also admonished Washington about the advisability of building boats with wheels amidships, because driftwood tended to clog them, despite their powerful engines.[8]

In the meantime, Union General John Pope, operating in Missouri, had plans of his own; New Madrid was his fixation. This fort was surrounded by bayous and swamps with only a few roads leading in, all of which were covered by Rebel guns. He planned to take 20,000 men, march along Sisketon Ridge, take the town and then move south to establish a stronghold 12 miles downriver. Pope also thought that if a gunboat or two could slip by Island No. 10 they could cover his crossing of the river to the vicinity of Tiptonville, 12 miles south of the island. His troops could then march north, invest the island and force its surrender.

The handsome General Pope, with a wide face and full-flowing beard, was a strong personality and no novice at war. He graduated from West Point in 1842 and had served bravely in the Mexican War, during which he earned two brevets. He became a brigadier-general in June 1861. An outspoken man, he voiced his opinions to Generals Halleck, Grant and Flag Officer Foote about the problems of New Madrid and Island No. 10. Eliminating these bastions would clear the Mississippi all the way down to Memphis, and at the same time pinch off large Confederate forces (10,000 at New Madrid along with 50 guns).

But as the Union men planned their next move, on March 9, 1862, an incredible battle was taking place in the east, off Hampton Roads, Virginia. This clash would echo not only in the west, but around the world.

When Virginians, after their seccession from the Union, occupied the Norfolk Navy Yard, they discovered the steam frigate *Merrimac* with its lower hull and works intact, and the decision was made to convert her into an ironclad. The man picked to rebuild her was one Lieutenant John Brooke, C.S.N., a former Chief of Ordnance and Hydrography in the U.S. Navy, and the inventor of the Brooke cannon widely used by the South throughout the war. His finished work resembled a barn roof on a raft and she sported a flat keel, a light-draft screw propeller, case-mated battery and inclined iron-plated sides and ends. The hull extended beyond the shield, and the revolutionary warship was designed to operate in shallow-water harbors.

When finished, the (renamed) *Virginia* was 236 feet long with 4-inch wrought-iron plating on her sides which had a 35-degree slope. When underway, her fore and aft decks were awash so that only her enclosed deck was visible. Her armament consisted of six 9-inch Dahlgren smoothbores and four rifled guns of 6- and 7-inch bores each. A four-foot iron prow was fitted on the bow so that she would be able to ram. Her two 600-horsepower, back-acting engines were designed to push her along at nine knots, although her bulk and weight allowed only four.

The *Virginia* was commissioned on March 5, 1862, and on the 8th she steamed into Hampton Roads to attack strong elements of the Union fleet that were congregated at the mouth of the James River. She first approached the 36-gun sloop *Congress* and proceeded to simply pound her beneath the waves, the Union gunners' response seemingly having no effect. Then she faced off against the *Cumberland* and battered her into a fiery wreck, inflicting 200 casualties. A request for the Federal ship's surrender was refused; instead the *Virginia* hammered her into a charnel house. The proud steam-frigate *Minnesota* came on the scene and was maneuvered aground; however, by this time it was getting late and the *Virginia* retired, intending to return in the morning to finish off the *Minnesota*.

News of the carnage inflicted by the Rebel warship spread like a flash through the Union Navy and high command. Gideon Welles, from his office in Washington, D.C., kept looking out his window for fear that the juggernaut would come churning up the Potomac. Of course he was in a position to know that the Union had an answer to the *Virginia* which was even then en route. In fact, even as the Rebel ironclad was retiring for the night, the new ship had arrived on the scene at Hampton Roads: an even stranger-looking vessel than the *Virginia*, called the *Monitor*.[9]

The *Monitor* was a radically new concept conceived by the Swedish engineer John Ericksson, and was later derisively tagged "Ericksson's Folly" and a "Cheesebox on a Raft." The ironclad, as built, was 175 feet long, 41 feet wide with a displacement of 1,000 tons. She had a flat hull with very little freeboard, and in the center of this "raft" was a spindle-type, revolving turret with 8-inch plating. Armament consisted of two 11-inch, smoothbore Dahlgrens, and her two Ericksson, vibrating-lever engines drove her at nine knots.

When the *Virginia* returned to Hampton Roads on the morning of March 9, it became clear that Confederate naval supremacy in the Civil War had lasted only one day. The North's "wonder weapon" had arrived and was now standing guard over the helpless *Minnesota*. *Virginia*'s captain, Franklin Buchanan, nevertheless gave it his best effort as the two ironclads dueled for four hours, neither ship able to sink, or even seriously damage, the other. It would only be the advent of ironclad ships that would give rise to the next step in military innovation: the armor-piercing shell.

In any case, the *Monitor*—which had barely been able to make the trip down from New York—would eventually flounder while trying to get to Charleston. The *Virginia* would be scuttled by its crew to keep her from falling into the hands of advancing Federal troops.

But the first battle between ironclad ships heralded an entirely new stage in the evolution of naval warfare. Alone, either ship could have destroyed any enemy vessel in the area, with the exception of each other. As some historians have concluded, both vessels were victorious in their battle—which was called a draw—in that together they doomed the venerable old, wooden man-of-war. The development of the *Virginia* also signaled that the Confederate Navy was capable of creating vessels that would be a match for any others afloat. The epic battle between the *Monitor* and the *Virginia* (or the *Merrimac*, as she is more commonly known) foreshadowed the gunboat struggles yet to come on the Mississippi.

In the west, Flag Officer Foote and General Grant had already recognized that the day of new water-fighting craft had dawned. Their flotilla had proven its mettle, and was about to be put to a greater test: the pounding into submission of a powerful, heavily fortified island. Fort Henry had already been shown the power of the gunboats. And at Fort Donelson Grant and others gave the gunboats much credit for the final victory, in spite of the beating they took in the process.[10] Everyone was looking to the gunboats for greater victories.

Cooler heads prevailed in the fleet. Foote, Captain Walke and the ironclad skippers all knew from experience that attacking a fort from the river, or any body of water for that matter, was risky because of danger from plunging fire, as shown at Donelson when they ventured too close to the Confederate gunners above. Military men agreed that the ironclads should have been built with heavier armor topside but, hindsight being as it is, it was too late to drydock and refit them. It was hoped that gunboats of the future would be so constructed.

At Island No.10 the batteries were at water level, as were the batteries on the surrounding Tennessee shores. Surely this could be a job for the gunboats, if they could withstand the return fire. The stark, cold fact was that before General Pope could control the river below New Madrid, the one big obstacle in the way was Island No. 10. The Confederates had to be dislodged.

1. Birthplaces of the "city" ironclads—above, the Eads shipyard at Carondelet, Missouri.

2. The soggy naval yard at Mound City, Illinois.

3. The Western Gunboat Flotilla anchored off Mound City early in 1862.

4. Union gunboats *St. Louis*, *Cincinnati* and *Mound City* at anchor off Cairo Naval Station.

5. A gun exploding in *Carondelet*'s casemate at Fort Donelson, as illustrated by Rear Admiral Henry Walke.

6. The most famous ironclad in the western fleet, *Carondelet* is shown here in a contemporary photograph in between exploits.

7. The gunboats attacking Fort Donelson on the Cumberland River. The Confederate gunners more than held their own against the ironclads, but the fall of Donelson nevertheless marked the first major Union victory of the war.

8. The Union "timberclads" *Tyler* and *Conestoga* bombard Confederate positions at Shiloh while in the background transports bring up Union reinforcements.

9. Flag Officer Andrew H. Foote, U.S.N., was the Western Gunboat Flotilla's first battle commander. He eventually succumbed to a wound received at Fort Donelson.

10. The ironclad *Essex* was completed in January 1862, just after the "city" gunboats.

11. The U.S.S. *Baron de Kalb* (originally named *St. Louis*) eventually fell victim to Confederate mines in the Yazoo.

12. Commander Charles H. Davis, U.S.N., took over the Western Gunboat Flotilla at the "siege" of Fort Pillow.

13. Union gunboats and mortar boats bombarding Island No. 10.

14. *Carondelet* and *Pittsburgh* rampaging against Rebel shore batteries below New Madrid.

15. The battle of Plum Point, where the Confederate River Defense Fleet sunk two Union ironclads.

16. The Union gunboats approach the Rebel fleet at Memphis, determined to avenge Plum Point.

17. *General Bragg,* the first Confederate vessel to hit *Cincinnati* at Plum Point.

18. *General Price* also rammed the Union ironclad, before a shot from *Carondelet* disabled her.

19. The demise of the Confederate River Defense Fleet at Memphis.

20. A panoramic view of the action at Plum Point, described by Henry Walke as "the first purely naval action of the war."

21. A bird's-eye view of Farragut passing the protective forts of New Orleans. Note the odd-looking Rebel ironclad ram *Manassas*, toward the lower right, roaming the battle area for targets.

22. The Union steamer *Mississippi* bearing down on the *Manassas*.

23. The unfinished Confederate ironclad *Louisiana* explodes.

24. *Manassas* taking on the *Brooklyn* at New Orleans.

25. *Governor Moore* fires through her own bow to get at the Yankee ship *Varuna*.

26. One of Porter's mortar schooners in action against Fort Jackson.

27. On the deck of a mortar schooner. These weapons could lob projectiles three miles, however Farragut eventually chose to take on the New Orleans forts directly.

28. Farragut's flagship the *Hartford.*

29. Farragut on the deck of the *Hartford.*

CHAPTER EIGHT

Genesis of
Island Hopping

On March 14, 1862, during a high flood stage on the Mississippi, Flag Officer Foote, in his flagship *Benton*, cast off and led a flotilla of the gunboats *St. Louis, Cincinnati, Pittsburgh, Mound City* and *Carondelet*, with 11 mortar boats in tow,[1] down the Mississippi, plumes of black smoke billowing from their tall stacks and heavy paddlewheels thrashing the turgid waters. The assault on Island No. 10 was about to begin.

Earlier, Pope had occupied Missouri's New Madrid, which commanded the river at the hairpin turn where it flowed northward for a spell after rounding the bend containing Island No. 10. (The island, though upriver from the town, was actually geographically south of it.) Enduring the Union siege for eight days, the harried Confederates at New Madrid finally melted into the night of March 11th, leaving behind a huge amount of supplies and materiel. Pope moved in and immediately set about establishing gun positions covering both approaches from the river.[2]

Island No. 10 was an elongated, egg-shaped piece of real estate, a little over two miles in length and about a mile wide. It commanded the river from the north and south and was so named because it was the tenth island down from Cairo. The Confederates had fortified it with 6,000 troops, 123 heavy guns and 35 field pieces. Though it would seem, in view of the Union victories in Tennessee, that Island No. 10 was too far north to be strategically viable in the Confederate scheme of defense, the fact was that the island was simply too good a blockage point—the Yankees weren't going anywhere on the Mississippi as long as the Rebels held there. More batteries had been established behind the island and above it, on the Tennessee shore. (Today the island no longer exists because the river has washed it away.)

On the 15th, Foote's powerful flotilla stopped at Columbus to pick up troops, then proceeded downriver to a position just around the bend, above the island and opposite Island No. 9. There, the mortar boats were moored to the shore, the gunboats anchored in the river. All awaited an appraisal of the situation by the top brass and the expected order to attack.

Finally, the mortar boats were ordered to open fire on the island, but their shells merely splashed in the mud, much to the delight of the Confederates.[3]

Besides his physical discomfort—his leg wound from Fort Donelson was still bothering him and he was dependent on crutches—Foote was faced with a new dilemma. The river was at flood stage, with a strong current. At Forts Henry and Donelson, he was headed upstream, against the current, so in case of crippling damage his vessels would drift downstream and out of harm's way. But here the situation was reversed; he was going downstream with the current, and that meant a disabled vessel would float down under the guns of the enemy. It was a perplexing problem, so he decided to move cautiously.

On the 17th, he gave the order to attack. In view of the strong current, he had his flagship *Benton* lashed between *St. Louis* and *Cincinnati*.[4] This combination offered a potential for ten-gun salvos from the bow—four from *Benton* and three each from the others. This floating juggernaut was to steam on the east bank of the river and the rest of the craft off the west bank, giving the flotilla a line abreast on both sides. However, just before the order to fire was given, *Pittsburgh* also moved to the east side.

At a little under 2,000 yards, the gunboats opened fire; the fort answered back. The river and surrounding area reverberated from the thunderous duel of over a 100 Yankee and Rebel heavy guns. In the flotilla all was bedlam with white geysers shooting up around and among the vessels, as the enemy probed for range.

A round shot struck the *Benton*, but with little damage. So far it was the only harm done to the fleet. Then a rifled gun on the *St. Louis* exploded, causing casualties among the gun crews and prompting Foote to comment later that "the guns furnished the Western Flotilla were less destructive to the enemy than to ourselves."[5]

Finally, as nightfall approached, Foote called the flotilla back to the anchorage. The truth must have dawned on all that the bombarding of this island into submission would not be an easy task. The wary Flag Officer decided on a temporary siege tactic: the mortars would stand off, just out of range, and shell the island relentlessly.

The mortar boats themselves were a curious lot. Each was a mere raft, 60 feet long, 25 feet wide, with one 13-inch mortar mounted between sloping, ironclad sides. The sides were equipped with an escape hatch through which the crew would retire after loading the mortar and fire it by a long lanyard, because the reverberations within the sides would be deafening. The shells would be arched over a distance of two miles, and were capable of dealing out a considerable amount of destruction. For the time being, Foote was content to let the mortars pound the island into submission and his crews settled down for a long siege, watching the shots arch high in the air and plunge down toward the island.

Meanwhile, General Pope was not one to wait for developments; he was creating them on his own. After he occupied New Madrid, he set about gathering his 20,000 troops for a push down the west side of the Mississippi to cross it and advance on Island No. 10 from the south, blocking the island garrison's only escape route, the Tiptonville Road. It was a sound plan and strategically correct. However, a river crossing in enemy territory was not to be undertaken lightly. First he needed transports to be gotten down past Island No. 10 and then he needed gunboats to protect them. Foote, having already sampled the Rebel batteries, was reticent about sending his precious gunboats past the island, so an impasse occurred during which both commanders seemed stalemated, the mortar boats continuing to lob shells at Island No. 10, or at least into the mud surrounding it. Finally, it was up to Pope to break the deadlock. He had been given a plan to bypass the island and therefore exclude a running fight with the island's guns.

It appears that one Colonel J.W. Bissel, while reconnoitering the western bank above the gunboat anchorages, spotted an opening in the timber-lined shore that proved to be an old wagon road leading a half mile into the woods. On a hunch, he decided to explore his find. Two miles farther in, he found a bayou. After learning it was called Wilson's Bayou, and that it emptied into the Mississippi below New Madrid, he was struck with an idea: why not cut a canal into the bayou and float armed vessels and transports into it, completely bypassing Island No. 10? It was a perfect answer and it would not require much materiel and or many men to complete.[6]

Bissell approached Pope and Foote with the idea and the general immediately sanctioned the scheme. A stream of telegrams flew back and forth from headquarters to St. Louis, as Pope and Halleck exchanged ideas. Halleck became convinced, and sent orders for the project to begin. Steamers, tugs, barges and an engineering regiment were dispatched to the scene; no time should be wasted. Bissell had ordered, in addition to the barges and steamers, six coal barges, one Columbiad cannon, six siege guns with carriages and two million feet of lumber with which to build rafts.

The canal was a brilliant feat of engineering. Crews on small rafts were first sent in to cut off trees eight feet above the water. Other crews followed in boats and removed the remaining trunks, using block-and-tackle arrangements. After this, a large raft moved in with a crew and a large circular saw which was attached to the tree stumps and, with a see-saw motion, sawed them off four and a half feet below the surface. Huge trunks had to be snaked aside and thrust among the standing trees.[7]

The Confederates knew about work on the canal but were not overly concerned; in fact an officer on the island reported to Richmond that "the canal was being cut, but it will fail."[8]

After eight days of continuous work, during which not a man was injured or lost, the two miles were breached and the waters from the Mississippi flowed into Wilson's Bayou through a canal 50 feet wide and 4½-feet deep. Shortly after, a fleet of boats,

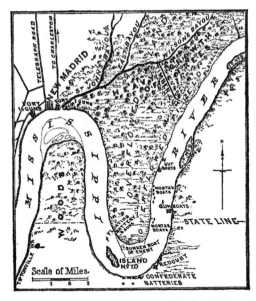

A map showing the position of Island No. 10.

small steamers, tugs and makeshift gunboats—field pieces mounted on rafts—steamed into the bayou and toward New Madrid.
Unfortunately, the canal was not deep enough for the actual gunboats to navigate; it was an ingenious project but it did have its
limits. Transports for Pope's troops were ferried through the canal
and out into the Mississippi, just below New Madrid.

However, now the Union forces were curiously imbalanced.
The formidable Western Gunboat Flotilla was blocked upriver;
downstream Pope's motley fleet of transports and ad hoc gunboats was vulnerable to a sudden Confederate sortie from the
South. In between the two elements of the Union forces remained
Island No. 10, loaded with firepower. It became obvious that
there must be a gunboat run past the island, however the question remained as to how it could be done without the vessel being
blown out of the water. On March 20, a conference was called on
board the *Benton*, attended by Foote, his staff and commanding
officers of the ironclads. The Flag Officer had also received word
from General Halleck who was now anxious to support Pope; the
dilemma needed to be resolved.

It was Captain Henry Walke who came up with a practical

solution. He would run his *Carondelet* past the island under cover of darkness. By taking certain precautions, the gunboat could be properly prepared. First, he would cover the decks with planks, from the wreck of an old barge; these would resist plunging shot. Surplus anchor chains would cover exposed areas topside, and an 11-inch hawser would be wound around the pilothouse up to the port holes. The boilers would be protected by piles of cord wood. Because the port side would be vulnerable to the island, he would have a barge loaded with coal and hay lashed to that side. Then bales of hay would be stacked on the stern, to protect it after his vessel ran past the island. To prevent the characteristic popping noise of all river craft, caused by the pop valves of the boilers, Walke would have the escaping steam piped aft into the wheel-house to muffle the sound.

Then there was the problem of repelling boarders. That problem would be solved by bringing aboard some of General Pope's best sharpshooters and equipping the gunboat's own crew with muskets, boarding pikes, cutlasses and hand grenades. In addition, a hose connected directly to a boiler would be available to scald prospective boarders. No lights would be used, except for a single engine room lantern.[9] If something went wrong Walke would immediately scuttle the vessel to prevent her from falling into enemy hands.[10]

In considering that the run would be made past the batteries on the Tennessee shore above the island, Foote decided on what is known today as a commando raid. On April 1, Colonel George Roberts, of the 42nd Illinois Regiment, took 50 hand-picked men and, during a night pummeled by a fierce electrical storm, put them on board barges that were then towed to a position two miles above the six-gunned emplacement the Rebels called Battery No. 1. The troops were then transferred to boats and rowed to the shore. They had hoped to make their approach under cover of darkness, but a flash of lightning exposed them, alarming the sentries. However, for the Rebels it was too late; the invading forces swarmed over the battery, overpowered the defenders and spiked the guns, primarily using large nails or rat-tail files pounded into the ignition vents. All returned to the fleet unharmed; it was a daring and successful raid. With that potential danger point out of the way, preparations then proceeded on the *Carondelet* for her run past Island No. 10.

At dusk on April 6, sharpshooters from the 42nd Illinois Regiment came on board. They were mustered and sent to their assigned stations. Crew members carried out a long hose, the one connected to a boiler, and coiled it against the casemate, within easy reach.

Around 8:00 P.M., the *Carondelet* moved a mile upstream where the coal barge, brought up by two steamers, was made ready. The weather, which up to this point had promised a worrisome moonlit night, turned cloudy and ugly, and Walke must have breathed a sigh of relief. In fact there was a thunderstorm approaching.

An hour later, First Master Hoel came on board. Having recovered from a wound suffered at Fort Henry while serving aboard the *Cincinatti*, he had been picked for his vast knowledge of the river and its idiosyncrasies. Meanwhile, the coal barge had been brought alongside and lashed to the port side. (Curiously, what is commonly labeled as the "port" side on all seagoing vessels, from time immemorial, was called "larboard" on the western rivers, though not by the U.S. Navy men there.)

When 10:00 approached, the *Carondelet*'s lines were cast off and pilot Hoel eased the odd-looking, floating entity into the channel. After the *Carondelet* cast off, the vanguard of the storm appeared. Soon the gunboat, the river and the island were engulfed in a furious tempest that whipped the water into a froth, unearthly flashes of lightning adding to the crew's apprehensions. For Foote and his crews, the darkness and the rain were heaven-sent, but the lightning could possibly betray their position to the enemy. It was fervently hoped that the sentries were hunkered down against the furious, slashing rain.

It was impossible to cover every contingency. Suddenly, the stacks of the *Carondelet* flared up with sheets of flame. Apparently, when the exhausts were bypassed into the wheelhouse, the soot in the stacks dried and the heat from the boilers ignited it. And, as the gunboat passed Battery No. 2, she matched the storm with fireworks of her own. Fortunately, the lightning must have hidden the streamers of fire from the stacks, because there was no response from the Confederates.

As she came abreast of the island, the stacks flared up again and this time a sharp-eyed sentry spotted it and spread the alarm. Rockets streamed into the air, warning all batteries that a Union boat was on the river, and the Rebel batteries on the island, as well as those on shore, opened up. Enemy round shot crashed all around the *Carondelet*.

It was now or never. Full steam ahead was ordered and the gunboat, encumbered by the barge, plowed ahead, although not with the speed for which she was designed. One enemy ball plopped into the barge. According to a newspaperman who was aboard the gunboat, what with the storm and the cannonading, it appeared that "all the forces of heaven, hell and the Confederacy were concentrated on the destruction of the audacious intruder."[11]

Walke immediately ordered the *Carondelet* moved in closer to shore. It was a case of expediency—either run the risk of running aground, or face the possibility of being blown to bits by the enemy. The gunboat was unable to duel with the shore batteries, her guns having been run in and the ports sealed shut. The gamble paid off. The *Carondelet* ran so close to the island that the Confederate gunners could not depress their pieces to get at her. Most of the shots arched harmlessly overhead.

It must have been a frustrating event to the Rebels. An officer who had just moved with his command to the island reported that one of the enemy's large gunboats passed one of his batteries, amidst a severe storm. He wrote that the island's guns were "fired from nearly all batteries, but owing to the intense darkness intervening [we] could not so much as disable her."[11]

At one point, the *Carondelet*'s barge scraped the bottom, and a hard-a-port rudder was called for. But the plucky gunboat and its burden plowed on. The *Carondelet* passed the south end of the island and returned to the main channel. One more obstacle remained, however: that of the floating battery which was supposed to be anchored at the foot of the island. It was discovered that the barge had earlier been cut loose from its moorings by the bombardments, and was grounded on the Kentucky shore. The *Carondelet* steered toward the Missouri side where she quickly passed the obstacle. The Rebel gunners made only a token effort at the gunboat by firing a few shots that fell harmlessly into the water. The *Carondelet* was now out of danger.

Walke ordered prearranged signals to be lit, lest the artillerists in and around New Madrid mistake her for an enemy vessel. Then in a triumphal parade of one, the gunboat passed in front of New Madrid's waterfront, receiving the accolades of the soldiers there. From then on the *Carondelet* was back in her element. After divesting herself of the barge and the other encumbrances to her guns, she proceeded to steam up and down the Mississippi, blasting enemy batteries out of action, one by one, opening the way for Pope's troops to cross the river.

William Onstet, who was aboard the Rebel steamer *McGill*, at the time of the momentous run, wrote his wife that the *Carondelet* had run past the island, by a "Yankee trick," that of using a barge full of hay and coal on her port side and the island artillery rained a "perfect shower of iron at him [Walke]." He predicted that the fate of the island was settled and the experiment was such a success that the run could be repeated by two or more boats at least.[12]

Onstet was right. On the 8th, the gunboat *Pittsburgh*, repeating Walke's successful feat, successfully ran past the island at night and joined her sister at New Madrid. Together they rampaged downriver, pounding all Confederate resistance down close to Fort Pillow.

When Pope swarmed across the Mississippi and marched his troops on the Tiptonville Road, the Confederates on Island No. 10 realized the game was up. They capitulated to Union forces and surrendered all their guns, amounting to 158 pieces, plus 7,000 stands of muskets, 700 horses, tents for 12,000 men, huge quantities of ammunition and three brigadier-generals, MacKall, Gantt and L.M. Walker and their staffs. It was a resounding victory for the Federal cause—at low cost—and another defeat for the Confederacy.

The action that followed the Island No. 10 affair resulted in spoils other than those at the island itself. Walke reported that enemy vessels captured or sunk in action on the Mississippi immediately following the capitulation were the *Red River, Ohio*

Belle, DeSoto, Admiral, Champion, Mars and a large wharfboat. Vessels sunk included the *Grampus, Devil Jack,* the "fastest gunboat on the waters," the steamers *Yazoo* and *Mohawk,* plus other small craft. An elated General Halleck wired General Pope, congratulating him on the great victory, adding, "It exceeds in boldness and brilliancy all other operations of the war."[13]

The surrender of Island No. 10 meant the Mississippi was now open as far down as Fort Pillow, and Union strategy decreed that, once that obstacle was removed, Memphis would be the next Confederate stronghold with which to contend. In Washington, General Pope was now so highly regarded that he was soon transferred east to match his skill against the commander of the Army of Northern Virginia. At Second Bull Run, he would fail to duplicate his earlier success.

Two gunboats of the Union fleet, the timberclads *Lexington* and *Tyler,* were not present at the Island No. 10 triumph; the night *Carondelet* made her daring run they were miles away, up the Tennessee River at a place called Pittsburg Landing, where General Grant was trying to hang on to his army. Named after a church on the site, the Battle of Shiloh was one of the bloodiest engagements of the Civil War, and a watershed in the war in the west.

A look at the Confederate position in April 1862 will shed some light upon the reasons for the attack on Grant's forces at Pittsburg Landing. After Forts Henry and Donelson were surrendered in February, General Albert Sidney Johnston was forced to withdraw from Kentucky and most of Tennessee. He formed a new line of defense at Corinth, in northeastern Mississippi, where the Mobile & Ohio Railroad ran from Columbus, Kentucky to New Orleans, bisecting the Memphis & Charleston line, which connected Memphis with Chattanooga. It was a railroad ganglion vital to the Confederacy that had to be defended at all costs.

In addition it should be remembered that, after one year of war, the greatest Yankee gains in the west had come in their river battles, usually against fixed positions. The fall of Confederate river forts had vaulted Union land armies deep into Southern territory, but the Rebels had still yet to be defeated in a major land battle. Most of their men, in fact, had yet to even see a Yankee, even as huge swathes of their territory were being lost. When Johnston determined that Grant's army was lodged on the "Confederate side" of the Tennessee River, its back to the water, a palpable fervor spread through the Rebel ranks. This, finally, was the opportunity the Southerners had been waiting for.

After a rather clumsy forced march—during which many troopers fired off their guns, just to see if they would work—Johnston's army roared into the Union position. Grant's men had not fortified their camp and many units were caught unprepared. Others had used their few minutes of warning to form line. Still others were warned and in line but were simply overwhelmed by the first Confederate rush. In any case, the battle soon became a gigantic melee, about 40,000 men on a side, directed by unit officers who had the enemy in sight; in Grant's words, "A case of Southern dash versus Northern pluck and obstinacy."

Though the Union men were pushed back, they exacted a terrible cost. In the "Hornet's Nest," a Yankee division held through most of the afternoon before its remnants finally surrendered. The Confederate command seemed to lose their overview of the battle and failed to exercise tactical control. Nathan Forrest and his cavalry, not otherwise directed, simply attacked the nearest Union formation they saw. Albert Sidney Johnston, the commander-in-chief of Confederate forces in the west, died after leading a gallant charge on horseback against a Yankee line. By the time darkness fell, both sides were battered and bloody, and the Federals were pressed against the river—but the Union men were also about to receive heavy reinforcements.

Grant, it must be said, was never anything but calm throughout the day, though he did express irritation that Lew Wallace's division had not come to assist in the battle (he later learned Wallace had mistakenly marched toward where the Yankee lines had been in the morning, not realizing they had been relocated). Among Grant's moves was to call the gunboats into action. Captain Gwin, aboard the *Tyler*, ordered his gunners to enfilade the Confederate lines. The *Lexington*, Captain Shirk commanding, also moved up and joined her sister in the bombardment. Although Grant, in his memoirs, credits the timberclads with laying down a barrage of fire that helped to slow the Confederate onslaught somewhat,[14] their influence on this quintessential Civil War battle has sometimes been exaggerated. The truth is, with a shifting front of 40,000 Confederates spread out through wooded and undulating terrain for seven miles, the effect of the two gunboats' fire could not have been a decisive factor, and it would be remarkable to find that the ships even knew what they were aiming at. Nevertheless, every participant in the battle remembered their presence, if only because, all night long, they kept on firing every fifteen minutes.

During one sortie, the gunboats moved in closer to the battle area and laid down a withering fussilade of shellfire into a ravine in which a Confederate charge was threatening a Union position. The Confederate charge was stopped cold. During the night, Don Carlos Buell's army had come up and was ferried across the river. By the time morning broke, including Wallace's division, which had finally found the Union lines, Grant had at least 30,000 fresh troops with which to renew the battle. The Confederates also seemed to realize that the situation had changed. On the second day of Shiloh, they essentially executed a slow, fighting withdrawal from the field. William Sherman, who had held the Federal left throughout the first day, attempted to pursue with his reinforced division but he ran into Forrest's cavalry and that was the end of the pursuit.

Today few question that Shiloh was one of the turning points of the war. The Confederates fell back on their shaky stronghold at Corinth and, for the time being, could no longer threaten Kentucky and Tennessee. The eruption of violence was unprecedented in the battles of the war so far. One observer, H.L. Patterson, wrote that the carnage was terrible. He said the battle was "the last fitful gasp of Secession." Then he continued: "I think this battle must end the war in the west."[15]

The idea that Shiloh was a Union victory, however, has always been subject to debate in the many years since the event. The Union army, with its back to a river, was surprised and very nearly crushed. After the first day's fighting, an entire Federal division (Prentiss' in the center) had been annihilated, the flanking divisions were mangled, and the banks of the Tennessee River were crowded with at least 5,000 blue-coated refugees from every unit, looking for escape from the Rebel onslaught. That Grant's army was reinforced by some 30,000 effectives after dark caused the Confederates to quite sensibly withdraw from the field on the second day. Nevertheless, the Union had suffered some 12,000 casualties (as had the Confederates) and, after the battle, Grant was removed from command.

Still, whichever side is credited with victory on the battlefield itself, the fact remains that, strategically, the South had been foiled at Shiloh. After Belmont, Donelson and Island No. 10, its great attempt to turn the tables in the west had not succeeded, by writ of superior Yankee strength. Clearly, the Confederates had failed to regain the upper hand in this theater of operations. As their territory continued to be seized and their arteries of commerce choked and occupied, the Confederacy's best hopes for ultimate victory now seemed, more than ever, held by their indefatigable armies still undefeated in the east.

A chagrined President Davis downgraded the part played by Union gunboats at Shiloh. He maintained that their fire was ineffective, because they were unable to depress their guns low enough.[16] Ironically, this was the same problem that faced Confederate gunners at Island No.10, the night *Carondelet* slipped by. President Lincoln, on the other hand, issued a proclamation, stating that it pleased Almighty God to "grant signal victories to the land and naval forces engaged in suppressing an internal rebellion. . . ."[17]

On the Upper Mississippi, the Western Gunboat Flotilla had cleared the river past Kentucky and Missouri and now had as its objective Memphis, across from Arkansas in the southwestern corner of Tennessee. But first the flotilla had to subdue Fort Pillow, a fortification located some 40 miles north of Memphis, consisting of heavy armament on high bluffs that extended south for five miles.

After a year of the Civil War, the Union's brown-water navy had exceeded expectations, blasting its way into Southern territory; the armies in the west had supported its gains. But now the blue-water navy would take a hand, attacking an objective some

1,400 nautical miles away from the combatant's respective capitals, where no field armies had yet ventured. While in the east General McClellan continued to gear up for his great assault on Richmond, the largest population center in the Confederacy was about to fall. The U.S. Navy had arrived in force at the mouth of the Mississippi.

CHAPTER NINE

Assault on Crescent City

New Orleans is a name that has contradictory overtones: a rowdy city, sometimes dangerous, but full of fun, music and good food, in the past not unlike today. Visitors flock to the city, especially at Mardi Gras time, during which all stops are pulled for a season of gaiety that at times borders on the decadent. An anomaly among American cities, its population embodies a cultural mix of French, Spanish and Caribbean, as well as black and Anglo-Saxon. In New Orleans, religions from Catholicism to voodoo are combined with antebellum Southern culture to create a flamboyance and sensuality considered curious by Americans and foreigners alike. At one time in its history, it was called "Hell on Earth,"[1] though the city is perhaps more often referred to as the "Big Easy."

Located in a swooping bend made by the Mississippi as it flows south, then to the east and south again, also earned it the nickname "Crescent City." Because of its strategic position, New Orleans was a mecca for craft plying the river. Colorful steamboats came to the city to unload products from the Mississippi Valley above and these cargoes were then loaded onto ships that voyaged to the Gulf and thence to the world's oceans.[2] Furthermore, New Orleans contained 170,000 souls and was the largest city in the Confederacy. It had more machine shops, trained workmen and busy shipyards than any other Confederate metropolis. Along with Mobile, Alabama, New Orleans was not only a funnel for river commerce but was an interstate rail hub, allowing it to transfer both imports and exports throughout the South.

In Washington, D.C., the strategic value of the Crescent City was recognized from the start of the war, and by late 1861 the U.S. Government was brainstorming the possibility of capturing it. Though the prime imperative for the blue water ships was the coastal blockade, the fleet was growing rapidly and would soon be able to concentrate enormous firepower on any spot of its choosing. Assistant Secretary of the Navy Gustavus Fox suggested a plan whereby the U.S. Navy would subdue the forts guarding the approaches to the city, capture New Orleans and then steam upriver to join the Western Gunboat Flotilla that was fighting its way down. He argued that New Orleans was strategically more important than Mobile, because capturing the latter would not contribute to the opening of the Mississippi River.[3]

Fox's opponents argued that it was foolhardy for wooden ships to tackle a stone fort, as pontificated by Britain's Admiral Lord Nelson. But Fox pointed to the successes of the Union Navy at Hatteras Inlet and Port Royal, during which wooden ships had successfully bombarded Confederate strongholds. The fact is, the advent of the modern age had not just brought advances in guns; the best new asset to naval bombardment was steam. In Nelson's day, ships were dependent on the wind and couldn't sustain accurate fire on a fixed position. By the Civil War, ships possessed their own power to maneuver, or to stay in place. Fox went to President Lincoln and got his approval of the plan, but with the proviso that all concerned wait until more intelligence was gathered on the strength of New Orleans' protective forts, St. Philip and Jackson.[4]

In Richmond, the ambitious Union naval plan was simply not anticipated. In the words of historian Chester G. Hearn, "Jefferson Davis and [Confederate Secretary of War Judah] Benjamin just weren't too concerned about New Orleans. They thought it was secure, and so turned their attention elsewhere." Louisiana troops were in fact being sent north for the battles in Virginia and Tennessee. To the north, after all, the way was blocked by a series of strongholds: Island No. 10, New Madrid, Fort Pillow, Memphis and Vicksburg. To the south, 100 miles downriver, the way to the city was blocked by two formidable facing forts, Jackson and St. Philip. These were located 20 miles above the Head of the Passes, a deep-water anchorage that capped three major entrances to the Gulf: Pass a Loutre, South Pass and Southwest Pass. Two of the channels were fairly shallow, ranging from 6-foot to 17-foot depths. Pass a Loutre was the deepest and was navigable for deep-draft vessels.

In the fall of 1861 Confederate vessels from New Orleans scored a remarkable victory over Union blockaders at the Head of the Passes. In September Captain John Pope had led a small fleet of warships, including the sloops *Vincennes* and *Preble*, the 1,900-ton screw sloop *Richmond* and some auxiliary vessels through the Southwest Pass and into the Head of the Passes, where they anchored, completely dominating all traffic in and out of the three entrances.

The defenders of New Orleans found this move intolerable and assembled a small fleet of flat-bottomed towboats, each with two guns, plus a former revenue cutter and—most important— their new ironclad ram the *Manassas*. This ram, converted from an old 387-ton towboat, was built with convex iron plating designed to deflect cannon shot. With a 143-foot length and a 33-foot beam, she was armed with but a single 64-pounder that could only fire through a forward port. Her one inclined engine and screw drove her at a painfully slow speed of only four knots. To observers, she resembled a large cigar or, as some put it, a whale—nevertheless, she was the flagship.

During the night of October 11, the *Manassas* led the little flotilla down the river to challenge the Federal squadron, towing three fire rafts that were but flatboats crammed with pine knots and other combustible materials to be used against the enemy. The skipper of the *Manassas*, Lieutenant A.F. Warley, instructed his force that the flagship would charge first, then fire a rocket to signal the other crews to light off the fire rafts, sending them downriver toward the enemy vessels.

Under cover of darkness, the cigar-shaped ram slid down the river toward the unsuspecting *Richmond*. Instead of the ship, she rammed a barge lashed alongside. And, although his ram received damage from the blow, her machinery was damaged and her smokestack knocked askew, Warley sent the rocket aloft, and down the swift-flowing river came the fire rafts, resembling a series of floating infernos.

The Union fleet fled in panic, even though the rafts never touched them and the flagship hadn't been damaged. In the melee, *Richmond* and *Vincennes* went aground, and the latter's captain, Robert Handy, actually passed the order to abandon ship. (His men were ordered to get back on their boat.) The little fleet of Rebel gunboats opened fire on the rest of the flotilla, inflicting little or no damage, and then withdrew upriver. They left behind a red-faced, much-chagrined Union force that meanwhile had seen a third vessel run aground.

Recriminations came thick and fast for a flotilla that allowed itself to be caught napping. Commodore David Porter called it "the most ridiculous affair that ever took place in the American Navy."[5] The Confederate Mississippi River commander, Commodore Hollins, labeled the skirmish a "complete victory," although the *Manassas* had to return to New Orleans for extensive repair work.

Besides the Confederates' ad hoc fleet, guardians of the Crescent City consisted of powerful batteries in the two forts that stood between the city and the Gulf.

Fort Jackson, shaped like a broken cogwheel, sat on the west bank of the river and mounted 74 guns, including some 10-inch Columbiads, the heaviest cannon in the Confederate arsenal. Upstream about a half mile was the smaller Fort St. Philip, an open installation consisting of brick walls covered by thick layers of sod through which glowered 52 guns. Each of the two forts was manned by about 700 troops and both were well-stocked with food and supplies. Their locations, at a slight bend in the river where ships had to slow down before proceeding upstream, were well chosen (by the Federals before the war), and constituted a serious obstacle to any Union vessels which dared to venture that far.

In addition to the forts' heavy armament, the Confederates strung eight old hulks across the river, connected by chains and a raft of logs that ran from Fort Jackson to the hulks. This raft could be swung aside to allow passage of friendly craft.[6] And still another precaution involved the old fort called "Chalmette," the site of Andrew Jackson's spectacular victory over the British during the Battle of New Orleans on January 8, 1815. Armed with 20 guns, any enemy fleet that could fight its way past Jackson and St. Philip would have to contend with this bastion, and in the meantime, the theory went, troops could be brought up.

In Washington, it finally took one man, the aforementioned David Dixon Porter, son of the renowned Commodore David Porter, to come up with a sound plan by which the forts could be breached and New Orleans taken. Having made some thirty trips up and down the Mississippi and through the passes, he had a close familiarity with the region and knew whereof he spoke.

Porter's plan called for a naval force to be fitted out with vessels mounting an aggregate of 250 guns, but with drafts of no more than 18 feet, plus mortar boats and supply vessels. The mortar boats would be constructed from 20 large schooners fitted out with one 13-inch mortar and two 32-pounder guns for each. The army would provide 20,000 troops for the occupation of New Orleans and then to fortify the heights above Vicksburg, which would be the next objective.[7]

The task of appointing a commander for the campaign was next, and Porter, surveying the list of 35 available captains, had a strong recommendation: his own foster brother, David Glasgow Farragut.

Farragut was a Tennessean by birth, but he remained intensely loyal to the Union, whose cause he joined early in the war. At the age of six he had been adopted into the family of Commodore Porter and at the age of 12 he served in the War of 1812, and thereafter in the Caribbean and the Mediterranean. When the Civil War broke out he was 59 and a hardened navy veteran. Although Farragut had married a Virginian, and made his home there, seccession caused him to move. He packed up and took his family north.

After his appointment to head the New Orleans Expedition, Farragut tackled his task with energy and resolve, a lifetime of navy experience behind him.[8] For a base of operations, he chose Ship Island, in the Mississippi Sound, guarding the entrance to Lake Pontchartrain. It was nothing but a "sprawling sand dune" with a smattering of marsh grasses, scrub oaks and pines. Originally, the island was to have been a coaling station for light-draft gunboats of the Union blockade that were to halt the Gulf traffic between Mobile and New Orleans.[9] There, Farragut set about assembling his fleet of two steam frigates, five screw sloops and a dozen gunboats—together mounting a total of 243 heavy guns.

The captain chose as his flagship the magnificent screw sloop *Hartford*. She displaced 2,900 tons, was 225 feet long, with a 44-foot beam, and her two boilers and two horizontal, double-piston engines drove her at a top speed of 13.5 knots. The *Hartford*'s 17.2-foot draft would also allow her to navigate deep and shallow waters alike, especially the great-depth channels of the Mississippi River.

On February 20, he brought his powerful fleet to Ship Island, awaiting the mortar schooners and assorted supply vessels. In addition to the *Hartford*, this fleet included the 4,700-ton *Colorado*, with 44 guns; the *Mississippi*, a 3,000-ton sidewheeler with 10 guns; three light steam corvettes of 10 guns each; 11 gunboats, tugboats, coalships; and assorted supply vessels.[10]

The Confederates, for their part, were not unaware of the power being arrayed against them. They were busy planning to defend their city with everything they had. General Mansfield Lovell was appointed commander of the defenses of New Orleans, and that included the fleet, because at that time all Rebel naval forces were under army command in this sector of the war.

Lovell was a West Pointer who had fought in the Mexican War, was wounded and was later appointed one brevet. He resigned in 1854 to become an iron manufacturer, Superintendent of Streets and finally Deputy Commissioner of Streets in New York City. When war broke out, he resigned his job and threw in his lot with the South. After being appointed a major-general in October 1861, he was assigned the New Orleans post, where he found himself commanding 4,000 raw recruits without arms, because the armory had been depleted to equip Confederate soldiers at Shiloh. When Farragut's powerful Union fleet loomed to the south, he set about creating plans to meet the threat.

Those elaborate plans were hamstrung by a lack of guns, ammunition and auxiliary equipment.[11] However, Lovell set about rectifying that situation: foundries were ordered to cast guns, a powder factory was built and a ragtag fleet assembled that would soon be augmented by the powerful ironclads *Mississippi* and *Louisiana*, then under construction. But the aforementioned manufacturing problems plagued Lovell in his efforts, including shortage of parts, wood, armament, iron plating and shops in which to build machinery. At one point, money became the most serious of all the General's problems, until Richmond finally recognized the Union threat and relaxed its purse strings.

By the middle of March, Farragut had assembled his fleet of 18 ships, plus mortar schooners and auxiliaries, off the Mississippi passes and was preparing to take it into the Head of the Passes, but the draft of one of his ships stood in the way. The *Colorado*, with a deep draft of 23 feet, would have to be snaked over the bars. After much labor, she was unloaded of guns and equipment and laboriously pulled over, her keel at times gouging out a couple of inches in the mud.

After two weeks, the fleet had assembled in the anchorage. Finally, Farragut decided to take a personal hand in operations. He boarded a gunboat and steamed up the river toward Fort Jackson. When the Confederates opened fire on the vessel, a crewman described the flag officer as calm and placid as a "spectator in a mimic [sic] battle."[12]

The mortar schooners were brought up, spars removed and foliage draped over mast tops, in order to blend in with the forests on shore. They were placed just below the bend south of Fort Jackson and on April 18, 1862, they commenced a relentless bombardment of the fort that was to last for five days. 16,800 shells were expended, but without any noticeable effect.[13] In the meantime, transports carrying General Benjamin Butler and 18,000 troops were brought into the Head of the Passes, where they anchored, awaiting their turn in the action.

At this juncture, the disagreement between Farragut and

Porter over the effectiveness of the mortars came to a head. Frustrated in the failure of the bombardment, Farragut announced that he was going to fight his way past the forts, convinced as he was that, once New Orleans was occupied, they would certainly die on the vine from lack of food and supplies. But first the raft of anchored schooners would have to be breached.

The task fell to Lieutenant Charles H.B. Caldwell, skipper of the gunboat *Itaska*. He steamed up, planted a charge on the chain, hopefully to sever the line holding the vessels together so they would drift apart and allow a passage for Union ships to slip by, one by one, in order to engage the forts. However, the charge failed to go off. Caldwell then had his gunners fire into the hulks, but the *Itaska* itself became entangled in the chains and was forced to go aground. The determined skipper then took his vessel upstream, close to the east bank, until she was above the obstacle. Using full power and the swift current, the plucky gunboat bore down on the chains and, using her weight much like an icebreaker today, parted them. She successfully plowed through the gap, and Caldwell proudly announced to Farragut the obstacle had been removed.[14]

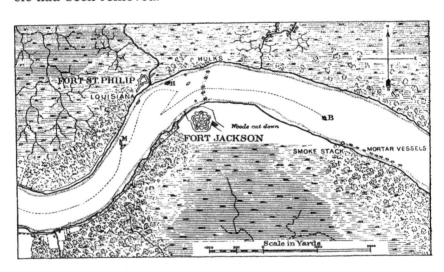

Map of the gauntlet run by Farragut on his approach to New Orleans, in this case indicating the approach *Brooklyn* made to the *Manassas*.

Farragut had taken great pains to prepare his ships for the ordeal of running the forts: anchor chains were draped over hulls to protect boilers and engine rooms; Jacob's ladders were slung to allow carpenters to quickly effect repairs; tubs of water, for dousing fires, were scattered throughout the vessels and fire crews were equipped with grapnels to better fend off fire rafts. And ships' hulls and upper works were smeared with mud, lest enemy gunners spot his vessels. Now all was ready.

The Confederates were ready, too. They had sent down the uncompleted *Louisiana* and the *Manassas,* along with 14 armed vessels of all sorts, including two Louisiana State gunboats and six river defense craft. The *Louisiana,* with workmen still aboard, tied up to the shore above Fort Jackson. It was hoped that, in spite of the incomplete installation of a driveshaft, she could still act as a floating battery with her 16 guns, in defiance of the mighty armada arrayed against her.

All together, arrayed against Farragut were the gunboats *Governor Moore, McRae, Jackson,* the ironclad *Manassas,* the *General Quitman,* and the river defense boats *Warrier, Defiance, Stonewall Jackson, Resolute, General Lovell* and *R.J. Breckenridge.* Added to these were the 128 guns of the forts, so the opportunity for a knock-down-drag-out fight was in the offing.[15]

At 2:00 A.M. on April 24, two vertical red signal lights went up on the *Hartford's* mizzen mast, and the fleet got underway. The battle for New Orleans was about to begin.

The fleet was in three divisions, led by the 1,370-ton screw gunboat *Cayuga,* followed by the screw sloops *Pensacola* and *Mississippi;* the corvettes *Oneida, Varuna;* the gunboats *Katahdin, Kineo* and *Wissahikon.* Following were the screw sloops *Hartford, Brooklyn* and *Richmond.* These vessels in turn were followed by screw gunboat *Sciota,* screw sloop *Iroquois* and gunboats *Kennebec, Pinola, Itaska* and *Winona.*[16]

The brig-rigged *Hartford* was in the Second Division, because the crews prevailed upon Farragut to place his ship there, fearing he might be killed or wounded, leaving the fleet without its leader.

Farragut might have been criticized for not having the fleet steam in two columns, as would have been the practice otherwise. But it must be remembered that the river was narrow at the bend below the forts and, in addition, the passage cleared through the boom of hulks was narrow in itself. The fleet had to steam single column, even if it meant that chances of straggling would occur, putting such vessels in jeopardy.

The tonnage in metal to be thrown by the fleet was 10 tons from all vessels, as opposed to $3^{1}/_{2}$ tons from the fort.[17] Farragut was flying in the face of the rule of thumb that stated "one gun ashore was worth four afloat."

The van of the fleet easily cleared the sunken hulk obstacle and bore down on the forts. One of *Cayuga's* officers wrote that although it was a starlit night, the ships were not discovered until well under the forts and then "they opened upon us a tremendous fire."[18] The vessels answered, followed by salvos from the mortars. The Confederates lit off a series of brush fires on the shore, plus fire rafts on the water, and the whole scene was lit up as if it were a stage play. Farragut had stationed himself high in the mizzen mast of the flagship and described the scene as if "the artillery of heaven were playing on earth."[19]

Poor *Cayuga* got the worst of it, being in the van and first in line. She found herself above the forts, but came under attack not only from the shore batteries but by three enemy gunboats—one astern, one off the starboard bow and one abeam. With her 11-inch Dahlgren she holed the boat astern, sending her to the bottom; a Parrott rifle holed the one off the bow, and the one abeam was taken care of by her sisters *Varuna* and *Oneida,* who had come up on the scene.

Meanwhile, *Hartford* was having her troubles. When her helmsman attempted to dodge a fire raft pushed by a tug, she headed for a mud flat above Fort St. Philip. Farragut gave the order "Hard a-Port!" but it was too late; she ran aground and the tug rammed the fire raft into her flank. Flames pounded over her bulwarks and climbed halfway up the masthead, aided by shells from the fort. Some of the crew panicked, but the cool-headed flag officer walked up and down, giving orders, totally oblivious to any personal danger.

The crew, inspired by Farragut's coolness and self-discipline, quickly rallied and set about dousing the fire. Farragut pointed at the tug and ordered a gun crew to sink her, which they did. One shot through the boiler and the little tug disappeared into the depths of the river. The *Hartford* backed out in the stream, and for a moment presented her broadside to any enemy rams which might have been in the area, but, fortunately, none were present. The big ship turned and continued her course upstream.

At this point, the ram *Manassas* joined the fray. She came up, struck the *Mississippi*, however that sturdy sidewheeler could not be budged. Then she turned on the *Brooklyn*, which was following the flagship, and inflicted a gash that was not a serious wound. When the Rebel ram backed off and hove to, an officer was seen to emerge from her hatch to inspect any damage. Suddenly, he staggered and fell headlong into the river. The captain of the *Brooklyn* called to a leadsman in the chains and asked if he had seen the officer fall. The leadsman replied that he not only saw the man fall, but in fact assisted by hitting him in the head with his leadline.[20] The *Manassas* swung about and headed downstream for another target. The gunners in the forts, thinking her to be a disabled Union vessel, opened fire on her, adding to her damage.

However, lying in wait upstream was the Confederate sidewheel steamer *Governor Moore*, armed with two guns—one fore, the other aft. Spotting the *Varuna*, now in the van, she opened fire on the unsuspecting Federal craft. The *Varuna*'s gunners responded, inflicting many casualties on the Rebel steamer. The *Governor Moore* was close enough to use her bow gun, but, because the craft was head-on, the bow was in the way. The captain then ordered the gun depressed and fired through his own bow. The first shot glanced off a hawse pipe; the second went through and hit the forward gun on the *Varuna*, inflicting heavy casualties. The Confederate vessel then rammed the *Varuna* hard amidships, sending her to a river bank, where she sank in shoal waters.

Flushed with success, the Rebel captain wanted to take on the entire Union fleet with his damaged vessel; however, one of his officers who was at the helm disobeyed, and swung the vessel to starboard, declaring that she and the crew had enough. In so doing, he exposed his flank to the oncoming Federal fleet. A volley of shots sieved her; she exploded and went to the bottom, taking most of the crew with her, ablaze and with colors burning at her peak.

The *Manassas* was still on the prowl for victims, though her gun had been disabled. Farragut ordered the *Mississippi* to run her down but the ironclad managed to evade and went up on shore, her crew escaping into the swamp through a hail of grapeshot. By this time, Farragut had most of his fleet past the forts. One vessel had been sunk and two of the gunboats damaged—the *Itaska*, having taken a shot in her boiler while trying to pass the boom, drifting helplessly downstream.

Farragut had his fleet pause while he assessed casualties. He had suffered 37 dead and 149 wounded, and there was little comfort in the fact that in the forts there were 12 dead and 40 wounded, in spite of Porter's relentless mortar shellings.[21] But the Confederate flotilla had ceased to exist and, upstream, New Orleans lay helpless, ready for the plucking.

Commodore Porter, sitting downstream, was gratified to see the charred remnants of the Rebel fleet come drifting down, including the *Manassas*, which exploded after being set afire by its departing crew. Encouraged, Porter immediately demanded the surrender of the forts. When he was rebuked, he opened fire with his mortars again. The troops in the forts held on doggedly. It was another case of Union fighting men learning about the grim resolve of their Confederate counterparts.

In spite of the immense amount of metal poured into it by Porter's guns, Fort Jackson remained in fairly good shape. Its commanders reported after the surrender that, although considerable damage had been done, there was a surprisingly low casualty list. The same was reported for Fort St. Philip. Morale was still high, but it was not to last for long.

The river battle was over. The Union fleet had run the gauntlet and, having lost only one vessel, proceeded upstream. Behind it, the crews aboard the *Louisiana* realized the jig was up so they set her afire. When the flames reached her magazine, she disappeared in a horrific explosion, ending her short career.[22]

Only three Confederate vessels, out of the original flotilla, remained afloat, helpless to do anything to stop the inexorable advance of the powerful Union fleet. The two ironclads were in essence dead-aborning, because they were useless in the struggle. Even the beached *Louisiana*, with the obvious intent of acting as a stationary battery, was helpless to affect Farragut's fleet, because of her weak firepower.

An interesting sidebar to this river struggle is the fact that on board the Confederate gunboat *McRae*, her commanding officer, Lieutenant T.B. Huger, was killed by a shot from the *Iroquois*. The irony is that he was serving in that U.S. vessel when war broke out, and that he decided to resign his commission and join the Confederate cause.

Farragut lost no time. He sent a vessel into a bayou called the "Quarantine," to inform General Butler, who had his transports there, that he could send his troops in to cut off the forts from any assistance from upriver. Butler did so, stationing them on each side of the river above the forts.

The victorious fleet moved upriver toward the prize, New Orleans. When it reached the Chalmette fort, just beyond the bend, called "English Bend" by some and "Slaughterhouse Bend" by others, they discovered that the Rebels had erected batteries on both sides of the river, mostly fieldpieces. The works looked formidable, but they proved to be a couple of paper tigers.

The *Brooklyn* unlimbered her huge Dahlgren 80-pounder and sent 21 shells after the defenders on both sides, silencing the batteries, scattering the crews and removing the last obstacle to taking the city.

When the citizens of New Orleans saw Farragut's massive fleet wheel around the bend and pulverize Chalmette's batteries, pandemonium reigned. Alarm bells rang throughout the city—four strokes repeated four times—and the populace, fearful of falling into enemy hands, went into a panic. General Lovell ordered the destruction of all the cotton on the wharfs in the hapless city, along with tons of provisions, many of these soon confiscated by the mobs. Lovell's troops tried to stop the looting, but the mobs ignored them and continued looting until everything had been cleared away, except for the cotton bales that were afire.

Meanwhile, Lovell was loading steamers with guns, ammunition and other military equipment and sending them upriver to safety, himself along with them.[23] Scores of citizens lined the levees and glumly watched as Farragut's fleet steamed up and anchored, crews either standing to their guns, or up in the rigging for a better view. One gunner's mate, on the *Hartford*, patted the breech of his Dahlgren 9-inch gun and grinned at them defiantly.

Farragut sent two officers ashore to receive the surrender from the mayor. These brave men proceeded toward the city hall, followed by a howling mob, unmindful of any danger to their person and with a determination to fulfil their mission.

The mayor refused to surrender, and even had the audacity to challenge Farragut to come and take the city. But the frowning batteries of the warships threatened a devastating bombardmentt, and the Union flag was soon flying from the customhouse, protected by a contingent of sailors and marines with howitzers.

During a reconnaissance mission above New Orleans, one of Farragut's vessels discovered the remains of another boom the enemy had built to throw across the river, in defense against Foote's Western Flotilla from the north. It consisted of logs lashed together with heavy chains. It might have proven to be a dangerous obstacle but for the fact that steamboat crews were unable to stretch it completely across the river. The strong current swept it away and dashed it against the bank where it was abandoned. The river at this time was close to flood stage, the water being only a few inches below the levees around the city.[24]

Upon receiving word of the surrender of New Orleans, the occupants of Forts Jackson and St. Philip decided, as Farragut had anticipated they would, that their position was untenable. In spite of their officers' protests, the enlisted personnel mutinied, spiked the guns, forced the officers to surrender, and then abandoned the forts. With the city cut off from them, things appeared hopeless.

Farragut and his crews were pleased to see the unfinished ironclad *Mississippi* come floating down the river from her berth. She exploded, scattering burning debris.

Later, General Butler marched into the city with his troops and the occupation of New Orleans was to begin. There were probably worse jobs in the Union Army than overseeing the conquests won by Farragut's fleet. For his repeated captures of Southern silverware in many of the wealthier enemy households, the general soon earned the nickname "Spoons" Butler. Unfortunately, the occupation of New Orleans was also to be marred by an inept administration and by charges of cruelty placed against Butler in the months to come.

In retrospect, the fall of New Orleans was a triumph for the Union and a tragedy for the Confederacy. Except for an area extending from Baton Rouge to Vicksburg, Union vessels were moving freely up and down the river, unchallenged. Strategic New Orleans now assured a passage into the Gulf for Federal vessels and assured a Confederacy slowly being torn asunder.[25]

The run past the forts earned Farragut acclaim and a promotion to admiral, the very first full admiral in the U.S. Navy. He was being compared to U.S. Grant as a commander who moved swiftly and could bring to bear decisive force. His decision to pass the forts was based partly on his disdain of Porter's mortar bombardments, but mostly on his unerring sense of strategy and technical sense, which told him that a straight-on run past the forts under cover of darkness, coupled with the mighty broadside capabilities of his ships, would net success. Had he waited much longer for the mortars to subdue the forts, the enemy would have gained time not only to bring up more strength, but to finish the construction of their two ironclads.

Had the Rebel ironclads been ready, the vessels would have been a formidable threat to the Union flotilla. The *Mississippi* was to have 20 guns in a hull of 1,400 tons and a 270-foot length. Her armor would have been covered with 3-inch iron plates, and her prow would have been equipped with an iron beak. The three-engine powerplant would have propelled her at 14 knots. The *Louisiana,* as planned, would have been armed with 20 guns in a 264-foot hull, with a 62-foot beam and a speed of 14 knots. Together, these vessels might have charged down and raised havoc with Farragut's magnificent ships, not unlike the *Merrimac* in Hampton Roads.

The ironclads were not built at the regular New Orleans facilities; instead, new shipyards had had to be built at Jefferson City outside the limits of New Orleans. One yard, in which the *Louisiana* was constructed, was under the management of E.C. Murry; the other, in which *Mississippi* was to have been completed, was under the management of the brothers Tift, agents of the Confederate Navy Department. However, an incredible parade of difficulties dogged the construction of these men-of-war from the start. It was a misfortune for the South that they were not finished in time to meet Farragut's fleet. As it happened the Union vessels had enough problems with the brave and homely one-gunned *Manassas*.

As would be expected, the fall of New Orleans caused a great deal of consternation in Richmond. Much criticism was placed on Lovett, Mallory and some on Davis himself. As for the latter, the President was reported to have buried his face in his hands and wept.[26]

Brigadier General J.K. Duncan, the commander of coastal defenses, reported to President Davis that Farragut's great success in running the forts was due to the darkness, a lack of lighting the river, plus a veritable fog of gunsmoke that obscured vision. He petulantly concluded that "the enemy's dash was successful mainly owing to the cover of darkness, as a frigate and several gunboats were forced to retire as day was breaking."[27]

Major General M.L. Smith, commanding officer of the Chalmette defenses, was a bit more appreciative of Farragut's tactical genius. He mentioned that a possible lack of communication between the command in the city and the forts was a big problem and, once that communication was swept away, the city was doomed.[28]

The fact remains, however, that the Confederate "army" in New Orleans was tiny and ill-equipped, and no match for the Union fleet once they had gotten past the forts. Earlier, General Lovell had been ordered to send 4,000 troops to Columbus, Kentucky, after Grant had taken Fort Henry—a deprivation that fatally wounded his chances of opposing Butler's and Farragut's forces.[29] Likewise with the naval defenses: 14 steamers had been pulled from New Orleans to meet the onrushing Federal gunboats to the north who were on their way to Memphis.[30]

Meanwhile, after the fall of New Orleans, Farragut cast his

eyes on Mobile Bay on the Gulf; surely a worthy (saltwater) objective for his elegant *Hartford* and the rest of his powerful fleet. But Washington had other ideas. The great strategic goal of splitting the Confederacy was now within sight, and by capturing New Orleans, Farragut had complemented the efforts of the Union Navy storming down from the north. The sea-going fleet from New Orleans was now about to join hands with the "turtles"; Farragut was going up the Mississippi.

CHAPTER TEN

Harvest at Plum Point & Memphis

While Farragut at New Orleans had removed a huge piece from the Confederate chessboard, and the Western Gunboat Flotilla was knocking off rooks and pawns on the Upper Mississippi, two events were taking place in Arkansas and northern Mississippi that would have a profound effect on the river campaigns to come.

During January 1862, General Samuel Curtis had routed Confederate troops under the command of General Sterling Price out of Springfield, Missouri, and pursued them into Arkansas. There, however, Price had teamed with the forces of General Earl Van Dorn, and the combined Rebel army was planning to strike back at Curtis at its first opportunity.

Curtis moved cautiously, until he reached a prominence called Pea Ridge, in the Ozarks, where he hunkered down to consolidate his forces and to reconnoiter the enemy positions. Van Dorn in the meantime had collected 17,000 men (including three regiments of Indians) for an assault. Throwing part of his army around Curtis' flank, he attacked the dug-in Union troops on March 7 but the Yankees held fast. At the height of the fighting on the following day Curtis launched his reserve in a counterattack and the Rebels broke. Van Dorn pulled back his army to the Arkansas River where he received orders to head east to buttress the Confederate defenses along the Mississippi River. The Battle of Pea Ridge (also called Elkhorn Tavern) ended any serious

Confederate threat to the State of Missouri.[1]

Curtis then marched further into Arkansas, extending his lines, but was unable to forage from the countryside due to counteraction from the locals. He found himself seriously overextended and in deep trouble. Finally, he moved his forces to the upper extremity of the White River, wired Halleck about his situation and waited for help.

Meanwhile, shortly after the retreat of the Confederate army from Shiloh, Tennessee, General Beauregard fell back on his base at Corinth to await an expected assault by Federal forces, convinced he could not be driven from his strong position. He did, however, call for additional troops, and soon had 60,000 men under his command, after the Confederate government had scoured all army detachments in the field. He was ready for Grant. But it was not Grant who would attack him; it would be Halleck. The supreme commander himself had come down to Pittsburg Landing, shortly after the Battle of Shiloh, relieved Grant of command and taken over to personally lead any attack on Corinth. Under this arrangement, there was no major place for Grant, who was given a corps and stripped of army command responsibilities.

Halleck gathered the combined forces of generals Pope, Grant and Buell until he had 100,000 men at his disposal. On April 29, he advanced ever so slowly toward Corinth, entrenching at the end of each day while fending off the impatience of his subordinates. His troops were convinced they were going to dig their way to Corinth—Halleck took an entire month to travel 20 miles. Later, President Davis remarked that the reason for Halleck's slowness was his conviction that Beauregard's forces were more formidable than they actually were, rather than due to the bad roads about which the Union commander complained.[2] Others speculated that one of the reasons he took so long was his dislike of the hot, steamy Mississippi weather. In any case Union initiative in the west temporarily became subordinate to one plodding, united advance.

Meanwhile, Beauregard dug in and awaited his adversary. Corinth commanded the junction of the Mobile & Ohio and Memphis and Charleston railroads—arteries that linked eastern and western segments of the Confederacy. However, by May 25, Halleck had finally arrived at the place and was ready to lay siege. Faced with the overwhelming horde Halleck had surrounded himself with, and influenced by the fact that a fever epidemic had meanwhile broken out in the town, the Confederate commander skillfully evacuated Corinth and fell back 60 miles, to the town of Tupelo. Not one piece of military hardware was left behind, although Halleck was able to claim some 2,000 prisoners, nearly all of them sick.

Jefferson Davis, unhappy over the evacuation, impatiently awaited Beuregard's explanation, but none was forthcoming. The general finally explained to a Mobile newspaper that the evacuation was in effect "equivalent to a brilliant victory."[3] Later, Beauregard was removed from his command and Braxton Bragg assumed command of the Confederates in the west.

While the desultory campaign for Corinth was taking place, the Western Gunboat Flotilla was once more seizing the initiative. Flag Officer Foote launched his plans for a thrust down the Mississippi against Fort Pillow, the only major Rebel obstacle remaining between his flotilla and Memphis. But this time the gunboats would not simply be fighting a fort—they would have a naval battle on their hands.

From its brief northward flow at the hairpin turn at New Madrid, the Mississippi River meandered south again for about 50 miles until it made another hairpin turn, below which was the Confederate Fort Pillow, on the Tennessee shore. Located on a high bluff, the fortress position consisted of a five-mile-long line of breastworks with guns tiered up from the water's edge to the main works.

In all, the Rebel defenses contained around 40 guns, including 10-inch Columbiads that could fire a 50-pound shot 600 yards.[4] For the Confederates, the fort was important in that it would bar any riverborne assault against Memphis—the terminus, on the Tennessee side, of the vital Memphis & Little Rock Railroad that originated at Madison, Arkansas. At Memphis the tracks continued on as the Memphis & Charleston Railroad to Chattanooga and then as the Chattanooga & Atlanta Railroad connecting to Savannah, Georgia as the Georgia Railroad. It linked the produce-growing regions of Arkansas to the eastern edge of the Confederacy, supplying Southern armies and populace with food and troops. It was a vital artery for the Confederacy, and their belief was that Fort Pillow could block—or at least slow down—any Union move downriver, until reinforcements could be brought up from Beauregard's army.

On April 12 Flag Officer Foote, aboard the *Benton* at New Madrid, ran up a "Get Underway" signal. The gunboats *Cincinnati, Mound City, Cairo* and *St. Louis* then joined the flagship in a single column downstream. At Tiptonville, where they were anchored, *Carondelet* and *Pittsburgh* joined the column.[5] It must have been an inspiring sight: seven gunboats plus auxiliary vessels—coal barges, dispatch boats, tugs and supply ships—all moving to the fluttering beat of their paddle wheels, with high smokestacks belching ebony smoke and bright flags flapping from jackstaffs and flagstaffs.

At night the flotilla anchored just above the fort, outside the range of its guns, to await General Pope's troops aboard transports due the next day. The troops did arrive, but so did some Confederate gunboats called "cottonclads," which had been engaged in chasing a Yankee steamer upstream. They were so called because they had compressed bales of cotton around their vital parts and only one-inch iron plating placed over four-inch oak for protection against shot and shell.[6] When five of them came up to challenge the flotilla it seemed like a case of gnats against elephants and scarcely a challenge to the latter. After firing a few salvos at long-range, and receiving some in return from the ironclads' big guns, the Confederate vessels turned tail and fled downriver to safety below Fort Pillow. The gunboats remained blissfully unaware of what was in store.

The Union fleet stayed at anchor, awaiting the arrival of 16 mortar boats which, upon arrival, were secured at a bend just above the fort and out of range of its guns. These eight-inch "mortars on a raft" were capable of raining destruction with 44-pound projectiles that could arc over a thousand yards.

During a conference between Foote and Pope, it was decided that a plan of attack similar to that used at Island No. 10 would be employed: Pope's troops would be landed above the fort and would work their way around to encircle it. When all was in place, the gunboats would commence a heavy bombardment, after which the troops would move in and capture the fort. It was to be a classic river/land campaign that, given the relative forces involved, could only be defeated by one man: General Halleck.

For the great move upon Corinth, Halleck opined that Pope's forces would be essential to his success.[7] In fairness to "Old Brains," a further Confederate withdrawal to the south would have left Fort Pillow hanging, untenable by the Rebels in any case. Nevertheless the gunboats were now faced with a Confederate fort and its garrison that they could attack, but were simply not equipped to occupy. With the invasion plans gone awry, Foote settled down to a lengthy siege. The mortar boats were put into action and ordered to lob shells at the works—bombardments that had little effect. It was beginning to look, in fact, as if these much-vaunted weapons were not living up to expectations.

Meanwhile, Foote was being worn down by the river battles, his gaunt appearance shocking to some visitors who had known him before the war. One can speculate, too, that the loss of adrenalin he suffered when the attack on Fort Pillow was relegated to a siege may have influenced his health. Officially he stated that his leg wound had reached the stage at which he could no longer operate efficiently and he wired Secretary Welles for a leave of absence.[8] The Secretary sent Captain Charles H. Davis to relieve him for what was thought to be a temporary assignment. Davis, who was slated to be a bureau head in the Navy Department, was under the impression that he would be in charge only until Foote's return to duty.

But fate would not have it that way. Foote was given an administrative position in Washington for a time; then later was appointed to command the flotilla besieging Charleston, which would have granted his heartfelt wish to return to the blue waters of the ocean. He died on June 26, however, before fulfilling his duties. Davis was then designated Flag Officer of the Western Flotilla, with the rank of Commodore.

The 55-year-old Davis had entered the navy as a midshipman

in 1823 and had served in the Pacific, the Mediterranean and the South Atlantic. Appointed a captain, he had become Chief of Staff and Fleet Officer at the time of the Port Royal expedition off the South Carolina coast on November 7, 1861.[9] Welles knew his commanders; Davis was to prove an excellent choice during the months to come. And no sooner had Davis stored his gear in the wardroom of the *Benton* when the Confederates made their move.

The "siege" of Fort Pillow basically consisted of Union mortar boats moving each morning to within range of the works (around the bend from the Confederate guns) to lob projectiles that would hopefully do some damage. An ironclad gunboat from the flotilla would stand alongside for protection.

On May 10, the assigned escorting gunboat was *Cincinnati,* commanded by Roger Stembel, and the mortar boat was No. 16, under command of Acting Master Thomas B. Gregory. The mortar boat was passing the early morning hours firing its heavy weapon at regular intervals, when Gregory spotted huge volumes of smoke downriver. He warned Stembel and the *Cincinnati* began trying to get up steam when suddenly, around the bend, appeared J.E. Montgomery and the Confederate "River Defense Fleet."

James Edward Montgomery, commander of the Rebel flotilla, was not a career navy man. Originally a steamboat captain on the rivers, he tried to impress upon the Confederate Congress his plan to convert steamers to rams, each protected by cotton bales and armed with one or two guns. The crews were to be rivermen and not navy personnel, because they were more familiar with local waters than regular navy men. When the Navy Department, not surprisingly, turned him down, Montgomery instead obtained the backing of the War Department and proceeded to outfit the vessels that would protect Memphis from the dreaded Union gunboats.[10]

The components of the River Defense Fleet were: *Little Rebel,* flagship; *General Bragg,* a 1,000-ton, brig-rigged former Gulf steamer; *General Sterling Price,* a 483-ton, converted sidewheeler with four guns; *General Earl Van Dorn,* a former towboat with one 32-pounder; *General Sumter,* 460 tons, with four 32-pounders and one 12-pounder; *General M. Jeff Thompson,* of unrecorded tonnage and armament; *General Beauregard*, 454 tons, with four 8-inchers and one 42-pounder; and *General Lovell*, of unknown tonnage, but with one 32-pounder. These were all acquired from New Orleans.

The flotilla was no match for the Federals from a gunnery standpoint, but the Confederate vessels were fitted with rams, and had speeds of from eight to ten knots with remarkable maneuverability. As an example, the *General Beauregard* had dimensions of 161-foot length and 50-foot beam and, at 454 tons, the capability of delivering devastating attacks.[11]

The element of surprise and speed worked to the benefit of the Southern flotilla, and their captains were determined to take full advantage. *Cincinnati* slipped its lines and moved to midstream, while her black gang poured oil in the firebox to quickly build up steam. Before she could get up to speed, however, *General Bragg*, the first of the River Defense Fleet to come around the bend, steered straight at her, smashing into her starboard side. *Cincinnati* answered with a point-blank broadside into *Bragg*. But before the heavy ironclad could maneuver further, *General Sterling Price* slammed into her stern, knocking off her rudder.

The rest of the Union flotilla was now heading downstream to join the battle. *Carondelet* and *Mound City* were the first to arrive, and they poured devastating shots into *Bragg*, which was now already crippled by the salvos from *Cincinnati*. The Confederate vessel floated downstream, disabled and unmanageable, her tiller ropes gone.

Meanwhile, *General Sumter* was next to hit the reeling *Cincinnati*, opening that vessel up to the shell room. During the melee, Commander Stembel and Acting Fourth Master Reynolds were wounded by Confederate sharpshooters.

On mortar boat No.16, Acting Master Gregory had turned his mortar on the advancing flotilla by reducing the charges and lowering elevation. The mortar shells exploded over the Confederate vessels, showering them with shell fragments and causing many casualties.[12] *General Van Dorn* raced up to the mortar boat and fired two 32-pounder shells through its blinds. Then *Van Dorn* turned to *Mound City*, which had just been rammed by *General Sumter*, and struck her a glancing blow.

By this time the river was a seething mass of vessels with

clouds of gunsmoke obscuring vision. *Benton* was now in the fight, firing first at *General Lovell* and then *Van Dorn*. *Cairo* and *Pittsburgh* were steaming down looking for targets. *Mound City* was unable to stem her flooding and headed for the shore, where she sank in 12 feet of water. *Cincinnati* had already gone down in 11 feet. *Carondelet*, who had blasted her way through the crowd, found *General Sumter* with a 50-pound shot that penetrated her boilers. The Rebel ship exploded, and what was left of her drifted off downstream with enormous casualties.

By this time, the entire Union fleet had drawn up and were shelling the Confederate vessels mercilessly. Montgomery, figuring to quit while he was ahead, signaled a withdrawal and his force returned downriver, pursued by *Carondelet* and *Benton*.

When Davis recalled the two gunboats the battle was over. It had lasted a little over an hour. Confederate casualties were heavy, with one vessel lost and two damaged. Union casualties included no loss of life, but several men were wounded and two vessels sunk. Later, Commander Phelps, of the *Benton*, reported to Welles that the battle was the Union gunboats' "first purely naval action of the war."[13]

The Battle of Plum Point, as it was designated, appeared to be a Confederate victory. After all, they sunk two enemy ironclads and relieved the pressure on Fort Pillow, at least for a time. But it was a hollow victory in that the sunken ironclads were quickly raised and put back into commission. The steamer *Champion*, in the flotilla's train, had immediately been brought up with 20-inch pumps in her hold and been put to work pumping out the two ships. Also, for the first time in the river war, one of James Eads's submarine bell boats was brought into action to help raise the stricken vessels. *Mound City*, in fact, was raised the next day; *Cincinnati* was back in action within two months.

Later, in Cairo, Fleet Captain Pennock reported to Davis that Captain Stembel was expected to recover from his wounds. He had been transferred to the ordnance steamer *Great Western*, under the care of a fleet doctor, then sent to Cairo. Pennock also expressed the opinion that the Confederate attack was not intended to be a general one, but rather was an attempt to sink the *Cincinnati*, then cut the mooring lines of the mortar boat, allowing it to drift downstream where they would capture and have it for their own purposes.[14] In any case, Fort Pillow became a moot point when Beauregard withdrew from Corinth as Halleck's huge army bore down on him, thereby outflanking the fort. The garrison evacuated the works and systematically destroyed it, in a spectacular series of explosions, during the night of May 29, thereby ending the siege.

As for Montgomery and the Confederate River Defense Fleet, even though they couldn't match their Union counterparts in tonnage or weaponry, they had given an amazingly good account of themselves. The fleet fell back to Memphis and, with the addition of more gunboats from downstream, was determined to make the Union pay for every inch of the city and its adjoining water. All eyes were now turned toward Memphis as the next battleground in the river war. But one consequence of Plum Point was an increase in expectations for the Union's own ram fleet, which had already been in the making. In time for the battle for Memphis, the U.S. Army ram fleet was about to take center stage.

Colonel Charles Ellet, Jr., a civil engineer and an expert on building bridges, dams and locks, with additional expertise in river navigation, was commissioned a colonel and ordered to build a fleet of ram vessels to augment the growing Union river fleet. Ellet had become fascinated with the ram concept while an observer in Russia during the Crimean War. He attempted to persuade the Russians about the potential of a ram fleet, but they disdained it.

The ram concept, to be sure, was nothing new. The Greeks had rams on their triremes; warcraft with three banks of oars, a crew of 200 and a large, reinforced prow for ramming. It was the only method of fighting in those days, considering there was no ordnance. During the Battle of Salamis, in 480 B.C., the Greeks used their triremes to devastating effect. An observer, Aeschylus, reported that the Greek rams "smite them [the Persians] till their hulls overturned."[15]

At first the U.S. Government was no more enthusiastic about the idea than the Russians. In fact, it took the celebrated battle between the *Monitor* and the *Merrimac*, during which that

Confederate vessel did so much damage with her ram prow, to awaken the sleeping giants of government.[16]

The Navy still could not be sold on the concept but, like the Rebel Montgomery, Ellet found a patron in the War Department. They commissioned him to build his ram fleet, which would join the Western Gunboat Flotilla, but would remain under Army jurisdiction.

Ellet began working feverishly on his proposed fleet. He assembled nine vessels, former side-wheel palace boats and stern-wheelers for conversion. The rams were converted at different shipyards on the Ohio: *Lioness, Samson* and *Mingo* were outfitted in Pittsburgh; *Lancaster* and *Queen of the West* at Cincinnati; *Switzerland* at Madison, Indiana; *Monarch* was fitted out at New Albany; and the *Mingo* and the *T.D. Horner* at Cincinnati. As they were completed, they were rushed down the Ohio and completed at New Albany and Mound City.

Using braces and timber guards, Ellet strengthened each vessel's hold bulkheads with oak braces, from 12 to 16 inches thick and 4 to 7 feet high from stem to stern. These bulkheads were secured by cross-braces, in order that the entire weight of the vessel would be used upon impact. The bows were strengthened with iron sheath over solid oak, and the boilers and machinery were protected by a bulwark of squared timbers and iron braces.[17]

It was theorized that because of their weight of around 400 tons and speeds of from 11 to 12 knots, the rams would not be armed; however, a contingent of 15 sharpshooters with breech-loading carbines would be placed on board each vessel, with steam hoses for repelling boarders.[18] Ellet was convinced his vessels could sink any river craft they might encounter and that their speeds would protect them from shot and shell from shore batteries and gunboats. He even talked Washington into appointing his brother, Alfred, as the skipper of one ram.

Their effectiveness would depend on the ability to strike adversaries squarely. Ellet wrote: "No ram could stop to ram twice"; in the process it could possibly take a beating from a slightly injured adversary.[19] As an aid for identifying his vessels, he had the names of each painted on her paddlewheel box and huge initial letters on the spanner cables between the stacks.

After they were finished, Ellet took his rams, plus the *H.T. Horner*, acting as tender for the flotilla, to the area above Memphis where Davis' vessels were anchored. They moored just above the ironclads, where they received a cool reception from the flag officer, a man who had little respect for the rams, and especially their army commander. The rams, he ordered, would bring up the rear of the column.

Using the interim during which Union occupation of abandoned Fort Pillow was accomplished, Ellet had his crews work on strengthening their charges. Each night they would anchor about 20 feet from the shoreline. During the day, the boats would be pulled to the shore by means of heavy lines secured to large trees. Ever alert for the possibility of hostile boarders, Ellet deployed sharpshooters around the work area.

One night, as Currie relates, an alert sentry heard suspicious noises in the woods. Fearing a Rebel attack, Ellet immediately called an alarm. All hands quit working, went to general quarters and lay to their guns, ready to repel intruders. Instead of Confederates, the intruder turned out to be a lone cow, attracted to the site by the lights and noises. The animal stood, chewing its cud and staring balefully back at them. Everyone had a hearty laugh over the incident.[20]

Finally, on June 6, an order was issued by Davis for the entire fleet to get under way and steam downstream. The assault on Memphis was about to be launched. The huge fleet moved out, the heavier and slower ironclads in the van. The rams, each towing a supply barge, steamed at half speed and the rear was brought up by a train of auxiliary craft, including a small hospital steamer. Destination of the fleet was a sand bar, the designated anchor site known as "Paddy's Hen and Chickens," four miles above Memphis. Three miles below that site waited the Confederate River Defense Fleet. Montgomery's force of eight vessels lay line-abreast, anticipating their next opportunity to challenge the Union fleet.

Memphis, with a population of 33,000 in 1860, was, in addition to Vicksburg, one of the south's most important riverports, hosting junction of four railroads: the Memphis & Ohio, which ran north into Kentucky all the way to Louisville; the Memphis & Charleston, which connected the Mississippi with the far eastern reaches of the Confederacy; the Mississippi & Tennessee, which ran southward to New Orleans, furnishing another outlet to the Gulf; and the Memphis & Little Rock spur across the river in Arkansas. These lines, except for the Memphis & Ohio, which was in Union hands to the north, funneled food, supplies and recruits from the states west of the river to the eastern and southern regions of the Confederacy.

Named after the ancient Egyptian capital of the pharaohs, Memphis was incorporated as a town in 1826, and as a city in 1849. When plantations burgeoned around the city, Memphis prospered as a riverport and became a main outlet for one of the South's most important commodities, King Cotton. In addition to cotton and the rail and water links, Memphis was also host to an important shipyard, established in 1844, at which many assorted river craft were built.

Civil War shipyards, especially those on the Mississippi River, in no way resembled the shipyards of later years, with their dry-docks, paved roads and docks, huge supply buildings and forests of cranes. The shipyard at Memphis, according to extant photos, was a cluster of wooden sheds with lumber and supplies piled haphazardly below the bluff, at water's edge. The usual system of wooden ways that led up from the water, like those at Cairo and Mound City, were absent.[21] Apparently, a vessel's keel was laid parallel to water's edge, because the limited space along the river below the bluff would not allow a craft to be launched head- or stern-on. Afterward, the ribs, stern and bow posts and planking and, in the case of ironclads, iron plating were added, after which the machinery was installed by means of long, powerful booms mounted on steamers moored parallel to the building site. After her completion, the vessel was launched sideways into the river, using crude ways of greased lumber or logs, assisted by winches from steamers.

The Confederates lacked the sophisticated ways of an Eads shipyard, for example, but they managed to build and launch a number of boats, in the Mississippi and other rivers, including some ironclads. In June 1862, the only vessels being constructed at the Memphis shipyard were the ironclads *Tennessee* and the soon-to-be-famous *Arkansas.*[22]

After the fall of Island No. 10 and Fort Pillow, the partially constructed *Arkansas* was taken downriver, and towed to Greenwood up the Yazoo River, north of Vicksburg. The *Tennessee* was moved across the river to the Arkansas shore to be finished at a makeshift facility. There she was to await manpower and supplies necessary for her completion.

The morning of June 6, 1862, dawned sunny and clear, and as the dank river mists lifted, hordes of Memphis residents could be seen lining the bluff to watch their River Defense Fleet dispose of the Yankee invaders. Before the sun rose, the river resounded with the ringing of bootheels over iron decks, the sharp whining of tackles opening gunport covers and the furious rasping of coal shovels over iron plates as the stokers fed their gorged boilers. The fleet, with paddle wheels turning and stacks belching smoke, got under way, moving upstream toward the enemy flotilla, which was still anchored or moored at Paddy's Hen and Chickens.

At 5:00, the Confederates came into view of the Union vessels and opened fire. Davis, in *Benton*, signaled all vessels to get under way stern first, because any vessel with serious damage could churn upstream, and not float down into enemy territory. He hoisted the signal to "follow his motions," then opened fire on the oncoming Confederate flotilla. The battle for Memphis had begun.[23]

Ellet, aboard his flagship, *Queen of the West,* saw his opportunity to demonstrate the prowess of his rams. Using his hat, he signaled his brother Alfred, who commanded the *Monarch,* to round to and follow. Both rams rushed downstream, swiftly passed the lumbering ironclads, and headed straight for the enemy. Ellet stood on the hurricane deck, between the stacks, in disregard of his own safety, and directed the movements of the rams by continuing to wave his slouch hat.

On through a heavy pall of coal and gunsmoke over the river, the *Queen* and the *Monarch* plowed forward, using their superior speed, their stacks belching black smoke and swirling clouds of sparks. As more fuel was thrust into the boilers for flank speed, the hissing of steam from escape valves echoed over the river.

For their part, the ironclads could only open fire with their stern guns at the Confederate fleet to cover the fast-moving rams which carried no bow or stern guns. Those would be added later, after the rams proved their mettle and their effectiveness in combat. As first designed by Ellet, the heavy guns would have been a detriment to their speed.

Spotting the *General Lovell* ahead, Ellet headed his vessel directly at her, while he motioned his brother to steer for the *General Price.* As the *Queen* closed on her target, the *Lovell*'s captain lost his nerve and made the fatal mistake of turning at the last minute, exposing his vulnerable flank to the ram. The *Queen* hit her squarely amidships, in a crash that thundered across the river. The impact was so hard that furniture and pantryware were thrown around inside the *Queen*. It also caused the *Lovell* to roll over to starboard, her stack falling across the *Queen*'s bow. Most of the Confederate crew leaped overboard before the ram sank, taking the rest with her.

For her efforts, *Queen of the West* was rammed hard by *General Beauregard,* and was temporarily put out of action, losing one sidewheel. Thus disabled, she limped over to the Arkansas shore to beach herself.

Meanwhile, *Monarch* bore down on the *General Price*. The *Beauregard,* after ramming *Queen,* turned and also headed for *Monarch* at the same time. The two Rebel vessels converged on the hapless Ellet ram in a deadly river waltz. However, she was too fast for them and slipped by. Their powerful momentums working against them, *Beauregard* slammed into *Price,* shearing off her sidewheel and putting her out of the fight.[24] Ellet's insistence on vessels of high speed was being proven before every observer.

Monarch, her paddlewheels thrashing furiously, turned and rammed *Beauregard,* which was now also taking a pounding from the heavy guns of the Union ironclads. The Confederate vessel staggered to the Arkansas shore to ground herself along with her sisters. Steam and smoke spouting from myriad holes, she sank in shoal waters. *General Lovell,* enduring a furious beating by both

Queen and the ironclads, also slashed her way to the shore, where she too sank, taking most of her crew with her.

Attention was now turned to the Confederate flagship *Little Rebel,* which, after being heavily battered by the gunboats, steered for the shore. Receiving a final shove from *Monarch* that drove her high on land, her crew scrambled over the sides and joined their fellow shipmates who, by this time, were melting into the Arkansas landscape.

The Arkansas shore was proving popular with the Confederate crews this day, as *Bragg* took her turn running aground and also losing her crew to the alders and willows lining the banks. Downriver, *Jeff Thompson* was beached and blown up with a thunderous explosion that broke windows all the way up to Memphis.

Captain Walke of the *Carondelet* later wrote a vivid description of the battle: ". . . screaming, plunging shells crashed into the boats, blowing some of them and their crews into fragments, and the rams rushed upon each other like wild beasts in deadly conflict. Blinding smoke hovered above this confusion and horror."[25]

The Union juggernaut continued on, and *General Sumter* was next to go. Holed by gunfire from the ironclads, she ran aground, and was later raised, refitted and commissioned in the Union Navy.

The only Confederate vessel to get away was *General Van Dorn,* which, because of her speed, made her escape all the way downriver to safety under the glowering batteries of Vicksburg. *Monarch* and *Switzerland* were ordered to pursue, and chased her for about ten miles until they had to call it off; the enemy steamer was simply too fast.

The triumphal *Monarch* then made lines fast to the crippled *Beauregard,* and towed her to a bar where she settled on the bottom, and was later considered not worth salvaging.

Back in the arena, as the smoke of battle dissipated, it became obvious to the crowds on the levee that Memphis would soon fall. There was an exodus out of town by many citizens, as well as military personnel, who could not face the conquering Yankees. The Confederate River Defense Fleet faded into history.

On June 6, Flag Officer Davis sent a message to John Park,

Mayor of Memphis, requesting that he surrender the city. After acknowledging Davis' note, the gentlemanly Park answered: "In reply I have only to say that the civil authorities have no resources of defense, and by the force of circumstances, the city is in your power."[26]

It was to be some time before Union personnel learned of the wounding of Colonel Ellet. He had been hit by an enemy ball while directing his rams from the hurricane deck of the *Queen*. At the time, his wound was not considered too serious and he continued to give orders. When a white flag appeared on the Memphis shore, he sent his son, Medical Cadet Charles Rivers Ellet, Lieutenant W.D. Crandall and a sharpshooter contingent, Cyrus Lathrop and William H. McDonald.[27]

As the party wended its way through the crowded streets, with a Union flag to run up the flagpole over the Post Office building, they were followed by a jeering and threatening mob. After the flag was raised, the mob sealed off the exits, trapping the party on the roof. It was not until the mayor was sent for by Ellet and an implied threat made of bombardment that the party was allowed to leave. It was an unhappy echo of the treatment of the flag-bearing party that landed in New Orleans, some time before, and was graphically indicative of the deep, patriotic feelings of the Southern people at that time. As in New Orleans, the Memphis citizens reacted bitterly.

Two regiments from Pope's army, hand-picked for just such a purpose, were sent into the city, to be met by closed stores and deserted streets as the sullen citizens bowed to the occupation. When they were allowed to use Confederate money for a time, things got back to normal and Memphis once again came to life as a riverport center. In fact, an occupying soldier, enjoying his stay there, wrote that Memphis was a "most pleasant town."[28]

The victory was a cataclysm for both antagonists. Currie submitted his opinion that, as a naval battle, "The Memphis fight was one of the greatest ever fought on inland waters," and as a victory, he maintained that "it was most advantageous, because it opened the Mississippi to Vicksburg, a passage essential to our army and it struck the severest blow the Confederacy had yet received." He went on to laud the part Ellet and his rams played in the battle.[29]

Jefferson Davis wrote that the possession of Memphis was no longer disputed, and that "its occupation by the enemy promptly followed."[30]

The battle, according to Alfred Ellet, "was one of the most remarkable naval victories on record." He marveled that two unarmed, frail, wooden river steamers, with hardly enough men on board to handle the machinery and keep the boiler fires going, would rush into the enemy's advancing columns, sinking one ship, disabling and capturing others. The event was a sight never before witnessed. Ellet also speculated that if the enemy had pressed the initial charge at high speed upon the moored Union gunboats, the result might have been different.[31]

Naval historian H. Allen Gosnell speculated that the battle was a "wild and disordered melee, contested under a pall of heavy smoke. Accordingly it is hopeless to make any positive determination of the movements and performances of the fifteen vessels involved, let alone their relative positions at any time."[32]

The slowness of the ironclads at Plum Point to respond to his surprise attack gave Montgomery the courage to gamble his fleet in defense of Memphis. His error lay in the fact that he had surprise on his side at the former but not the latter.[33] In fact, at Memphis it was Montgomery's force that were taken by surprise, when Ellet's rams came out of nowhere and charged headlong into his flotilla. Of course at Memphis, as at New Orleans, the Confederates were desperately trying to build full-fledged ironclad gunboats, but these had not been ready in time.

Colonel Ellet's career was to be short-lived. Although he continued to function as a commander in the ram fleet, his strength waned and he became seriously ill. He was placed aboard the hospital ship *Switzerland* and sent up to Cairo for further treatment, but he didn't make it, passing away on June 21. His government, wanting to honor him publicly, gave him a state funeral at Independence Hall in Philadelphia. Meanwhile, his brother, Alfred Washington Ellet, who was now senior commander, took command of the ram fleet.

One result of the fall of Memphis was the capture of a great number of spoils of war harvested by Union forces, including six river steamers that were tied up at the city's wharfs. The Confederate forces, however, had pulled out; only 100 prisoners were taken.

After the battle, Commander Phelps of the *Benton* obtained a Confederate flag that flew from the peak of the captured gunboat *General Bragg*, and sent it to Ohio's governor, David Tod. In his letter he remarked: "I feel great satisfaction in being able to present to the state of Ohio, this trophy taken 'in action' which terminated so disastrously to the Rebel cause."[34]

It was now the early summer of 1862. In the east, General McClellan's peninsula campaign had failed, however in the west Union forces had scored triumph after triumph. One more push would be required and the Confederacy would be split.

CHAPTER ELEVEN

Eyeing Vicksburg from the South

After the fall of Memphis, combined with the Federal coup at New Orleans, the fate of Vicksburg, Mississippi now seemed to hang by a thread. To this Rebel citadel David Glasgow Farragut turned his attention, but only because Washington willed it. Personally, he had no desire to submit his ships to the swift currents of the river and its shallow drafts. Summer was approaching and the river would soon fall. Too, up the Mississippi enemy batteries were placed on bluffs from which his ships would be subject to plunging fire and his guns unable to elevate enough in order to fire back. Farragut commanded a different sort of fleet from the kind that had stormed out of Cairo, Illinois. His were bluewater ships, wooden, not ironclad, and, though powerful, weren't created for river fighting.

One can sympathize with Farragut's position. He had just epitomized the strategic importance of naval supremacy. Now he was being charged with taking frigates across sandbars into brown water, deep in enemy territory, into unknown (shallow) depths during a hot Mississippi summer. Lord Nelson, after all, may have won the Battle of the Nile, but he wasn't asked to sail upriver to the Sudan. Farragut related his doubts to Secretary Gideon Welles and wondered aloud as to the feasibility of attacking the Gulf port of Mobile, Alabama instead.[1]

In New Orleans, an alarmed General Butler also wrote Welles concerning Farragut's indecision about moving upstream. There was a flurry of anxiety in Washington over whether Farragut was on the team, with several redundant dispatches sent. In any case, the Admiral soon realized the error of his thinking, and made plans to move against the next largest city in the state of Louisiana: Baton Rouge. On May 6, he sent the *Iroquois* upriver to demand the surrender of that city, although there was no Rebel garrison or batteries there. The *Brooklyn* was to follow a few hours later.

Baton Rouge was named after a red cypress tree that marked the boundary between Indian tribes. In 1719, a fort was established there by the French, and in 1763 the area was ceded to England at the conclusion of the French and Indian War. Later the area came under Spanish control, then went back to the French again and finally became a part of the United States, via the Louisiana Purchase of 1803. Baton Rouge was incorporated as a city in 1817, and became the state capital in 1849. During the Civil War, the capital of Louisiana was moved to other sites: Opelousas, Alexandria and Shreveport. It was returned to Baton Rouge only in 1882, long after hostilities had ended. From the rich farmlands around it came cotton, rice, fruit, vegetables and sugar. These staples became vitally important to the Confederacy during the early days of the war.

The city was never fortified, because the Confederates had considered it protected by the strength of New Orleans to the south and Vicksburg to the north. With the former fallen, however, Baton Rouge was now slated as the new citadel to hinder Yankee control of the lower Mississippi. From the Union perspective it was imperative that Baton Rouge be occupied before any attempts at fortification could take place.

The *Iroquois*, and supporting craft, reached the area on May 7, 1862, and dropped anchor abreast of the city. Commander James E. Palmer, captain of the *Iroquois* and commander of the force, sent an officer ashore to summon the mayor to a conference on board. A young girl, Sarah Morgan, living in the city, saw the "graceful young Federal" as he stepped ashore and asked her for instructions to the mayor's office. She maintained that the Federals "had disarmed me by their kindness," continuing "I admire foes who show so much consideration for our feelings."[2]

Nevertheless the mayor was "out of town," and would not surrender the city. His vice mayor would, it was offered, come in his place.[3]

Frustrated and angered by the obvious snub, Palmer wrote his flag officer: "Here is a capital of the state with 7,000 inhabitants acknowledging it is defenseless, and yet assuming an arrogant tone, trusting to our forbearance."[4] However, with the arrival of the *Brooklyn*, Palmer took a bolder tone. He sent a message to the village hall, laying down the condition that the city must be surrendered to the naval forces of the United States, while he assured them that the rights and property of all citizens would be respected.

Palmer further demanded that all Confederate state property be turned over to him and that the United States flag be flown over the arsenal in town. Frustrated by this demand, Mayor B.F. Bryan, who was not out of town after all, shot back a letter stating that his city would not surrender voluntarily to any power on earth. He denied any influence over the arsenal.[5] Finally, Palmer's patience ran out; he sent an armed party ashore whose members raised the flag over the arsenal. That settled that.

Captain Craven of the *Brooklyn*, now commander of the expedition, left some vessels to watch the city, and sent a force upriver toward the Union fleet's second objective, Natchez.

Natchez, the epitome of the antebellum South, was the oldest city along the Mississippi. It was founded by Pierre Lemoyne d'Iberville, who built a fort on the site in 1716. Destroyed by the Natchez Indians in 1729, it was re-established in 1771 and rapidly grew to become a center of wealth and influence and a steamboat port of great importance.

Like New Orleans and Baton Rouge, Natchez had a mayor devoted to the Southern cause. On May 12 Commander Palmer had brought up the *Iroquois*, and dropped anchor off the city's waterfront, joining the *Oneida* and some gunboats which had been sent ahead of him. He summoned the mayor and, once again, as at Baton Rouge, a city official refused to meet with him. The recalcitrance of river cities was beginning to wear thin with the Union commander.

The angry Palmer seized a ferryboat that had been coaling

and, armed with a force of sailors, marines and a couple of howitzers, he threatened to land, march on the town and seize it by
force. The mayor quickly recanted and sent a couple of frightened
representatives carrying an apology from himself to Palmer.
Natchez was surrendered and occupied by a token force, until
army troops could arrive, in order to prevent any Confederate
attempts to take back the town.[6]

With Baton Rouge and Natchez now in Union hands,
Farragut decided to take the *Hartford* and accompanying vessels
on a foray up the river to reconnoiter the defenses of Vicksburg
itself. He found those defenses formidable: heavy batteries to the
south and north of the city, 29 guns in all; 8,000 troops and a fleet
of gunboats lurking under the protection of those guns.[7]
Considering that there was nothing he could do, Farragut returned to New Orleans, once again considering an attack on
Mobile. There he was greeted by another flurry of messages from
Washington ordering him to assault Vicksburg, in coordination
with Charles H. Davis' fleet to the north. President Lincoln, as
ever, held his eyes on the prize: splitting the Confederacy by taking the Mississippi.

On May 24, Farragut returned to a point below Vicksburg to
again study the military capabilities of the city. And once again,
he found the defenses seemingly impregnable. As he had anticipated, the batteries on the bluff were too high for his ships' guns
to elevate. He returned to New Orleans again, after almost strand-
ing the *Hartford* at high water because of her deep draft—a problem that plagued him often on the Mississippi.

At this point in time, Confederate batteries were active along
the river from Port Hudson, just north of Baton Rouge, to
Vicksburg. Farragut's ships were only able to move up and down
the river because of their superior armament and mobility, and
they still had to fight their way past these batteries each time.
Also, the Red River, between Port Hudson and Vicksburg, was
still under Confederate control, and it connected the eastern half
of the Confederacy with the vast resources of Louisiana and
Texas. Over this river flowed food, raw materials, supplies and
over 100,000 recruits for the Southern armies.

To the north of Vicksburg were high hills, or bluffs, upon

which gun batteries could command the northern approaches of the river and stand as a deterrent to riverborne landings and challenge any bombardment attempts by Union forces. One rise in particular, Haynes Bluff, contained Confederate fortifications that would play a vital part in the siege of Vicksburg during the difficult days ahead.

As the navy and army commanders and General Halleck argued endlessly over the merits of assaulting Vicksburg, its defenders, under the leadership of General Van Dorn, were busy preparing defenses against an attack from all sides. Unfortunately, the foot-dragging by Union commanders lost for them a golden opportunity to take Vicksburg early on, when troops at Corinth and New Orleans were available and when the Vicksburg garrison was seriously undermanned.

CHAPTER TWELVE

Treacherous
White River

G eneral Samuel Curtis was still in trouble in Arkansas. Having marched into the northeastern sector of the state, he found himself and his army without supplies and without food for his animals. Harassed by Confederate General Thomas C. Hindman's cavalry, Curtis was unable to forage the countryside without troop protection for the foraging parties. In addition, Curtis had reason to believe that Hindman had received reinforcements from Texas and was much stronger than he actually was.[1] Curtis pulled back to Batesville on the White River, where he fired off messages for help.

A worried Halleck called upon Flag Officer Davis to dispatch several of his gunboats, with steamers of supplies and troops, to go to Curtis' aid. Davis, in fact, had already formulated his own plan to sweep the Arkansas and White rivers in order to seek out any remaining Confederate gunboats that might have escaped from the battles at New Orleans and Memphis, including the fast gunboat *General Van Dorn*. The flag officer readily agreed to Halleck's expansion of the mission and began to make preparations. Unfortunately, he only had a few of the gunboats of the Western Flotilla on hand, so he called upon Colonel Charles Ellet, the commander of the ram fleet, for assistance. Ellet demurred, however, citing the temporary disabilities of his vessels after the recent battle for Memphis. His force lacked provisions and maintenance.[2] He did, nevertheless, promise three of his rams to Davis for the expedition. Lt. Colonel Currie would command the ram contingent, but would not be under navy jurisdiction.[3] After all, Ellet reasoned, wasn't the recent victory at Memphis due to the independent action of the rams?

An annoyed Davis declined Ellet's offer, because he resented the colonel's insistence that he remain independent of Navy control. The Western Flotilla, he decreed, would go it alone without the rams, but with a train of troop transports and supply vessels. The vessels picked by Davis for the mission were: *Mound City*, as flagship for the new commander, Augustus H. Kilty; *St. Louis*; the timberclad *Lexington*; and the armored tug *Spitfire*.

On the morning of June 12, Kilty ordered the squadron to get underway. By early afternoon they had reached the mouth of the St. Francis River. There was a brief interlude, during which the *Spitfire* sortied up the river on a reconnaissance mission. Inasmuch as there were no threats to the convoy on those waters, the tug returned, but not before the skipper had spotted a considerable amount of cotton bales on a wharf. Kilty was pressed for time, so he decided to leave the removal of the bales to another flotilla. At 1500 he gave the order to get under way, and the force proceeded upriver once more.

At Helena, Arkansas, the squadron came upon a large steamer, the *Clara Dolsen*, moored to a wharf. The 939-ton, 268-foot-long vessel was one of the finest and fastest river steamers on the Mississippi. Upon spotting the flotilla upriver, she cast off and, with flank speed, fled downriver pursued by *Lexington*, the fastest vessel in the flotilla. But the *Clara Dolsen* was a bit too fast even for the swift timberclad, and got away.[4]

On June 14, Kilty's squadron reached Montgomery's Point at the mouth of the White River, 180 miles south of Memphis. There they moored while the *Spitfire* went upriver on her usual reconnoitering mission.

The White River, while not as long as the Arkansas, flows into the Mississippi just below the latter, but is joined to it by a channel called the Arkansas Cutoff, just above the Mississippi. The White rises in the depths of the Boston Mountains in northwestern Arkansas, detours for a bit through southern Missouri before turning south again, where it winds, meanders and finally empties into the Mississippi. In 1862, its major tributaries were the Black, Cache, Little Red and North Fork rivers. The White River is around 685 miles long, drains 28,000 square miles of Arkansas soil and is navigable for large craft up to 300 miles from its mouth. General Curtis had picked his campsite well.

After regrouping his force, Kilty signaled all vessels to follow his *Mound City* up the narrow river in single file. Then to everyone's pleasant surprise, the *Spitfire* came around the bend with a prize in tow, the *Clara Dolsen*.[5] The tug had captured the steamer a short way upstream, where she had been moored. It seemed that the river had not been wide enough for the vessel to go any further so she had became stranded.

At the Arkansas River Cutoff, Kilty ordered the squadron to anchor and wait for the expected convoy containing a contingent of troops from the 46th Regiment of the Indiana Volunteer Infantry. This convoy, under the escort of the timberclad *Conestoga*, arrived shortly, accompanied by the big transport *New National*, a 317-ton steamer captured from the Confederates at Memphis; a small steamer *Jacob Musselman*; and the supply vessel *White Cloud*. The troops were under the command of Colonel Graham M. Fitch.

The entire fleet now steamed up the White, in single column, with *Mound City* in the van, followed by the *St. Louis*, the other gunboats and train vessels following. The trip was uneventful except for a report from army scouts indicating that the Rebels had established artillery batteries on the bluff and had blocked the river near St. Charles. The fleet halted for the night, while Kilty and his commanders formed strategy for the assault on the enemy stronghold the next morning.

The Confederates at St. Charles were planning a warm reception for the flotilla. Earlier, after the fall of Memphis, Confederate General Hindman, concerned that the Federals might sortie up the Arkansas and White rivers, had his engineers survey them for possible obstruction sites. Inasmuch as the Arkansas was low, attention was then turned to the White. The engineers determined that St. Charles, between two bends in the river and with high bluffs, was the best choice for a site, not only to obstruct the river, but to establish artillery positions to cover the obstructions.[6]

The site, from a tactical viewpoint, was an ideal one. Confederates soldiers and civilians (and also slaves) were put to work on the battery sites: one was high, the other at riverside. Logs were rafted in and pounded into the river bottom by two pile drivers. On the bluff, Hindman placed two 32-pounder rifled pieces that were brought up on the gunboat *Pontchartrain* under the command of Captain J.W. Dunnington. In addition, two 3-inch rifled pieces, brought from the arsenal at Little Rock, were placed into position. Later, the captain of the 399-ton gunboat *Maurepas*, which had been moored at St. Charles, removed his armament of two rifled 3-inchers and a brass 12-pound howitzer; they were then placed into position on the lower battery.[7]

It was next decided to scuttle the *Maurepas*, along with the transports *Eliza G.* and *Mary Patterson*, in the center of the river as obstructions. The theory was that an enemy flotilla would be forced to halt at the obstruction and thereby be subject to enfilading by the batteries. The Confederates sat back and waited for the Yankees to come up the river. They did not have to wait long.

On June 16, The Union flotilla column consisted of *Mound City, St. Louis, Lexington* and *Conestoga* abreast, with transports following and the train vessels to the rear; it moved upriver toward Hindman. About two miles south of St. Charles, Kilty halted, allowing the transports to disgorge Colonel Fitch's troops.

Once this force formed and began marching on the fort, the gunboats got under way, shelling the woods in front of and to the rear of the troops, to drive away any lurking enemy forces.[8]

Slowly and surely, the gunboats moved upriver, blasting away at the underbrush with cannister and grape ahead of Fitch's advancing columns. As they rounded the bend, they sighted the superstructures of the scuttled vessels in midstream and the bluff containing the batteries just below. The Confederates opened fire on the leading vessel.

Kilty, not wanting to risk the timberclads to any masked batteries along the riverside, ordered them to anchor and to give his ironclads cover as they moved up to engage the batteries head-on. The *Mound City* and *St. Louis* turned their big 8-inch bow guns on the lower battery and commenced blasting away, but the Rebel gunners, slackening their fire a bit, held to their guns and continued with answering fire.[9] Then, for some reason, Kilty thinking he had the upper hand and the lower battery under control, ordered more steam and moved his vessel to within point-blank range, pounding away at the upper battery even while it pounded back at the gunboat.

Then the disaster happened. A 69-pound shot hit *Mound City* on her port side, smashing through the iron plating and heavy timbers underneath, exploding her steam drum. The carnage was horrible; steam filled the casemate, scalding many of the crew and sending some overboard. As the crippled gunboat drifted downstream, her sisters lowered boats to pick up survivors. She came to rest on the right bank near the lower battery. The Confederates demanded the striking of her colors, but the crew refused. Some of the Rebel soldiers from the lower battery rushed down and placed hands on the anchor stocks, declaring victory. Then, frustrated over the refusal of the crew to surrender, they turned their attention to the men in the water and shot them in cold blood.

The elated upper battery then sighted the *St. Louis* and launched a barrage of shots at her. The ironclad answered in kind with her bow guns, and a raging duel ensued.

Meanwhile, Fitch's troops had reached the fortification, swarmed over the parapets and driven off the defenders, killing and wounding some, including the commander of the lower battery, a Captain Fry, who was taken prisoner. The Battle of St. Charles was over. Battered *Mound City* was taken in tow by the *Conestoga* and the *Spitfire* and hauled away out of further danger.

Because Kilty was scalded along with his crew, First Master John E. Duble took command of the vessel. After an inspection, he was dismayed to discover the remaining crew members drunk, along with crewmen from other vessels. The officer's quarters had been broken into and personal effects strewn about. Many items had been stolen, even from those dead or wounded.[10]

Another disaster was narrowly avoided when the *New National* kept getting in the way of the *Conestoga*. At one point she was alongside the *Mound City* when a badly scalded gunner's mate aboard the ironclad, while in his death throes, accidentally pulled the lanyard of a loaded and primed 8-inch gun. The shot slammed into the transport, injuring one man and severing a steam line.

In his report to the flag officer, Duble remarked that he would never again be placed in such a position where he was compelled to see such misery, such depravity and so much disorder.[11] The casualty list on the *Mound City* was heavy. Out of a complement of 187 officers and men, 125 men were either killed by steam, drowned or shot in the water, and 25 were wounded, including Captain Kilty.

After the battle was over, Davis wrote a report that the victory had given the Union command of the White River and had secured communications with General Curtis and that he would be "unalloyed with regret but for the accident to the steam drum and heater of the *Mound City*."[12]

The next day, after the transports had left to take the wounded back to Memphis, the gunboats moved 65 miles upriver to a place called Crooked Point. But when it was determined that the river was dropping too fast, the flotilla moved downstream to avoid being stranded in shallow water.

In retrospect, the White River campaign had some important ramifications. On the plus side, the river was opened up to Union traffic, allowing supplies and men to reach the beleaguered Curtis; three Confederate vessels were also destroyed, including a gunboat. It was unfortunate that the *Pontchartrain* had already made her escape up the Arkansas River, to the protection of Little Rock.

On the minus side, it was obvious that the heavy damage to *Mound City* could have been avoided. The flotilla commander should have remembered the lessons learned from Fort Donelson that gunboats should never get too close to gun emplacements on a bluff. Captain Kilty was a brave man who had stood on deck, fully exposed to direct fire, as he ordered his ship right into the mouths of the Rebel batteries. But he had tried to win the battle by himself. With Union troops about to attack the fort from the rear, he could have exercised more caution.

The Confederates had proven anew the effectiveness of covering a river obstruction with heavy guns trained on vessels forced to halt before them. This lesson, acquired about river obstructions such as those at the forts below New Orleans, had stuck and was successfully used at St. Charles. The Union fleet had halted and been pummeled, losing one gunboat in the process. It took troops on land to spike the gun batteries, something the gunboats were not able to accomplish.

However, the Union had re-proved a thesis of its own, that of coordinating a simultaneous land and river assault against a strong fortification. Bombardments from vessels alone would not do the trick; land forces had to be used in coordination with those on the water. Also, better methods of dealing with the obstructions themselves would have to be worked out, without men exposing themselves to lethal fire from enemy batteries. This and other hard lessons learned would be put to effective use in coming campaigns.

Meanwhile, on the Mississippi, Admiral Farragut had reluctantly come up to Vicksburg for the third time, now with Porter's flotilla of mortar schooners and a contingent of 3,000 soldiers, on loan from General Butler at New Orleans. On June 26 the mortars commenced bombarding the town and for two days caused a great deal of fascinating pyrotechnics, but little or no serious damage. It was plain to Farragut that Vicksburg was an entirely different matter from New Orleans and that the guns on its high bluffs were not about to surrender to his ships. The Union army needed to take a hand. Nevertheless, rather than stand by passively observing both the mortar boats and the rapidly falling river, he decided to run past the batteries.

At 0200 on June 28, Farragut raised his famous "get-underway" signal of two vertical red lights up the mizzenmast of the *Hartford*, and the fleet got underway, the *Iroquois* in the van. At 0400, the Confederates spotted the flotilla and opened a withering fire. The guns of the fleet answered with salvos, backed by the incessant rounds of the mortars. By daylight, the fleet was safely past the city although the *Brooklyn* and two other ships didn't get through. Damage to the fleet was light; only a few vessels, including the flagship, had been hit. The *Hartford* received a cannonball directly in the captain's cabin, a few moments after Farragut had left it.

Farragut wired Gideon Welles that his run past Vicksburg was "to no purpose" but that the fire of his ships was "tremendous" and that he had managed to get most of his flotilla of big ships through unscathed.[13] In divining the military situation around the town he wrote Welles that he was "satisfied it is not possible for us to take Vicksburg without an army force of twelve or fifteen thousand men. General Van Dorn's division is here and lies safely behind the hills."[14]

Once past Vicksburg, Farragut's fleet did have the pleasure of encountering their counterparts from the north. The Western Gunboat Flotilla never snuck up on anyone, filling the air as it did with smoke and noise as it churned downstream from Memphis to join hands with the squadron from the Gulf. When the two disparate fleets met, amid great celebration in both flotillas, the Mississippi, in theory, if not in practice, had been taken.

Commodore Davis and Farragut held a conference, however, at which they both agreed that naval forces alone could not subdue Vicksburg; it would take a large force of troops, in coordination with mortars and naval guns. Both commanders wired Halleck to that effect, but the painfully cautious general informed them he could spare no men. He was still holding together the 100,000 strong Union forces at Corinth.

Twelve miles above Vicksburg the water was already too low for Farragut's large ships, and the river was receding farther every day. Farragut and Davis nevertheless formulated plans for a bombardment of the city, in prelude to any army assault. The mortar fleet continued lobbing shells into the city, but to no avail—Union troops failed to show up from the land side and, in the depths of the Mississippi summer heat, the fleet was beginning to suffer. One thing by now was certain: the conquest of Vicksburg was going to be a long and arduous campaign.

Meanwhile, Colonel Ellet, ever anxious to get his rams into action, and having been the vanguard of the fleet on the way down from Memphis, took the *Monarch* and *Lancaster* up the Yazoo River on June 28, to seek out and destroy any enemy vessels lurking there. The rams, comprising the first Union incursion into this sector, raised havoc with enemy craft and installations, although they didn't travel very far up the river.

The Yazoo had its beginnings at the confluence of the Tallahatchie and Yalobusha rivers, then flowed parallel to the Mississippi for 189 miles, emptying into it just above Vicksburg. It flowed through a fertile region known as the Yazoo Delta (or Basin, as it is called today) with Greenwood and Yazoo City the most important towns.[15]

The Yazoo River and Yazoo City were the center of much activity during the campaign for Vicksburg. And a part of this activity concerned a vessel that was about to take center stage in the Mississippi River war. The Confederates had already proven, with the *Virginia*, that they could build as formidable a warship as any other afloat. But in the west, their efforts, based as they were on their meager industrial infrastructure, had repeatedly been foiled by Federal encroachments and unexpected attacks. The unfinished *Tennessee* was burned at its dock at Memphis. At New Orleans, the *Louisiana* and the *Mississippi* hadn't been ready in time to meet Farragut's onslaught. Along the entire length of the Mississippi, only one ironclad-in-progress had been gotten away, up the Yazoo River, from the Union fleets converging from both north and south. And in July 1862 it was ready to fight. The U.S. Navy was about to meet the Rebel ironclad C.S.S. *Arkansas.*

Confederate Counterstroke

James Eads had his counterpart in Memphis, in respect to build-ing gunboats for his country. Although engaged in a project less expensive and ambitious, Captain John Shirley, a steamboat mogul from Memphis, had received a contract from the newly formed Confederate government, in the fall of 1861, to construct two ironclad men-of-war for the protection of Memphis from Federal assault. With contract in hand, worth $160,000, Shirley laid the keels for two vessels, *Arkansas* and *Tennessee*, at his ship-yard at Fort Pickering, 12 miles below Memphis.[1]

In spite of shortages of skilled shipyard personnel—most of them having gone north to Yankee shipyards where the money was better—work was commenced in earnest. As it progressed, the Confederates pinned great hopes on these vessels, believing they would be more than a match for Union gunboats. Lack of resources, however, finally forced Shirley to construct one vessel at a time and the work proceeded at a painfully slow pace. As late as March 1862, the hulls were far from complete; General Beauregard, now commander of the Army of the Mississippi, ordered that the vessels be completed and he sent a naval officer to inspect the hulls. The officer, Lieutenant John J. Guthrie, reported that of the two hulls one would take six more weeks to complete and that the other, the *Arkansas*, would soon be launched.[2]

After Island No. 10 fell to Union forces, followed by the fall of New Orleans, the *Arkansas*, commanded by Lieutenant Charles H. McBlair, was towed downstream by the steamer *Capitol*, along with barges loaded with equipment with which to complete the vessel. The hull of the *Tennessee* was destroyed on the stocks, to keep it out of Union hands. Because New Orleans and its shipyards were in Federal hands, McBlair took his charge up the Yazoo River to Greenwood, 12 miles upriver, where he hoped it would be completed. The inept McBlair was unable to finish the work, so he left her moored in a state of disrepair with engine parts, boilers, guns without carriages and assorted equipment strewn about her decks and her partly completed iron plating badly rusted. The rest of the plating lay on the bottom of the river in a sunken barge. What the Confederates had was a rusty hulk without any lethal iron teeth.

Furthermore, the *Arkansas* had no deckhouse and no engines. She was a floating wreck and not at all the juggernaut she was supposed to be. The citizens of Greenwood were upset to the point where they petitioned the Confederate Navy Department to send someone more competent to take charge. Even General Beauregard got into the act by urging Mallory to replace McBlair.[3]

The man picked to replace him was Lieutenant Isaac N. Brown, a Kentuckian and a 28-year veteran of the U.S. Navy, who had been in charge of the New Orleans shipyards at the time of Farragut's assault. He arrived at Greenwood on May 28, and after inspecting the hull, was so appalled at McBlair's "lukewarmness and inefficiency," that he actually considered shooting him.[4] McBlair took off for Richmond to protest his handling at the hands of Brown, but he must have met with a negative reception for there is no record of what later became of him.

Brown's first move was to establish his headquarters at a nearby plantation from which he requisitioned blacksmiths, carpenters and five machinists.[5] He then procured a contingent of soldiers from Fort Pemberton to assist in the raising of the sunken barge. This they did with the help of a diving bell. The site was not desirable, so the Arkansas was towed downstream to Yazoo City where she was moored to the south side below the loop made by the river as it passed the town.[6]

Yazoo City was an ideal spot for a shipyard. Founded in 1824 as Hanan's Bluff, it was incorporated in 1830 and named Manchester. Later the name was changed to Yazoo City, because of the Yazoo Indians who inhabited the region. By 1839, the town had become the largest community in the county with a population of around 1,000, and was also the state's largest marketing center.[7]

The people of Yazoo City gave their generous support to the *Arkansas* project. Blacksmiths were sent from surrounding plantations, iron was hauled down from a rail junction at Vaughan and wagon masters at Jackson built the gun carriages. Ordnance stores were brought up from Vicksburg, shot balls were forged in Jackson and some powder was made in Yazoo City itself.

With over 200 workmen and 12 iron forges active, the work continued around the clock with Brown tirelessly attending to every detail. During that time, he wrote his wife that his attention was entirely required in getting the Arkansas ready. In order to protect the gunboat, while under construction, Brown had a raft moored in the middle of the river, a few miles down, containing two 42-pounders and a contingent of militia.[8] He sent the craft down the river to watch for any Union excursions upward. All attention in the area was focused on the ironclad. Materiel was brought in by wagons from the railroad yard at Vaughan, 15 miles to the east. All day under the sun the crews worked, and at night they labored under pine torches.

When the two Union fleets converged at a point above Vicksburg—Farragut's from the south; Davis's from the north—Van Dorn, in command at Vicksburg, grew nervous. He insisted that the *Arkansas* be completed, put under his orders and sent against the powerful enemy fleet. "It was better to die in action," he maintained, "than be buried up at Yazoo City."[9]

Finally the *Arkansas* was ready to sortie down the river to meet the enemy, not because she was completed to everyone's satisfaction, but because of pressure from higher up and because the river was falling, prompting the fear that she would be stranded at Yazoo City, helpless.

Resembling a house on a raft, the hull was a viable ironclad ram, at least on the surface. Her crew affectionately labeled her "Bucket of Bolts," while others referred to her as "an hermaphrodite ironclad."[10] Nevertheless, she was 165-feet long with a 35-foot beam and an 11-foot draft. She sported a solid iron ramming beak 16-feet long, 10-feet wide bolted to eight feet of timbers. Her casemate consisted of charcoal iron plating, 18-inches thick with wood and compressed cotton backing, sloped at a 45-degree angle, with railroad iron added to the casemate; her pilot house projected only two feet above. The power plant, made up of two low-pressure engines with an output of 900 horsepower, raised from the sunken steamboat *Natchez*, powered the twin screws. There were no rudders; it was hoped that the screws operating independently would easily maneuver the craft.

The gunboat's armament consisted of two 9-inch smoothbores, two 64-pounders, two 6-inch rifles and two 32-pounder smoothbores.[11]

Finally, low water forced Brown to move his ram downstream, with a crew of 100 men. She cast off on July 12, with the citizens of Yazoo City on the banks to cheer her on. The vessel maneuvered to midstream and, with a top speed of eight knots, began the journey to her destiny. By the time she reached the town of Satartia, a broken steam line fouled her powder supply and she was forced to moor alongside a sawmill while the powder was spread out on tarpaulins to dry in the sun, atop piles of sawdust. By constant turning and shaking, the powder was finally dried by nightfall and placed in the aft magazine.[12] After dark, the *Arkansas* continued her brave odyssey down the river, toward the awaiting Union fleet.

The morning of July 15, 1862 found the ironclad approaching the Old River, a Mississippi channel that the Yazoo once followed, before changing its course many years before and now entering the Mississippi some 12 miles above Vicksburg. One of the crewmen described the scene as being almost "bucolic, warm and calm, allowing smoke to rise above the trees, allowing easy observation of oncoming river craft."[13] The men were at battle stations with guns primed and ready. Then a Union tugboat in the river spotted the smoke from the Confederate vessel's stack, swung around and ran downstream, her whistle blowing wildly.

Farragut couldn't see the danger in the approach of a lone

enemy gunboat, so he sent three ships, which, coincidentally or not, comprised a cross-section of the Union river fleet: the gunboat *Carondelet*, the army ram *Queen of the West* and the timberclad *Tyler*, each by now a renowned vessel. The trio steamed up the Yazoo to meet the oncoming "threat," while the fleet remained idle, conserving fuel at anchor.

At 0600, the antagonists came within sight of each other, and the Union personnel immediately realized that the rumored Confederate monster of an ironclad was no rumor; it was alive. What they saw was a house-like vessel colored a "chocolate brown," because of her layers of rust, with a huge smokestack belching volumes of black smoke. Projecting through two opened gunports on the bow were the black, ugly snouts of heavy guns.

The first vessel to open fire was the *Tyler*, at a range of half a mile. The *Arkansas* responded with her two bow guns. Commander Gwin of the *Tyler* stopped his engines and allowed his craft to drift downstream, keeping up a rapid fire from his own bow guns, until he reached a spot 100 yards off the *Carondelet*'s bow.[14] Together, the two Union gunboats poured a withering fire at the approaching ram, but the "monster" kept coming, projectiles bouncing off her casemate. Lieutenant Grift, aboard the *Arkansas*, reported that the gunnery of the Federals was excellent and that their rifle bolts [shots] rang on his vessel's armor, shifting some of the iron but not penetrating. One of his crewmen, with "more curiosity than prudence," thrust his head out a gunport, and had it taken off by an enemy shot.[15]

Then the *Arkansas* headed for the *Carondelet* which was blasting away rapidly, but only chipping at the Rebel ship's armor, no shots penetrating. The *Arkansas* in turn raked the gunboat with her 64-pounders, inflicting heavy damage. Brown tried to ram the *Carondelet* and missed. But as he passed the stricken gunboat, he poured a broadside into her waterline, cutting away her wheel ropes and destroying steam gauges and water pipes. The *Carondelet*, scourge of Fort Donelson and Island No. 10, was about to go down, but Commander Walke used her last gasp of momentum to run her aground, rather than let the enemy sink her in midstream. As the *Arkansas* roared past, Walke observed two shot holes in her side, with crews effecting repairs. The

Carondelet suffered four killed, 16 wounded and 10 missing, many of them having jumped overboard and drowned.[16]

The army ram *Queen of the West* was already hightailing it down the river to the safety of the fleet. The *Arkansas* charged at *Tyler* and Commander Gwin prudently steered his vessel downstream, ahead of the ram, keeping up a distance of 200 yards and pouring out fire from his stern guns, answering those from *Arkansas'* bow. Gwin gloomily reported that his and the *Carondelet's* shots had repeatedly hit the Rebel ram, but failed to do any damage. His own vessel suffered eight killed and 11 wounded, with relatively little damage.[17] He also bitterly excoriated the skipper of the *Queen of the West* for cowardice by his desertion of the two sister vessels locked in combat with the *Arkansas*.[18] It was later learned that some of *Tyler's* shots did penetrate the Rebel vessel, wounding Brown, damaging the wheel and mortally wounding the pilot.

The *Arkansas* pressed on, chasing the two Union vessels out to where the Yazoo met the Mississippi, where the fleet lay sleeping at anchor, in spite of the gunfire up the Yazoo. It had been assumed by many in the fleet, and no doubt by many of the commanders, that Union vessels returning down the Yazoo were emptying their guns into the woods, as was the usual custom. Upon hearing the gunfire, at least one captain, Commander Bishop of the *General Bragg*, ordered steam up, cables slipped and crew waiting for orders to get underway, but no such order was forthcoming.[19]

When the *Arkansas* slid into the broad Mississippi she was suddenly faced with a huge fleet of over 30 Union vessels: the gunboats anchored on the Vicksburg side of the river; the rams near the Yazoo, transports off the Louisiana shore and Farragut's fleet, plus the mortar boats, downstream. In addition, the tents of the Union encampment seemed to stretch for miles along the east bank. What to do and where to go? At this point Brown's options were limited; his only refuge would be beneath the Confederate guns of Vicksburg and that is where he headed, in the meantime resolved to inflict as much damage as possible. He was aware that his route would take him past the big ships and the ironclads, but he had no choice; *Arkansas* was already damaged with her stack riddled, forcing steam pressure to dangerous lows. The current of the Mississippi was now providing as much propulsion power as her engines. The Rebels gritted their teeth and pressed on.

By this time the Union fleet was alerted there was a tiger in their midst. Among the first to respond was the 3,000-ton screw sloop *Lancaster,* of Farragut's squadron, which steamed out to engage the ram, but a shot from the *Arkansas* penetrated her steam drum, scalded many men and put her out of the fight.

Then the *Kineo* and the *Hartford* itself both stood out and joined in the chase. The river was now alive and resounding with action. The usual smoke veil began to cover the scene. Many times Brown was forced to fire at gun flashes; he later described ". . . the realization of having steamed into a real volcano, the *Arkansas* from its center firing rapidly to every point of the circumference, without the fear of hitting a friend or missing an enemy." He also suspected that Federal rams trying to get near him were suffering as much from the Union men-of-war as they were from the guns of the *Arkansas*. The Rebel crew, however, did not get away scot-free. As she passed some of the heavier-gunned ships of Farragut's squadron, she received many hits, among them a shot from *Hartford* that killed three crewmen; a second shot killed a sponger; a third killed three more men and wounded three others.[20]

An action such as this, when the air is filled with the crashing of guns with volumes of choking fumes, plus the groans and screams from wounded and dying men, tests one's resolve. Gwin later related his frustration at anyone being idle during combat, while comrades elsewhere were being shot down and that was "trying to the extreme." "But," he admonished, "one must stand up and take what comes. On board a man-of-war there is no other recourse."[21]

As the *Arkansas* passed the anchored gunboats down the line, the formidable *Benton* and the *Essex* moved out to engage her. *Arkansas* took on the *Benton,* maneuvering to ram, but the Union vessel evaded the attempt, instead absorbing a starboard broadside from the Rebels as they passed by. That was the last shot fired by *Arkansas* in the battle, as she had now successfully run the gauntlet. The battered warship left the 30-plus dazed Union ships behind her as she continued downriver to Vicksburg and safety. And it was not a moment too soon: her smokestack had been nearly shot away, her hull holed in many places, and all but one gun was out of action. A little longer under fire and the *Arkansas* would have been sent to the bottom of the Mississippi, probably with all hands.

As the wounded Confederate ram staggered to the wharfs at Vicksburg, thousands of the city's citizens, including generals Beauregard and Van Dorn, crowded the bluffs to celebrate her arrival. They cheered, sang patriotic songs and some even danced. When she moored, crowds of people swarmed the area, wanting to see at first hand the plucky vessel. Some made the mistake of peering in through the gunports, and, upon seeing the grisly remains of dead crew members, recoiled in horror.[22] However, the gunboat had become a true folk hero—of an inanimate sort—to thousands on the Confederate side.

Both Farragut and Davis were mortified. It was a humiliating day for the Union Navy, allowing an enemy vessel to simply blast its way through their combined fleet. An annoyed Farragut declared that he was concerned over what would be said in the press about the debacle. He reported to Washington that the ram had taken them all by surprise.[23]

That night the Federals sallied down to Vicksburg to retrieve their honor. Meantime, the *Arkansas* had been swarmed by hordes of workmen and artisans, including many soldiers from Van Dorn's command. The dead and injured were removed and calls went out to replace crewmen. It was after dark when the Union ships came into view, but by now the *Arkansas* was not alone. In Brown's words, ". . . a number of our antagonists of the morning, including the flagship *Hartford* and the equally formidable *Richmond*, were seen under full steam coming down the river. Before they came within range of the *Arkansas*, we had the gratification of witnessing the beautiful reply of our upper shore-batteries to their gallant attack."

The Union ships' broadsides were guided by a fire set by Yankee soldiers on the Louisiana shore to mark the ram's position on the opposite side. But the *Arkansas* was not there; the wily Brown had moved his moorings downstream a bit, and the Union ships wasted ammunition, firing at the position where she was supposed to be. One 11-inch shot did find the ram, killing several crewmen and further disabling her engines.[24] However fire from the Rebel ship and the Vicksburg batteries holed the *Sciota*; the *Hartford* was hit, killing three men, and the *Winona* received a shot in her port side.[25] The raid was a flop, and the Union ships skulked back to their anchorage.

Flag Officer Davis vowed to get the *Arkansas* at all costs. The mortar schooners were ordered to bombard the wharf area where the ram was moored. The 13-inch shells, for the most part, fell harmlessly nearby—one shell throwing up a lot of fish on the deck.[26] This went on for a week, but it gave Brown time to repair his boat even as shells were plopping all around, sometimes spraying water on the men on deck.

During repairs, life aboard the *Arkansas* took on a different hue, as the Yankee shells thudded around them. The crew, part of which were volunteers sent from a Missouri regiment by General Van Dorn, were veterans of recent actions. At first they were eager to help when they saw the damage to the ram, but when the mortar shells started to fall, many of them took "shell fever" and turned themselves into the hospital.[27]

Finally, Union nerves wore thin. After a conference between Farragut, Davis and Ellet, it was decided to attack the Rebel vessel with rams, while the rest of the flotilla engaged the batteries on the bluffs. The *Queen of the West*, now Ellet commanding; *Essex*, William "Dirty Bill" Porter commanding and the *Sumter* were picked for the mission. The original plan called for the *Essex* to ram the *Arkansas*, grapple her and tow her out into midstream where the *Queen* would ram her, but it was not to happen.

On July 22, the flotilla came around the bend, hell-bent to put away the *Arkansas* once and for all. The Union rams were followed by three ironclad gunboats, *Benton*, *Louisville* and *Cincinnati*, which immediately took on the bluff batteries, while Ellet's rams headed for their target.

The timing of the attack was unfortunate for the *Arkansas* because most of her crew was in sickbed ashore and, as usual, one of her engines was disabled. The *Essex* took the first run toward the Rebel ship. The crew on board the Confederate ram, with officers helping to man the guns, poured shot after shot into the oncoming Union vessel, but to no avail. As with her sister ship, she was laden with cotton bales piled around vital parts to absorb shot and shell and, like a "mad bull, nothing daunted or overawed," came at the *Arkansas*.[28] Brown had his crews slip the lines and, using the starboard screw, maneuvered so that his bow faced the oncoming enemy vessel. As the distance closed both ships blasted each other with bow broadsides; the *Arkansas* was mangled, with eight dead, but the *Essex*, damaged and blinded, missed her target and went aground on the bank.

Every Confederate gun in the area was aimed at her. The *Essex* crew managed to back her off the shore, but not until she had taken a dreadful beating. "Dirty Bill" Porter came out of a hatch to inspect the damage, and a Confederate officer on shore drew his sword, challenging the naval officer. Porter poured out a stream of vitriolic oaths and went back in his vessel. The *Essex* was unmanageable and she was allowed to drift downstream to the safety of the mortar vessels.

Now it was the *Queen*'s turn. Ellet steered straight for the *Arkansas*, taking hits from batteries on the bluffs. Ellet overestimated the speed of his vessel, passed the enemy ship, turned and attempted to ram against the stream. The *Queen* hit the *Arkansas*, sending her almost on her beam. Like her sister, the Union ram then plowed up on shore, as the stern guns of the *Arkansas* raked her with fire. However, the crew managed to get her off the shore, and the *Queen* ran upstream to the safety of the anchorage.[29]

The *Arkansas* once again came through the efforts of the Federals to destroy her; her indomitable skipper, plus her brave crew, had staved off everything the Yankee fleet in the west could throw at them. To Farragut, not only had he been "defeated" by the infernal Rebel ship, but the whole Vicksburg campaign was turning out to be a failure.

With the river falling more every day, it was time for Farragut to take his deep-water ships south again, lest they find themselves grounded in Mississippi mud. Illness in the torpid Deep South summer had taken a heavy toll of crewmen in both fleets, putting entire vessels temporarily out of action. Sixty-eight of *Brooklyn*'s crew were sick; a third of *Louisville*'s crew were ill and one-fourth of *Benton's* were down with fever.[30]

On July 24, 1862 Farragut's squadron up-anchored and headed back to New Orleans and the Gulf. Davis took his flotilla back up to Memphis two days later, after sending four vessels down to Baton Rouge in case the *Arkansas* roamed downriver. By the end of the month, the Yankees had cleared out of an entire stretch of the Mississippi, leaving the Confederate ironclad and the defenders of Vicksburg without an enemy on their doorstep.

The actions had taken a heavy toll on Brown, too. Weakness from his wound, plus the grind of the past weeks, threatened to incapacitate him, so he decided to go to Grenada, Mississippi for a period of recuperation. First-Lieutenant Stevens was put in command with orders that, in Brown's absence, the *Arkansas* was not to leave the safety of Vicksburg, under any circumstances. Little did Brown know that he would never again tread the decks of his beloved ship.

CHAPTER FOURTEEN

Faulty Engines, Infernal Machines

When Admiral Farragut took his squadron south after the *Arkansas* debacle, he paused at Baton Rouge to drop off transports of troops under the command of General Thomas Williams to hold that city against any Rebel attempt to retake it. He also left the gunboats *Essex, Kineo, Cayuga, Katahdin* and *Sumter* to support Williams' troops and to watch for any excursions down the river by the *Arkansas*.

In view of the Yankee evacuation of the Vicksburg area, the Confederates did indeed cast their eyes on Baton Rouge with the aim of reopening supply lines to the west. The city's proximity to the Red River, as well as its locale on the Mississippi, made it a strategically desirable prize.

General Van Dorn decided to send a land force of 4,000 men down to make an assault on Baton Rouge, but the operation also required the presence of the *Arkansas* to handle the Union gunboats. Van Dorn and his commanders had every reason to believe that their vaunted ram, which had given the Yankees such a bad time at Vicksburg, would be able to handle the assignment with ease. It was a good plan, except that it failed to take into account one factor—the wretched engines of the *Arkansas*.[1]

Van Dorn assigned the land task to Major General John Cabell Breckenridge. A Kentuckian by birth, Breckenridge had studied law and had served in the Mexican War. After mustering out of service he became a politician and was elected Vice

President under James Buchanan. When his four-year term was up, he ran unsuccessfully for president against Lincoln. Because of his Southern political leanings he went south at the outbreak of war and was appointed as a brigadier general of the Confederacy in November of 1861, later serving at Shiloh.[2]

By the time Breckenridge reached Baton Rouge, many of his troops were down with fever and the mission appeared to be in doubt. But the intrepid general kept going, meanwhile urgently requesting the assistance of the *Arkansas*. The vessel, however, still moored to a waterfront wharf, was having trouble with her engines. Her engineers insisted that she needed further repairs.

In addition, the *Arkansas's* new crew had been recruited from artillery regiments in Vicksburg, and they had to be trained as sailors. When the ship's "creator," Captain Brown, had taken leave to recuperate from his wound, he had implored Commander Stevens not to take *Arkansas* into battle without him. Nevertheless, Stevens was under enormous pressure to support Breckenridge's attack, and when finally ordered to move out, Commander Stevens had to obey. He sent word to Brown at Grenada that he had been ordered to sortie to Baton Rouge. On receiving the news, Brown, though still recuperating, pronounced himself cured, packed his kit bags, and had himself taken to the railroad station where he "threw himself on the mail bags of the first passing train."[3] At Jackson, he arranged for a special train to take him to Vicksburg, only to learn that the *Arkansas* had left four hours earlier. He grabbed another train headed for Baton Rouge.

The *Arkansas*, meanwhile, was steaming down the Mississippi on her mission to take on the five Yankee gunboats. After being underway for 24 hours, however, her engines started to act up, so Stevens anchored the boat while the engineers attempted to make repairs.

While this was going on, Breckenridge's troops were already assaulting General Williams' garrison at Baton Rouge, and were driving the Federals toward the river where they came under the protection of the gunboats' big guns. Breckenridge could only advance so far without the *Arkansas* to keep the Union ships busy, so he withdrew to the suburbs to await developments.

The *Arkansas* had gotten underway again, and had reached a point just four miles above the city, when her starboard engine stopped and the torque of the port engine forced her aground amidst some cypress stumps.[4] Finally, the engines were coaxed into action, the vessel worked free, and she continued her journey.

When the Union vessels hove into sight, *Essex* in the van, the fight was about to begin. Stevens decided to turn upstream a bit, get enough headway and ram the *Essex*. He had barely accomplished his turn when both engines quit and the vessel drifted ashore, helpless. Stevens realized it was a desperate situation; the ship had broken down, run aground and the Union ships were shelling him. He gave the order to abandon ship, but first he and his crew began to dismantle it. Engines were broken up, powder and shells scattered around the decks and guns loaded and primed. All available flammable material was strewn about and set on fire. The crew scrambled over the bow and into the safety of the wooded banks; Stevens was the last to leave, jumping from the stern and swimming ashore.[5]

The burning hull went adrift with guns and ammunition exploding and the Federals scrambling to get out of the way. After an hour of drifting downstream, there was a thunderous explosion hurling fiery pieces of the ram all over the river. The *Arkansas*, which for a brief time had been the scourge of the Federal fleets, vanished into history. In the South she was lamented; in the North her destruction was hailed. Jefferson Davis referred to her demise as "a sacrificial offering to the cause she had served so valiantly in her brief but brilliant career."[6]

With his river support gone, Breckenridge had no choice but to withdraw his troops and abandon his assault on Baton Rouge. His forces returned to Vicksburg. The majority of the *Arkansas* crew managed to make their way to Port Hudson, 25 miles upstream. Some were taken to Vicksburg by Stevens, who, according to Captain Brown after the war, ". . . could not use that tender care which his [the *Arkansas*] engines required."

With his campaign for Baton Rouge thwarted, Van Dorn made prodigious efforts to fortify Port Hudson, in order to establish a bastion to prevent Union ships from ascending the river to Vicksburg, thereby putting that stretch of the river under his control. Breckenridge and his troops were put in charge of the place.

About this time there was another poor judgment call by Jefferson Davis in his appointment of his friend Theophilus H. Holmes to replace the able General T.C. Hindman, in spite of Van Dorn's urgent appeal not to replace him. "Granny" Holmes, as he was called by his troops, was soon to prove useless to Van Dorn, once again proving that Davis could be shortsighted in his choice of commanders.[7] And that choice was going to affect the coming Vicksburg campaign.

There was a lull until August 16, when Lieutenant-Commander Phelps threw off the lines of the *Benton, Mound City* and *General Bragg,* plus the *Switzerland, Monarch, Samson* and *Lioness,* and with transports of troops, under the command of Colonel Charles R. Woods, moved downstream to a point called Milliken's Bend, 30 miles north of Vicksburg, which was still under Rebel control.

There, the powerful Phelps force captured a Confederate steamer, *Fairplay,* and a sizeable cargo that consisted of 1,200 new Enfield rifles, 4,000 new muskets, a large quantity of ammunition for field guns, a small howitzer and large amounts of small arms.[8]

Colonel Woods learned that a Confederate force was in the vicinity; he landed his troops and captured the encampment of the 31st Louisiana Regiment. The enemy troops had fled, but left behind a cache of ammunition, provisions and some small arms.

That evening, the flotilla continued downriver until it came to the mouth of the Yazoo River where it anchored for the night. The next morning, after a brief reconnaissance of the Vicksburg area, the fleet steamed up the Yazoo. At a point 20 miles upriver, they came upon an enemy force constructing a battery of one 64-pounder rifled gun, two 42-pounders, some 32-pounder smoothbores, a 24-pound brass howitzer and a few 12-pounder field pieces. Some of the pieces were brought on board vessels of the flotilla. Because of their great weight, the majority of them were destroyed.

Once again the flotilla steamed northward, until it reached the mouth of the Big Sunflower River in which it was rumored that some Confederate vessels were lurking. Ellet took his rams 20 miles upriver to a body of water called Lake George where some Confederate steamers were moored, but low water forced him back, without any military action.

Later, for the same reason—that of dropping water levels— Phelps was forced to descend to the Mississippi. He was satisfied, however, that if he were unable to ascend the river and its tributaries, surely the Confederates couldn't either. He set course back to the anchorage at Helena, after leaving two boats to watch the river mouth. Along the way, he took time to destroy some Rebel wildcat batteries. Commander Phelps reported to Commodore Davis that his appearance so alarmed the Confederates at Vicksburg that they hastily assembled troops for its defense in the event there was an amphibious landing.[9]

In the Gulf, Federal forces had captured the Texas ports of Galveston, Corpus Christi and Sabine Pass. The latter, located at the Louisiana border, especially cut off a source of supplies for the eastern body of the Confederacy. As a result, the only remaining routes east were the Red River and the rail connections at Vicksburg, one of which served Louisiana.

It was to be the last naval action for some months. Meanwhile, the war as a whole had become a swirling array of maneuvers and battles, and its outcome seemed very much in doubt. On August 30, another battle took place at Bull Run in the east. This time, Lee had Stonewall Jackson pinning the Union army to his front, while James Longstreet came up to deliver a haymaker against the Federal left. The Union forces, under John Pope, fled in disorder from the field. Braxton Bragg had brought his army into Tennessee and Kirby Smith was operating in Kentucky, both Confederate armies reoccupying towns that had been considered securely held only months before. In September Lee took the Army of Northern Virginia into Maryland, where a horrific battle was fought on the 17th, at Antietam.

Even though the Union controlled most of the Mississippi River, Vicksburg was still intact and growing stronger every day. Port Hudson, as well as Port Gibson, had been newly fortified with guns and garrisons. The Confederacy's connection to its western states was as yet unbroken.

Another non-combatant event that occurred at this time was the replacing of Flag Officer Davis with Commodore Davis Dixon Porter, in October 1862. Porter had distinguished himself with his mortar fleet at New Orleans and Vicksburg and had been appointed a commodore in April of 1866 and a rear admiral at the time of his appointment as the commander of the Mississippi fleet, in October 1861.

With the lull in river action, Porter took his fleet to Cairo and proceeded to strengthen his boats. Meanwhile, the War Department transferred command of the squadron to navy jurisdiction where it should have been all the time. Porter was given full authority. Among his priorities was to recruit a force of marines to accompany the gunboats on missions, to go ashore and deal with enemy ambushers and guerrillas. Alfred Ellet, now a brigadier-general, was put in command of this effort and charged into the assignment with his usual creative energy. He dubbed the force the "Misissippi River Brigade," the members of which were to be recruited from invalids and convalescents in hospitals.

Ellet issued a series of handbills that advertised recruitment for the brigade, one of which stated that, with a bounty of $100, "the recruits would be provided with good cooks and bedding." Another trumpeted the fact the "Ellet scouts" would be furnished fine quarters and transports fitted out for their comfort. Prospective recruits were additionally promised no long marches, no camping without tents or food or carrying knapsacks, and "good facilities for cooking at all times." Another poster pointed out the advantages of not having to dig trenches, no prisoner guard houses to guard, no picket duty and no chance of short rations. Still another poster proclaimed that the brigade would be "famous in the annals of Mississippi warfare . . ."[10]

To transport his elite brigade, Ellet procured a fleet of seven vessels: the *Autocrat, B.J. Adams, Baltic, Diana, Fairchild, John Raine* and *Woodford*. The *Fairchild* would act as the commissary and quartermaster vessel and the *Woodford* as a hospital vessel. These boats were former New Orleans packets that were to be specifically rebuilt, according to Ellet's specifications: boilers protected by timbers and bunkers, barricades of 2-inch solid oak planking of double thickness for the decks with loop holes cut for muskets. The pilot house would be enclosed with sheet iron and a gangway large enough for two horses abreast. Comfortable quarters for officers and enlisted men were also high priority. A barracks compound was built at St. Louis for those times off ship.

Lieutenant Colonel George Currie was put in charge of the organization of the brigade and of whipping the men into shape. He organized and trained six companies of infantry and four squadrons of cavalry. The objective of the brigade, which foreshadowed the special forces units of World War II, was to keep the Mississippi free of roving bands of guerrillas which were continuing to harass traffic on the river. When pronounced ready, the men were put on board their special transports and, with gunboat escorts, proceeded to look for trouble.

Unfortunately, the brigade was involved in one of the most painful episodes of the war. According to Lieutenant Colonel Currie, the force had been called down to Helena and, along the way, were fired upon by a wildcat battery at Austin, Mississippi, on the east side of the river. The brigade was deployed ashore to look for the culprits whom they found and engaged in combat. After a short fight, the Rebels were driven off, through the town of Austin, with both sides suffering casualties. In an unexplained act of vengeance, and in spite of the pleas of the citizens and his own men, the Union commander of the force then decided to burn the town which was populated only with women and children, their men having gone off to war. Currie lamented the injustice of this act.[11] The brigade later went on to serve in the Vicksburg campaign.

Other events, of technological importance, were taking place at this time. Admiral Porter put into effect an idea he had long entertained, of lightly armed and armored shallow draft vessels to maneuver in river tributaries within which the ponderous gunboats could not maneuver.

These vessels were stern-wheeled steamers with light draft and armored with $1^{1}/_{4}$-inch iron plating around vital parts, hence their nickname "tinclads." The boats would prove to be of great value for navigating the tributaries that the deeper-draft and heavier vessels could not.[12]

One of the most famous of these tinclads, the *Black Hawk,* would soon be the Mississippi flotilla's flagship. She was a side-wheeler, 260-feet long, with a 43-foot beam, a 6-foot draft, and displaced 903 tons. Her armament consisted of two 32-pounders, two 30-pounder rifles, one 12-pounder smoothbore and one 12-pounder rifle.[13] Sixty-three of these vessels commissioned, and efficiently served with Admiral Porter's fleet in the months to come.

Advanced technology in warfare was not, however, the sole province of the Union; the Confederates were also coming up with innovations. Realizing that they couldn't match the Federal fleets in numbers or in strength, they set about designing methods of equalizing the disparity, including the torpedo boat, submarine and the torpedo. All three were ingenious methods, but the submarine and torpedo boats failed to live up to the expectations of their designers. The Confederate torpedo, however, gave a good account for itself, sinking a number of Union vessels.

In its own peculiar way, the torpedo managed to revolutionize warfare by directly influencing defensive weapons of the future. Nevertheless, the Confederacy did build and commission some torpedo boats and it is worth a look at them, because they were way ahead of their Union counterparts in this field. That invention, however, depended upon an earlier one.

In early 1862, a Confederate captain, Francis D. Lee, had invented the first chemical fuse. Glass vials of sulfuric acid were put into a cylindrical metal container. Between the phials and a very thin, rounded top, was a highly explosive mixture. When the top of the container was crushed, it in turn crushed the phials and the resulting acid spill would detonate the mixture. Lee theorized that, by screwing the tubes into a container of high explosives, he would have a devastating weapon—one that could be used against ships. The devices would be armed and floated out in a stream to be impacted by contact with a ship's hull. Accurately floating them out, he realized, would be a risky business at the very least. There ought to be another way to get them into the streams and against warships.

Lee came up with an idea for a craft that would travel underwater. It would have a turtle-like hull, iron-plated, with just a smokestack and pilot house above water. A long, wooden spar on the bow, to which was attached a container of gunpowder, made it an effective weapon against both iron and wooden ships.[14]

Theoretically, his craft would approach an anchored enemy warship, in the dark and unseen, ram the spar into the vessel's hull and sink her. The long spar would keep the craft far enough away from the explosions, and the iron plating would protect the crew from musket and small arms fire. In August 1863, this craft, named *David*, would later justify its existence by detonating a torpedo against the U.S.S. *Ironsides*. The explosion failed to sink the warship, but it caused her to be put into drydock for lengthy repairs.

The Confederacy developed a series of these boats, called Spar Torpedo Boats, that ranged in length of from 40 to 50 feet. In addition, three underwater craft, known as Submarine Torpedo Boats, were developed by the south. The most famous of these was the *H.L. Hunley*, named after its inventor, and which proved to be the first successful submarine. It was merely a boiler, 20-feet long, joined at each end and propelled by a screw propeller powered by cranks in the hands of an eight-man crew sitting in tandem. A long spar, upon which was placed the torpedo, was fastened to the bow. Unlike the torpedo boat, this vessel could submerge completely and was intended to approach an enemy ship, silent and invisible, ram the victim with the spar torpedo and sink it. Supposedly being "invisible," the sub would then manage to get away. Unfortunately, the *Hunley* underwent a series of misfortunes in her all-too-brief, but promising career.

The submarine floundered at a dock and was raised, only to sink again, taking a crew with her each time. The third crew of the *Hunley* (comprised of perhaps the bravest men in naval history) was lost too, but only after their sub had rammed and sank the Union warship U.S.S. *Housatonic*, in the fall of 1864.[15]

The Confederate torpedo boats and submarines played little or no part in the Mississippi sector of the war, however, the same cannot be said about the "torpedos," or mines, which were called "infernal machines" by the Federals. This instrument of destruction became a real thorn in the side of the Union Navy, and was to be responsible for the loss of three important Union warcraft in the Mississippi campaigns. The Confederates named this weapon after an oceanic electric ray of the family Torpedinidae which has the ability to attack and stun its prey by discharging a series of electric pulses from electric organs in each fin or wing. In some cases the shock produced is strong enough to stun a man.

The mine is an old invention. An American hydrogapher, David Bushnell, unsuccessfully tried to blow up a British ship in 1776, with a keg mine. Using the very first crude submarine-like vessel, the *Turtle*, the device consisted of 150 pounds of explosives in a wooden keg, to be fastened to the bottom of a ship using screws. The device would then be detonated by a timing device. It proved ineffective, due to the copper-sheath plates placed on ship bottoms, which were meant to retard the action of wood-boring marine worms.

Bushnell also devised a floating keg of gunpowder to be fired by a gunlock mechanism when contacted by a hull. That experiment also proved to be a failure, much like his later attempt to set loose a number of kegs among British warships in the Delaware River, on July 7, 1778. Once more the good plan went awry, when ice hampered the kegs and they failed to damage any ships. The resulting panic among British crews, however, caused the incident to be labeled in the annals of warfare as "The Battle of the Kegs."

In the 1800's, Robert Fulton sank some old hulks, using a mine device. Another crude submarine contraption, called the *Nautilus*, was demonstrated with some success, but no one seemed to be interested except for man named Jules Verne, who used the sub's name—and illuminated the concept—in his book "Twenty Thousand Leagues Under the Sea."

When the Confederacy revived the idea of mine warfare, the task of development fell to one Matthew Fontaine Maury. A Virginian by birth, and an officer in the U.S. Navy until the outbreak of war, Maury had been experimenting with an underwater explosive device since April 1861, and was anxious to try it out. His contrivance was made up of an oak cask full of powder with a trigger device attached to a long lanyard run to the shore, to be operated by personnel hiding in trenches or behind high river banks. After exploding one of these kegs in the James River, to the approval of the Confederate Navy Department, Maury was awarded with the title "Chief of the Sea Coast Harbor and River Defenses of the South."[16] In July 1861, he made a series of abortive attacks on Federal warships in the James River. Undaunted, and after consulting with Lieutenant Isaac N. Brown, C.S.N. (of *Arkansas* fame), it was decided that mines should be placed in Mississippi River tributaries to offset growing Yankee naval power. The plan was to place Maury's three-foot, cylindrical devices across a river, connected to galvanic batteries on shore, with insulated wires connected in turn to telegraph keys that acted as trigger mechanisms.[17]

There were several types of mines used by Confederates: pitch-lined, beer barrels filled with gunpowder, called "Rain's Keg Torpedos" by their admirers, and triggered by contact fuses; tin containers of various sizes and shapes; the "Fretwell-Singer" mine, the "Swaying" mines made of copper and the most famous of them all, a five-gallon demijohn (a bottle cased in wicker) filled with black powder, called "Fretwells," after their inventor. This latter mine was lashed to a floating block of wood and anchored in the bottom of the stream where it would be suspended between the bottom and the surface. The device would be detonated either by contact or by means of a long lanyard which ran to the shore.

These mines were responsible for the sinking of the gunboats *Cairo* and *DeKalb* in the Yazoo River. Isaac Brown personally claimed responsibility for the destruction of the *DeKalb* by placing two Fretwells in the Yazoo.[18] Jefferson Davis extolled the importance of the mine as a defensive weapon, saying that the device "was more effective than any other means of defense." Although the full potentialities of the weapon had been known for some time, Davis claimed that "it remained for the skill and ingenuity of our officers to bring the use of this terrible weapon to perfection."[19]

Union officers, on the other hand, thought that the mine was the most terrible weapon ever designed and used by man, and some admitted that it would be difficult to safeguard a port from a concerted mine effort.

The efforts of the Confederacy to utilize the mine, and other new inventions, have to be admired. Faced with the overwhelming superiority of the Union Navy, Richmond expended much time and money in trying to develop weapons that would give their navy some kind of edge. Ultimately, however, the South was unable to bring enough trained engineers and industrial resources into play. Also, constant bickering between leaders of the fledgling nation, whether political versus industrial, or army versus navy, shackled the Confederate efforts.

Nevertheless, one of the weapons they were able to employ was about to plummet a famous Union warship into the hallowed halls of naval history.

CHAPTER FIFTEEN

Long Live
the Cairo!

In January 1862, one of James Eads's original seven ironclads slid down the ways at Mound City, Illinois, and was floated out into the Ohio River. Christened the *Cairo*, after that important city at the heart-like tip of Illinois, she was commissioned on January 25, 1862, at a cost of $101,808 to the Federal government. Thereafter, she was towed to her namesake to be fitted out, armed and crewed. This process took some time, because there was a shortage of personnel. In addition, her appointed captain, Lieutenant S. Ledyard Phelps, was not able to take command; he was engaged in a sweep up the Cumberland and then the Tennessee River with the timberclad gunboats.

Lieutenant James M. Pritchard was appointed to temporary command.[1] As recruits and materiel poured onto the base, work began in earnest for the completion of this vessel for which Flag Officer Foote had predicted great things and which he claimed would be the fastest man-of-war in the river fleet.

Shortly, Lieutenant Nathaniel Bryant was given command, because of his seniority to Phelps. This was a good choice. Born into a Maine shipbuilding family in 1823, Bryant was appointed a midshipman in 1837 and was commissioned one year later. His service tenure took him to the Mare Island Shipyard and to the steam sloop U.S.S. *Richmond*.

Bryant put all his time and energy into training his new 175-man crew, of whom 17 were officers, and into overseeing the installation of the vessel's appointed 13 guns.[2]

The *Cairo* then served with the Western Gunboat Fleet and was active in the occupation of Clarksville and Nashville, Tennessee. She received her baptism of fire at the Plum Point action and in the big battle off Memphis on June 6. She was then ordered to patrol the Mississippi until November, when she joined the expedition up the Yazoo River. Prior to that action, Commander Bryant had been put on extended sick leave and a new skipper was slated to be appointed.

Lieutenant-Commander Thomas O. Selfridge, Jr., was the choice for command and thereby fated to guide this gunboat into history. The *Cairo*, as with her sisters, was not what one would call a handsome vessel, certainly not like many of those in today's navy. According to one extant photo, she was angular and squat, yet, to old salts, there was a kind of rough, purposeful beauty to her. She was designed and built for a specific wartime job, and she accomplished all that was required of her during her relatively short career.

Her overall length was 175 feet, with a 51-foot beam and a six foot keel draft. Her displacement tonnage was 512, and she was designed for a speed of 6 knots. She was well armored, with $2^{1}/_{2}$-inch charcoal iron plating on her casemate that had an inclination of 35 degrees on her sides and 45 degrees on her fore and aft ends. Her 28-foot-high chimneys sported regulation black paint, with a gray band, distinguishing her from her sisters.[3]

Whether she was the fastest of the "city" ironclads is debatable. Her planned 22-foot-diameter paddle wheels were propelled by two inclined, reciprocating, steam non-condensing engines with a 22-inch diameter cylinder and a 72-inch stroke. These engines were fed by five boilers, 35 inches in diameter and with 24-foot lengths, producing a pressure of 140 lbs./sq.in.; they were fed by 18–20 bushels of coal per hour by a complement of four coal heavers, with the boilers attended by 12 firemen.

An auxiliary engine, called "the Doctor," was located aft of the boilers and between the main engines. This machine was used for driving two coldwater pumps and two mainforce pumps to supply the boilers with water. It had a cylinder diameter of eight inches and had a 21 inch stroke.[4]

The effectiveness of a gunboat depends not only on her armor, or speed, but also on her armament. According to information made available after her resurrection from the Yazoo, *Cairo* carried 13 guns: three 7-inch bore 42-pounder army rifles; three 8-inch bore 64-pounder smoothbores; six 32-pounders; and one 30-pounder Parrott rifle. They were placed three on the bow, two on the stern and four on each broadside. Even today, on display at Vicksburg Military Park with ten of her original complement of guns poking through gun ports, she has a formidable look.

The crew of the *Cairo* were a homogenous lot: 49 percent of the men were Irish, British, German, Canadian and Scandinavian; 35 percent were native Americans and all together they can be summed up as being 27 petty officers, 111 seamen, one ordinary seaman, 12 firemen, four coal heavers, three landsmen and one apprentice.[5] A composite picture of the average crewman aboard the *Cairo* would have been a 26-year-old Caucasian with blue eyes and brown hair, 5'7" tall.

The majority of the crew were designated "seamen," in spite of the fact that only a few had sailing experience and one-third, at the time of the war, reported having no vocation whatsoever.[6] They wore typical uniforms of the riverine fleet of that time: some regular navy men wore traditional blues, others wore army uniforms and some civilian clothes. It was not until later, when the fleet came under Navy Department jurisdiction that all crewmen were required to wear regular navy uniforms. As for food on board, they lived off dry provisions of salt beef or pork, bags of beans, flour, jugs of molasses and, whenever possible, fresh food that would be foraged from nearby farms and plantations. Such was the *Cairo* in December 1862, before her fateful voyage.

With Union eyes on Vicksburg as the ultimate prize in the struggle to split the Confederacy, Grant, in his grand strategy, planned to trap the Confederate forces there between two armies, his and Sherman's. Grant was to march his army down the dry ground ridges east of the bayous of the Yazoo Delta to asssault the city from the east, first cutting it off from Jackson, which lay 40 miles to the east. At the same time General Sherman with 32,000 troops were to proceed up the Yazoo River, disembark, and move on Vicksburg from the north. The Confederate army around Vicksburg would have no hope of defeating both of the simultaneous attacks, and in fact was outnumbered by each of the Federal armies.

Sherman's immediate aim was to move his troops to a point where the Vicksburg & Jackson Railroad crossed the Big Black River that ran from the north and emptied into the Mississippi above Grand Gulf. With the railroad cut, the armies could then swing southwestward and assault Vicksburg, supported by Porter's gunboats on the river. But first of all, the Yazoo River had to be ascended and communications made with Grant, who would move south from his base at Holly Springs just over the border from Tennessee.[7] A previous reconnaissance was made up the Yazoo by the gunboats *Marmora* and *Signal*, and the river was reported to be full of mines and sunken barges. The flotilla descended the river and it was decided that a much larger naval force would be needed.[8]

Meanwhile, the great pincer movement was being disrupted by Confederate cavalry. After Grant left his Holly Springs base General Earl Van Dorn, with 3,500 horsemen, swept in behind him and seized the great depot there on December 15. They destroyed a track, a bridge and military supplies and equipment worth $1,500,000, and took 1,500 prisoners. At the same time Nathan Forrest was rampaging along the Union supply lines in western Tennessee, ripping up 70 miles of track. Grant, his lines of communication suddenly in jeopardy, was forced to withdraw north and he established a base at Grand Junction just over the Tennessee border.

Sherman and Porter, unaware of Grant's situation, were proceeding apace, concentrating their attentions on the Yazoo River and the Confederate positions at Chickasaw and Haynes Bluffs. When the *Marmora* and the *Signal* returned from their mission up the Yazoo, Porter then ordered the 207-ton *Marmora* and the 190-ton *Signal*, both sternwheelers, to ascend the river again, this time accompanied by the ironclads *Cairo* and *Pittsburgh* and the ram *Queen of the West*. Captain Walke, commander of the expedition, cautioned his captains to be careful about running their vessels in among the mines and to avoid channels where they were set. They were to haul any mines to shore, using small boats, and to detonate them safely.[9]

On board the *Cairo*, preparations were made for the expedition. The boilers were cleaned out and provisions were brought on board, including fresh beef, which was mostly obtained by foraging parties.[10]

On the morning of departure, December 12, the flotilla got underway and entered the mouth of the Yazoo, in a single column: *Marmora, Signal, Queen of the West, Cairo* and *Pittsburgh*. After pausing to bombard a Rebel sharpshooter position at the mouth of the Old River, the flotilla steamed up the chocolate-colored waters of the Yazoo. More nests of enemy sharpshooters were encountered and the vessels frequently shelled the woods on both sides of the river as they progressed upstream.

At one point, the *Marmora* overhauled a skiff containing two men, one white, the other black. The white man was an overseer of the Blake's Plantation nearby. When he was questioned, by Captain Getty, the man admitted he had knowledge of the location of the mines, whereupon Getty slapped him in irons.[11]

Finally, at a point 20 miles upstream, the flotilla came upon a cluster of mines. The rest of the vessels hove to while *Marmora* and *Signal* steamed ahead to deal with the threat. The *Marmora* halted and Captain Getty ordered a cutter launched which would drag a line from it to the shore, in order to ensnare any lines connected to the mines. When they came to the surface, they would be exploded by musket fire. The *Signal* and *Queen of the West* also moved up to join Getty. As the mines popped up, the crews fired away.

Meanwhile, the *Cairo* was beyond a bend in the river. When Lieutenant-Commander Selfridge heard the crackling of musket fire, and thought *Marmora* was under attack, he ordered his ironclad moved up to aid her, hammering the woods on either side of the river as she proceeded. Alongside the *Marmora*, Selfridge hailed Getty to ask him why he had stopped. Getty replied, "Here is where the torpedoes are."[12] Selfridge had grown impatient, so he ordered a cutter lowered for his own investigation.

His men, along with those from *Marmora*, busied themselves

snagging lines to be dragged toward shore for demolition of the attached mines. While this was going on, the bow of the *Cairo* drifted too close to shore; Selfridge ordered all engines reversed and the huge craft moved back into midstream. He then shouted for *Marmora* to move ahead, but Getty hesitated, fearing the mines.[13]

Gwin, on the signal, gave the order to get under way, and both vessels moved ahead. At that moment, Confederate batteries on Drumgould's Bluff, two miles to the east, opened fire on them; *Cairo's* forward gun captain ordered the bow guns to respond. The huge paddlewheel churned the murky water as the gunboat picked up speed, when suddenly two thunderous explosions ripped the air—the *Cairo* had hit mines. The first tore a hole in her starboard bow; the second shattered her port quarter and flooded the forward shell room. The force of the second blast was such that No. 1 port gun was lifted off the deck, its carriage shattered, leaving it in a canted position; the heavy port anchor was plummeted skyward. Three men were injured in the blast.

Crewman George Yost reported that the entire forward hold was full of water, and the gunboat began to go down by the head. "The water," he wrote, "rushed in like Niagara."[14] Yost later wrote that the explosion had taken place after a boat crew had picked up a small buoy, brought it on board and had commenced hauling in a line attached to it.

Since the blasts occurred as the ironclad moved ahead, it is possible to surmise that the mines were attached to the buoy and had floated under the gunboat, where they were either detonated by contact or by a battery on shore. No one will ever know.

For a few moments, confusion reigned on the stricken gunboat. Selfridge ordered the vessel run aground, and the crew secured a heavy hawser to a tree to keep her from slipping into the channel.[15] Hand and steam pumps were frantically put to work, but to no avail. Selfridge saw the hopelessness of the situation and ordered the ship abandoned. As a final act of defiance, one of *Cairo's* forward gun was fired at the Confederate batteries, just as the vessel was sinking. The crew took as many personal effects as possible and transferred them to boats from the *Queen of the West* that came up to assist. Yost lamented the fact that the

30. The Rebel ironclad C.S.S. *Arkansas*.

31. Today, the site of the Confederate shipyard at Yazoo City.

32. A depiction of the point-blank duel between the *Arkansas* and *Carondelet*, which ended unfortunately for the Union ship.

33. *Arkansas* blasting her way through the Union fleet near Vicksburg.

34. A depiction of the legendary Confederate ship under construction.

35. Death of the *Arkansas*. With her engines failed, she was blown up by her own crew as Union gunboats closed in.

36. Colonel Charles Ellet, founder of the Union river ram fleet. After dying from a wound suffered at Memphis, command of the ram fleet fell to his equally energetic brother Alfred.

37. Charles Rivers Ellet, son of the above, made his own reputation as a dashing commander of the brown water rams.

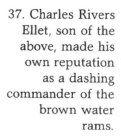

38. Chickasaw Bayou and the Vicksburg bluffs.

39. Rear Admiral Porter's flotilla passing the Vicksburg batteries.

40. Porter's battle beneath the Vicksburg bluffs, April 16, 1863.

41. Farragut's naval attack on Port Hudson, March 13, 1863.

42. David Dixon Porter succeeded Davis as commander of the Western
Gunboat Flotilla. After the fall of Vicksburg he went on to command
the North Atlantic squadron.

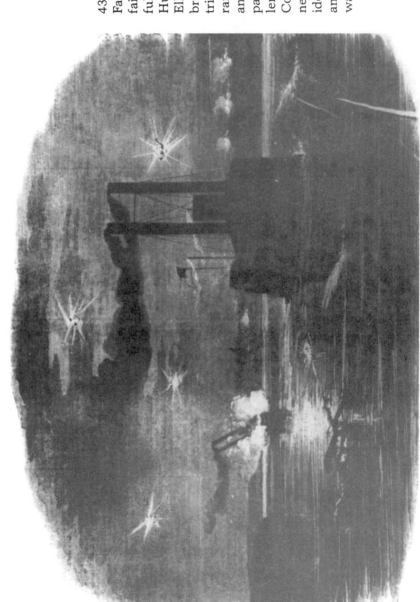

43. When Farragut's fleet failed to successfuly pass Port Hudson, Alfred Ellet and his brother John tried to run the rams *Lancaster* and *Switzerland* past Vicksburg to lend assistance. Confederate gunners had other ideas, however, and *Lancaster* was lost.

44.
The *Rattler*,
one of the shallow-
draft Union gunboats able
to traverse the waterways
off the Mississippi around
Vicksburg.

45. The state-of-the-art
Union ironclad *Indianola*
under construction. Lost in
battle, she was then "saved"
from Rebel salvage by
Porter's famous
dummy gunboat.

46. One of the original Eads iron-clads, the U.S.S. *Cairo* fell victim to Confederate mines in 1863, but is currently on display at Vicksburg.

47. The pilot house of the *Cairo*, after being raised from the Yazoo River in 1956. In conversing with a supervisor at the Vicksburg Military Park, the author happened to comment on the flag seen flying in this photo. "Well, we found her and now she's ours," came the matter-of-fact reply.

48. Casemate door of the the *Cairo* being raised from the Yazoo River.

49. Four of the five boilers, with steam drum, restored on the *Cairo* at Vicksburg Military Park.

50. (Cover illus.) "The Union Fleet Passing Vicksburg" by Tom Lovell.

51. Even today the *Cairo* looks to be a formidable man of war.

52. View on starboard aft deck of the *Cairo* showing paddlewheel spider, with pitman arm of port engine, and a restored 30-pounder Parrott rifle.

53. View of the Mississippi River today from Vicksburg's shore, looking north. Peninsula to the left contains Grant's Canal cut in the winter of 1862–63.

log book could not be saved.[16]

Finally, the hawser was unable to bear the massive weight and it snapped; the *Cairo* slipped backward into six fathoms of deep water, only her chimneys and jackstaff jutting forlornly above the surface.[17] It had taken only 12 minutes for the ironclad to sink. Some of her crew took down the flag from the jackstaff, and the crews of the *Queen of the West* fastened lines to the *Cairo*'s chimneys and pulled them down, lest the enemy discover her final resting place. There she was fated to lie, undisturbed, for the next 94 years. Selfridge later reported that it was with "deep regret and melancholy that I was forced to return downriver."[18]

For nearly a century the Cairo lay submerged in the turgid, muddy waters of the Yazoo, a few miles below Snyder's Bluff. It was in November 1956 that Edward Bearss, Vicksburg Military Park Historian, who had long been aware of her possible burial site, discovered her remains by means of magnetic compasses, just 30 feet down from the east bank of the river near Blake's Plantation. Additional years passed, however, before the finances, manpower and materiel necessary for the massive salvage effort could be put in place. Then, in the fall of 1964, after the agonizing task of siphoning a century of mud from her innards, huge cranes lifted the bow section of the gunboat out of the water. The *Cairo* was cut into three sections: bow, midships and stern, and placed on barges for transport down to a shipyard in Pascagoula, Mississippi, for restoration. (Technicians actually restored one of her reciprocating steam non-condensing engines and had it up and running!)

In 1977 the *Cairo* was shipped to Vicksburg and put on display in a specially built compound in the Military Park, completed in 1984. Today, in addition to the vessel itself, many artifacts taken from her bowels—guns, stoves, crockery, boots and shoes and many personal items of officers and crew—are also available for viewing.

Meanwhile, back in December 1862, crews from the *Pittsburgh* were sent ashore to find those responsible for *Cairo*'s sinking. At a place called "Blake's Levee," they discovered powder and the materials to make mines and promptly destroyed these, along with a dozen small boats. The Confederates had fled, leaving behind all the materials.

But this was of small comfort to Selfridge, who was criticized for being so impatient as to get his vessel sunk; one officer sarcastically wrote that the captain had removed two Rebel mines by placing his vessel over them. Selfridge admitted that he had been unfortunate in pushing perhaps a little farther than prudence dictated. Admiral Porter also observed that due caution was not observed, and that *Cairo* moved too fast.[19]

The flotilla, minus the *Cairo*, descended the river to the Mississippi. Selfridge and his crew were taken to Cairo and the captain promptly reported, with great trepidation, to Admiral Porter on board his flagship *Black Hawk*, to officially report the loss. Selfridge was in fear of a courtmartial. Porter waved his fears aside; he could not punish a captain who had only sought to confront the enemy.[20]

In a great show of magnanimity, Porter promptly assigned Selfridge command of the timberclad *Conestoga*.[21] The admiral then descended the Mississippi with the largest armada of war vessels yet seen on that river. When Porter reached the mouth of the Yazoo, he awaited more data supporting Sherman's planned assault on Haynes Bluff, in preparation for an all-out campaign against Vicksburg.

First, however, Porter decided that a task force be sent back up the Yazoo River to determine the strength of the Confederate batteries at Haynes Bluff, some 11 miles north of Vicksburg, and shell them into submission. The vessels chosen for this sortie were *Benton*, the flagship, carrying Lieutenant-Commander William Gwin, commander of the expedition; the timberclads *Tyler* and *Lexington*; and auxiliary vessels.

On December 23, the naval force moved upriver, taking sniper fire along the way and responding with broadsides of cannister and grape. On the 27th, they cautiously approached the bluffs and opened fire, receiving blistering volleys in return. The *Benton*, being the flagship and largest vessel of the flotilla, took the greatest amount of hits but suffered no serious damage. Unfortunately, Commander Gwin ignored the pleas of his subordinates and stood outside the pilothouse during the action.[22] A

Confederate sniper spotted him and put a rifle ball into his chest, mortally wounding the Union officer.

The entire expedition was a bust. Not only did the gunboats fail to silence the batteries, but the Union Navy suffered the loss of one of its most able commanders. In addition, the attack alerted the Confederate commanders in Vicksburg, and Pemberton promptly sent two more brigades to bolster the city's defenses.

Meanwhile, the loss of the *Cairo* to enemy mines did not escape the notice of Colonel Charles Rivers Ellet. He fully realized the seriousness of the infernal machines and the clumsy manner in which they were destroyed—by men in boats snagging the ropes holding the mines, exposed to relentless fire from enemy snipers. So he put his fertile inventor's mind to work creating a device to effectively accomplish this task.

On December 30, he explained to Admiral Porter the theory of the mine-sweeping device. It would consist of the strong frame of two heavy spars 65 feet long, secured by transverse and diagonal braces and extending 50 feet forward of a vessel's bow. A 35-foot crosspiece would be bolted to the forward extremities of the braces. Through each end and in the center of the crosspiece would be a heavy iron rod, $1^1/_2$-inch in diameter and 15 feet in length, which would descend into the water and have at its end an iron hook. An intermediate hook would be attached to each bar, some three feet from the bottom.

The theory, according to Ellet, was that the hooks would catch the ignitor cords attached to the mines, thus neutralizing, exploding or otherwise disabling them. The vessel would be protected from danger by 50 feet of water between the explosion sites and the bow.

Ellet's device was finished on December 30, after he had worked all night with his carpenters, and it was promptly attached to the bow of the *Lyoness*.[23] However, the device was never used, because strategic plans were changed, and the test expedition was eventually scrubbed. It was to have been the first serious attempt at developing a viable mine-sweeping device.

The next move in this deadly military chess game would now be made by William Tecumseh Sherman.

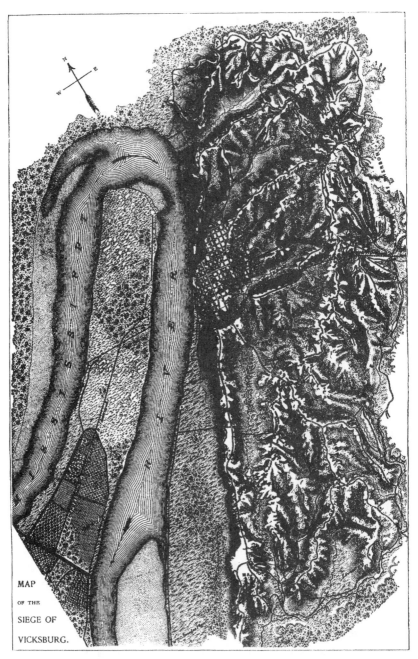

MAP

OF THE

SIEGE OF

VICKSBURG.

Sketch map of Vicksburg. One can easily identify with Grant's desire to cut a canal through the city's facing peninsula and thereby nullify the Confederate citadel's commanding position on the Mississippi.

CHAPTER SIXTEEN

Gunboats Come to Grips

The location that was the object of so much military activity in 1862–63 was first visited in 1718 by French adventurers, and in 1790 the Spanish built a military outpost there named "Nogales," which was later translated to "Walnut Hills." It became an incorporated settlement in 1825, and was later named "Vicksburg" after the Methodist minister Reverend Newitt Vick. The name Walnut Hills later reverted to those hills backing the city to the east and north.

In order to get a clear picture of the Vicksburg campaign, and the difficulties that were implicit for the Union, it is necessary to understand the terrain around the area at the time. The city sat atop a bluff 200 feet high which was part of an escarpment that runs parallel to the Mississippi for 300 miles from Memphis, skirts Vicksburg, then runs southward to Port Hudson in Louisiana. Vicksburg itself was on a promontory that was a part of the Walnut Hills escarpment and contained the Chickasaw Bluffs, named after a bayou at its base. To the east of these bluffs was high ground guarded from approach by rifle pits and gun batteries. To the north, the Yazoo delta's low land spread out toward the Mississippi and formed a crescent containing a morass of swamps, sluggish streams, stale bayou lakes and nearly-impassable swamps.

The region to the immediate north of Vicksburg was commanded by Confederate General Stephen D. Lee, a distant relative of Robert E. Lee. Stephen Lee was an 1854 graduate of the West Point academy and had served as his relative's aide de camp before being appointed a brigadier general in November 1862.[1]

The works at Chickasaw Bluffs were vulnerable up until Grant's withdrawal after the Holly Springs disaster. With Grant no longer a threat, however, Lee was reinforced by 6,000 men, swelling the overall Rebel forces to 14,000, making the position practically impregnable.

Sherman was unaware of these developments and, counting on Grant to do his part in his drive down parallel to the Mississippi Central Railroad and to keep Pemberton's forces at the Yalobusha line, Sherman would have been able to take the Chickasaw Bluffs bastion, join Grant's army and come storming down on Vicksburg from the east.[2]

Fully confident of victory in the two-pronged attack, Sherman loaded his three divisions of 32,000 men on transports: divisions under the commands of generals Morgan, Steele, Morgan Smith and A.J. Smith. Then, with Porter's entire fleet of ironclads, timberclads, tinclads and rams, he departed downriver on December 20, 1862. At Helena, Sherman picked up 12,000 more men.[3]

However, along the way, unknown to Sherman and Porter, a Confederate telegrapher was flashing the news to Vicksburg: "Great God, Phil, eighty-one gunboats and transports have passed here tonight." Philip N. Hall, the receiving telegrapher, raced to a home where Confederate General Martin Luther Smith was attending a Christmas ball. "The party," announced Smith, "is at an end."[4]

Porter's mighty flotilla, with his flagship *Black Hawk* in the van, finally reached the mouth of the Yazoo on December 25 and anchored while a raiding party destroyed the terminal of the Vicksburg, Shreveport & Texas Railroad across the river from the city. Then the fleet prepared to ascend the Yazoo for the assault on the Chickasaw Bluffs.

In the meantime, a series of events were taking place in Washington that were to affect the Yazoo River expedition. General John Alexander McClernand, a division commander who served with Grant at Forts Henry and Donelson and at Shiloh, had been up to political shenanigans behind Grant's back. In spite of a lack of formal military training, he was a powerful politician with considerable influence over Stanton and Lincoln. He managed to persuade the president that the West Point generals, particularly Grant, were hobbling the Mississippi campaigns, and that he himself should lead the investment of Vicksburg.

President Lincoln, for his part, was anxious to please the influential congressman from Illinois. After some consultation, Lincoln permitted McClernand to raise a force of volunteers from Illinois, Indiana and Iowa. The general managed to raise 30,000 recruits and he asked for permission to be put in charge of the Vicksburg campaign. Then he headed for Memphis, with his green recruits, to supersede Grant, who had already moved downstream. In a snit, McClernand loaded himself, a new wife and his sycophants on a steamer and went downstream after Grant.[5]

Meanwhile, General Halleck denounced McClernand's disruptive moves as cheap politics. He sought out Lincoln and convinced him that the man was absurd and asked that Grant be put in full command with McClernand subordinate.

While McClernand's steamer was chopping its way down the Mississippi, Porter's powerful flotilla of gunboats, transports and auxiliaries were moving up the russet waters of the Yazoo. The force paused at a place called Johnston's Plantation, now in ruins, which had belonged to General Albert Sidney Johnston, the Confederate general who was killed at Shiloh. It seemed that Porter's marines had burned the place, after a wildcat battery fired from it at a reconnaissance gunboat the day before. Here, Generals M.L. Smith and A.J. Smith landed their divisions and moved off in two columns toward the bluffs to the east. Just to the north of these, on a parallel course, also in two columns, moved the divisions of Morgan and Steele through a quagmire of water and foliage.

The four columns moved up to the bayou directly beneath the Chickasaw Bluffs, which at this point were crowded with 10,000 Confederate troops and 34 guns. The bayou was 100 feet wide and 15 feet deep. On December 29, supported by fire from the gunboats, Sherman's forces put up pontoons across the bayou and attacked the bluffs, coming under a withering fire from the entrenched Confederates. At one point, Union soldiers were pinned down and had to hand-dig protective caves in which to hide from the rifle fire from above.

A regimental captain of the 42nd Ohio Regiment wrote that the point of attack on the bluff was the interior of an arc, or semicircle. As the brigade moved up, it "found itself in the center of converging fire, a flaming hell of shell, shot, cannister and minie balls. It would be vain to attempt any description of the noise and confusion of that hour."[6]

After being nearly cut to pieces by the murderous enemy fire, Sherman withdrew his forces, while he boarded the flagship to confer with Porter. Together, they hatched a plan to move the remainder of the men up to attack Drumgould's Bluff, overwhelm the troops there, then advance down to higher ground to attack the defenders of the Chickasaw Bluffs. But a dense fog delayed the expedition on the evening of December 31, and the advent of a moonlit night destroyed any chance of surprise. On January 2, the entire amphibious force packed up and moved back down the river to the fleet anchorage.

Though the slaughter at Chickasaw Bluffs was not as great as at Fredericksburg, two weeks previous, where Union troops had similarly been launched against Rebel-held heights, the losses were grim enough: 208 killed, 1,005 wounded and 563 missing, out of 30,000 effectives. Confederate casualties were 63 killed and 134 wounded.[7] The attack was a dismal failure and Union forces pulled back to the junction of the Yazoo and Mississippi.

The defeated armada reached the mouth of the Yazoo in time to greet McClernand, who had just steamed up in the *Tygress*. The fretting general read the riot act to Porter and Sherman and took command of all forces, including those of Grant. Sherman issued an order to his troops to the effect that there had been a change in command, and thanked his men for their brave part in the expedition.

Unknown to McClernand, however, Lincoln's order to Grant to assume overall command in the theater and subordinate McClernand had been received and would soon be implemented. Grant was to divide his great forces into four army corps, one of which would be McClernand's, and McClernand himself would "be under immediate command of Grant's direction."[8]

With all the recriminations and wrangling behind them, the entire amphibious forces, under the protection of the gunboats, now steamed back to Young's Point, just below Milliken's Bend, where they had established a base of operations, while the main body of the fleet remained at the mouth of the Yazoo River, waiting for further orders.

The navy and land forces leaders went into conference and decided that something must be done to offset the fiasco at the Chickasaw Bluffs. But where? Sherman had learned that the steamer *Blue Wing*, loaded with mail and ammunition, and towing barges of coal, had been captured by a Rebel gunboat and taken up the Arkansas River to a fortification called "Arkansas Post," 40 miles upstream, and that the artillery works there were manned by about 5,000 enemy troops. The site was a danger to Union traffic on the Mississippi and it had to be removed before any more operations were launched against Vicksburg. McClernand, ever the one to see a chance for glory, agreed to the plan, so he joined Sherman and his staff on board the steamer *Forest Queen*. Together they paddle-wheeled down to Porter's flagship, anchored at the Yazoo, and went into conference.

The admiral announced that he would go along with the gunboats *Baron DeKalb* (formerly *St. Louis*), *Louisville, Cincinnati*, the ram *Monarch*, the gunboats *Black Hawk* and *Tyler*, plus the tinclads *Rattler* and *Glide*, and a fleet of transports ferrying 30,000 troops. This formidable military force would go against an estimated 5,000 men and eight guns as their objective on the Arkansas River.[9]

That river was and still is the largest river that feeds the Mississippi. Its course, from its beginnings at Leadville, Colorado in the Rockies, takes it through the states of Colorado, Kansas, Oklahoma and Arkansas and it flows 1,459 miles before reaching the Mississippi.

To the Confederates, Arkansas Post, a cavalry camp, also provided an excellent site for a fort to guard approaches from downriver that would threaten Little Rock. The fort was named Fort Hindman. It was 300 feet across, star-shaped, and contained casemates one of which housed three Dahlgren 9-inch guns; one with a single 9-inch Dahlgren and another that housed a 4-inch rifled Parrott and a 12-pounder smoothbore. The rest of the guns were mostly field pieces of various calibers. The parapets of this fortress were around 25 feet thick and were surrounded by an 18-foot ditch below and a mile-long line of rifle pits. The site was under the command of Confederate General Thomas J. Churchill.[10] The channel below the fort had been marked with buoys to be used as range markers for his guns.

Admiral Porter's task force weighed anchor on January 4, 1863, and sailed to the mouth of the White River, but in a "feint maneuver," to the south took the Arkansas River Cut-Off, and moved up slowly until it reached a point three miles below the fort. On January 10, troops were disembarked on both sides of the river; on the west bank to block any enemy retreat across the river, and on the east bank to assault the fort. The gunboats brushed the range buoys aside, moved up and drove sharpshooters from their pits at the river's edge. Meanwhile, one division of Union troops got lost in the swamps for a time, but managed to rejoin the main body in time to drive the enemy from their outer earthworks.

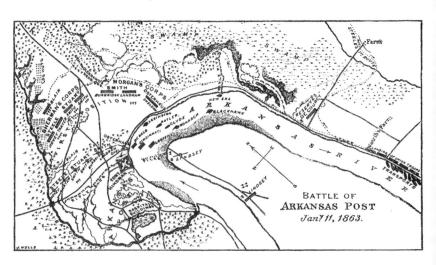

Map of the Union gunboats' approach on Arkansas Post (Fort Hindman).

Then the big guns of the war vessels were elevated, and the fort was given a firestorm of shot and shell. Meanwhile, on the 11th, the disembarked troops stormed the works. Providing support for them, Porter's guns again blasted away at the fort, silencing most of its guns.

The devastating powers of the flotilla's guns, combined with the overwhelming assault by Sherman's troops, proved too much for Churchill. He ran up the white flag and surrendered the fort, which had suffered considerable damage. Casualties amounted to 60 killed, 80 wounded, and a surrendered prisoner count of 4791. Union losses were 129 killed, 831 wounded and 17 missing.[11]

The expedition, after destroying what was left of the fort, re-embarked and went back down the river, and thence to Milliken's Bend on January 21 to await the arrival of General Grant, who at first thought the Arkansas expedition an unnecessary move, but recanted after hearing of the victory, thereupon putting his stamp of approval on the operation.

Union gunboats continued to dominate the Mississippi, in spite of the batteries at Vicksburg and Port Hudson. In one important sortie, the *Queen of the West*, with Colonel Charles Ellet commanding, ran the batteries at Vicksburg, receiving numerous hits, but managed to close with the Confederate steamer *City of Vicksburg*, which had been brought down from the Yazoo River.

This enemy steamer, along with others coming up from the Port Hudson/Red River area, was bringing supplies to Vicksburg.[12] The *Queen* was now strengthened with cotton bales around her vitals and her steering apparatus was moved forward behind the bow bulwarks, but the arrangement proved to be cumbersome so it was moved back to the pilothouse. The time consumed at this work resulted in a considerable delay that caused her to arrive at Vicksburg in daylight, instead of night as originally planned, giving enemy gunners a clear shot at her. Miraculously, she suffered only minor hits.

Ellet steered directly for the *City*; his ram's bow guns, loaded with incendiary shells, keeping a stream of fire directed at the unfortunate steamer at the wharf. Then *Queen* rammed her, but the force of the blow was tempered by large guards that were draped over the ram's bow and she swung parallel to the *City*, the ram keeping up an incessant stream of shells, causing considerable damage to the Rebel vessel and crew. Ellet then backed off and drifted downriver, past the lower batteries, dodging shots until he reached a point where he could anchor in order to effect repairs.

At 1:00 A.M., Ellet continued his journey downriver to Grand Gulf, which Farragut had earlier destroyed, then on to Natchez, where Ellet reported that "not a word of our coming had reached the place and people scarcely knew who we were."[13] The intrepid commander reaped a harvest of spoils below Natchez, where the Confederacy had a stream of supply vessels plying those waters.

There he captured and destroyed three Rebel steamers: one containing 110,000 pounds of pork, 500 hogs and a quantity of salt for the garrison at port Hudson; another, with 200 barrels of molasses, sugar, 30,000 pounds of flour and 40 bales of cotton; and the third with 25,000 pounds of meal. It was quite a day's haul for the *Queen*.

Presently, Ellet needed fuel, so he was preparing to dash upriver in the small steamboat *DeSoto*, which had been captured from the Confederates earlier, to get some. Meanwhile, however, Porter had thoughtfully dispatched an unmanned coal barge downstream so Ellet was resupplied. After leaving the *DeSoto*, which was now a tender, at the mouth of the Red River, he went south with the *Queen* down the smaller Atchafalaya River, destroying two enemy wagon trains and burning plantations along the way. Then he returned to the Red River and the awaiting tender.[14] His next foray took him up the Red, where he came upon the steamer *New Era*, which carried a load of corn and a passel of Confederate military personnel. So far it seemed that Ellet and his one-ship raiding flotilla had been reaping huge dividends in spoils. The *New Era*'s cargo was confiscated and the personnel taken prisoner; the Rebel pilot was pressed into service on the *Queen*.

But Ellet was bound to be challenged; the Confederates were not about to let him get away with his rampage for very long. In Jackson, military heads were put together, and as a result Colonel W.S. Lovell, C.S.A., was ordered to Alexandria, Louisiana, on the

Red River, to fit out as a ram the *Webb*, a riverboat steamer that had escaped Farragut's onslaught on New Orleans. This vessel, a sidewheeler, displaced 655 tons and was 206 feet long, with a beam of 32 feet. A former privateer, she was fitted with a 32-pounder on her bow and cotton bales around her two boilers. With this armed vessel, Lovell was prepared to challenge the *Queen* or any other Union vessel that might come along.

That other vessel did come along. Admiral Porter was anxious to supply protection for Ellet, so he sent down the new pride of the Federal Navy, the gunboat *Indianola*.

This war vessel was the result of the newest technology in the Union and was as fine a gunboat as ever plied the river waterways. Designed by Joseph Brown for the army, she was built in Cincinnati, in late 1862, at a cost of $183,662.56, specifically for use on western rivers. With an innovative sidewheel/propeller design, she was 175 feet long, had a beam of 52 feet, and housed seven engines: two for propelling her sidewheels, two for her two propellers, two for her capstans and one for supplying water for the bilge pumps and fire pumps. All were powered by five boilers that also produced steam for her top speed of six knots. Her casemate, which had an incline of $26^{1}/_{2}$ degrees, was covered with three inch iron plating and the hurricane deck was covered with one inch plating. As armament, this powerful vessel was fitted out with two 11-inch Dahlgren smoothbores forward, and two 9-inch Dahlgrens aft, which gave her a considerable arc of firepower.[14]

The *Indianola*, commanded by Lieutenant-Commander George Brown, slipped by the Vicksburg batteries on February 13, and anchored downstream to await further orders and learn the whereabouts of Ellet and his *Queen of the West*.

Ellet was still on his rampage up the Red River. On February 14, the *Queen* was churning upriver with the *DeSoto* for more prizes: three steamers that prisoners had told him were moored at Gordon's Landing, 30 miles away. The Confederates had a battery of four 32-pounders at the landing, but these, according to the prisoners, would give him little trouble. As the *Queen* reached a bend below Gordon's Landing, however, the captured Rebel pilot that Ellet had taken aboard ran her aground within range of the batteries. A deluge of 32-pound shots tore into the ill-starred ram, smashing machinery and severing her steam chest. Confusion reined on board, and crewmen jumped overboard to escape the terrible steam that was filling the vessel's innards. Bales of cotton were tossed overboard for swimmers to cling to, including Ellet, who were hoping to reach the *DeSoto* coming up from below. However, that vessel was having troubles of her own with an unshipped rudder whirling her out of control until she was hard aground and had to be destroyed. Ellet and the other survivors looked to their captured vessel *New Era* downstream for rescue.[15]

After she picked up the battered, water-soaked survivors, the *New Era* quickly vacated the Red River. Ellet and his men were heading back up the Mississippi when they were delighted to meet the *Indianola* coming downstream. Aboard, Ellet promptly reported the loss of the *Queen of the West*.

In the interim, the Confederates had repaired the *Queen* and made her seaworthy again. On the 26th, she, along with the *Webb* and the gunboat *Dr. Beaty*, all under the command of Lieutenant-Colonel F.B. Brand, exited the Red River and steamed up the Mississippi to within 30 miles below Vicksburg, where they came upon the *Indianola*, moored to the shore. The flotilla prepared to do battle.[16]

Captain Brown had been expecting supporting vessels to come down from Porter's fleet, but the admiral was engaged in the Yazoo Pass expedition and had failed to send any. Brown was on his own now, against three enemy men-of-war. But in true navy tradition, the undaunted skipper prepared to meet the challenge, in spite of two coal barges lashed alongside, which he had planned to use for any reinforcing vessels from Porter.[17]

With the advantage of a brightly moonlit night, the (now C.S.S.) *Queen* had the distinction of making the first offensive move. With considerable momentum, she headed for *Indianola*, who at the last moment maneuvered so as to present a coal barge to the onrushing ram. With a fearsome crunch, the *Queen* plowed into the barge, slicing it in half and indenting the thick plating on the gunboat's midship area.

The *Queen*'s impact was so forceful that the ram was stuck

against the gunboat's hull, unable to extricate herself. Her sharp-shooters fired away at any opening on their adversary's hull. The *Webb*, meanwhile, came up and plowed into the *Indianola's* bow, the force of the blow knocking everyone on both vessels off their feet.[18] The hit did little structural damage to the ironclad, but did manage to disable her starboard engine. *Indianola* swung around from the blow and, in so doing, shook off one of her attached barges. Thus unencumbered, Brown leveled his 11-inch Dahlgren at the *Queen*, which was just then rounding for another charge, but the shots missed. That gave the *Webb* a chance to swing around the *Indianola's* starboard side and strip away the other barge, laying her open to another ram attack. All during the fight, Brown was outside the casemate, on the hurricane deck, giving orders to the pilothouse, the gunners and, by kneeling on the iron grating, to the engineers below. He was completely oblivious to his own safety.[19]

Then the *Queen* came charging in and delivered another blow, glancing off just below the gunboat's pilothouse. As she drifted past, the 9-inch Dahlgrens on the stern of the *Indianola* opened up on her, killing two men and disabling three guns. The intrepid ram hove to again and crashed into the gunboat, this time doing some structural damage. Then her consort, the *Webb*, made a wide turn, bore down on and thundered into the unfortunate *Indianola,* which was by now reeling in circles.

The last Dahlgren blast had penetrated deep into the *Queen's* hull, permitting volumes of water to pour into her compartments. But by this time, the *Indianola* also had taken too much punishment and was shipping water fast; Brown steered her to the river bank and beached her. He lowered the flag to the *Dr. Beaty,* which had just joined the fray in time to receive the surrender. Confederate Major Brand, aboard the *Dr. Beaty,* reported that the *Indianola* was "one of the most formidable ironclads in their [Union] navy, protected in every way possible with thick heavy timber and heavy iron plates . . ."[20]

Major Brand then took command of the captured gunboat and was instructed to head south and run up the Red River for repairs and fitting out. Upon reaching the Jefferson Davis Plantation, the *Indianola* was run ashore and settled in 10 feet of water.[21] A detail was ordered to board her, remove all supplies, equipment and ammunition. But no sooner had the Confederates begun work on their prize when news arrived that another huge Union gunboat was fast approaching from upriver. With great reluctance the Rebels had no choice but to destroy the captured ironclad and exit the area. The *Indianola* was blown up, and the *Queen, Webb* and other vessels fled in panic.

When the "huge enemy gunboat" made its appearance, it was to be one of the most bizarre incidents in the Civil War, causing both consternation and joy, depending upon which side one was on. Later, there would be acrimonious inquiries into the incident.

The Union gunboat was a "dummy," a brainchild of Admiral Porter, who had committed a total of $8.63 to build the craft to run past the batteries at Vicksburg. It appeared that the intensely practical admiral had observed that some of the Confederate guns would burst while trying to fire at his vessels. Logically, the more vessels he could send past the batteries, the more Rebel guns would burst. A mortar vessel was brought up to shell the city, but it evoked no response.[22] Then Porter had the idea of building a dummy boat that he could sail past to tempt the Confederate gunners. Gathering some carpenters, he covered the hull of an old coal barge with lumber to resemble a casemate and two wheel houses. A chimney was constructed from old pork barrels. Large logs, "Quaker guns," which protruded from the fake casemate, were also installed. Two old canoes served as cutters on each side. A burning pot of tar and oakum, that poured out volumes of smoke, was placed in each chimney.

The fake ironclad was launched on the 24th and, with chimneys belching black smoke, drifted past Vicksburg. The batteries responded with a thundering barrage that prompted Porter to remark that those batteries had never opened "with such a din" and that "the earth fairly trembled."[23] Shots went through the contrivance, but otherwise it was not seriously damaged, leaving behind a parcel of shaken gunners who thought the Union had an invincible gunboat at last.

Down the river drifted the dummy gunboat, a flag flying from its fake jackstaff, causing alarm among Confederate sympathizers as it went along.

She finally came to rest, ironically enough, just above the plantation where Brand's crews were working on raising the *Indianola*. The Confederate crews on the sunken Union gunboat grew nervous as the big, silent monster lurked above them, not revealing any intentions. When the order came down from Pemberton at Vicksburg to destroy the prize, rather than have it revert back to Federal hands, the boarding crews were eager to comply. The guns were spiked, and dry powder was placed in the magazine.

Meanwhile, acting on suspicions that the ironclad was not what it appeared to be, a contingent of soldiers gingerly rowed out for a closer examination, and discovered it to be a hoax. By the time this information was broadcast about the dummy, it was too late—the *Indianola* had been blown up.

It appeared that the gunboat had tried not to die. On March 4, Confederate General Stevenson reported that the *Indianola* was not destroyed and that she could be raised. All that was salvaged, however, was one 11-inch Dahlgren and two 9-inchers. It was decided that the hull was beyond saving.[24]

In the South, as in the North, there was a storm of protest and criticism about the failure to raise the *Indianola*.[25] One Richmond editor expressed the opinion that the loss of the Union gunboat was more disgraceful than farcical.

One man who was less than amused by the whole affair was Admiral Farragut in New Orleans who, upon receiving news of the loss of *Indianola*, decided that it was time to send some of his fleet up to support Porter's movements.

However, Port Hudson stood in the way. This site, at an important hairpin bend in the river, was not considered a menace until August 1862, when it was discovered that the Confederates were emplacing heavy batteries. A week later, guns newly installed in the earthworks fired upon Federal vessels plying the river. It became obvious that this was now an installation of real importance.

General Banks, in early March, had brought up 25,000 troops from New Orleans to Baton Rouge and, after a conference with Farragut, decided to make a diversionary attack on Port Hudson to allow Farragut's fleet to slip past the batteries. Those batteries presented a formidable obstacle with two 10-inch Columbiads, two 8-inch Columbiads, three 24-pounders and a line of eight rifled guns along a bluff four miles long and from 80 to 100 feet high.

Undaunted, Farragut brought his naval force up to Prophets Island, five miles below Port Hudson. The flotilla consisted of the big ships *Hartford, Richmond, Monongahela* and *Mississippi*; gunboats *Albatross, Genessee* and *Kineo*; plus a contingent of mortar boats and the ironclad *Essex* assigned to shell the fort, in order to occupy its attention, while the run was being made. The side-wheeler *Mississippi* would bring up the rear of the flotilla. As further protection for the ships, a gunboat was lashed alongside the port quarter of each sloop for additional support during the maneuver.

The theory of this ship-coupling was that if the large warship were to be grounded or disabled in any way, the gunboat would assist it. Although the gunboats were lashed to the side of the sloops, they would be far enough aft to allow broadside guns clear access.[26] Boat howitzers were also placed in the rigging platforms of the mizzen masts of the sloops.

On the night of March 14, the flotilla got under way against a five-knot current, and their course was to take them past the batteries and around a 150-degree bend in the river. At first it seemed to be a textbook operation—until the Confederates pulled a surprise. They switched on a series of locomotive headlights on the east bank and lit a series of huge bonfires on the west side.[27] Thus illuminated and silhouetted, the vessels received a fusillade of angry shots from the Port Hudson gunners. Meanwhile, the mortar vessels opened up on the batteries.

In the van, lashed together, *Hartford* and *Albatross* moved upstream but, upon reaching Thomas Point, almost ran aground. Then they managed to free themselves, thanks to the additional power of the gunboats alongside. Next in line were *Richmond* and *Genessee*, followed by *Monongahela* and *Kineo* with *Mississippi* at tail end. The incredible accuracy of the Confederate gunners took its toll. A shot slammed into *Richmond*'s steam drum, causing her to drift back out of the fight. The *Monongahela*, with the *Kineo*, had her rudderpost holed and her propeller fouled.

The latter got off the shore, but had to drop back, also out of the fight. The *Mississippi* came up next, so far undamaged, but, as she approached Thomas Point, her pilot lost his way and she ran hard aground. Unable to get her back into the stream, and under heavy fire, her captain passed the order to abandon ship. After the crew spiked the guns and destroyed the engines, they set her on fire; she drifted downstream, blazing from stem to stern until she blew up. Out of a ship's complement of 297, 64 were reported missing; 25 were killed.[28]

General Banks was probing the city's defenses, but upon learning of the misfortunes of the fleet he withdrew to the suburbs to await further developments. He had not quite fulfilled his task of keeping the Rebel gunners occupied while the fleet slipped past. Instead he vowed to invest Port Hudson at a later date, when conditions were more favorable.

Admiral Farragut now had only two of his seven ships north of Port Hudson, and he felt they were not enough, so he sent a dispatch to Admiral Porter, asking for more gunboats to be used in patrolling the river between Vicksburg and Port Hudson. Unfortunately, Porter was at that time busily engaged in the bayous and waterways around Vicksburg. But then General Alfred Ellet heard of Farragut's call for help, and he had himself taken to the flagship for a conference with the admiral.

During the conference, Ellet proposed that he provide two of his rams for the naval actions downriver. Farragut protested that they were going over Admiral Porter's head on this plan. Ellet (not one to be dissuaded by such a technicality) assured him that Porter would have agreed with the plan were he present, so Farragut approved the operation.

Back in his flagship, Ellet ordered the *Lancaster* and the *Switzerland* to make the run past the batteries and thence to Farragut. Because of delay in getting stores on board, the vessels were not able to make the run until near daybreak. The *Lancaster* was commanded by Colonel John Ellet, brother of Alfred. Ellet's vessel, the *Switzerland*, was the pilot craft and the *Lancaster* was to follow to starboard. The two rams floated with the current partway, then got up power. When, unfortunately, the noise of steam popping from the rams'chimneys alerted Vicksburg gunners and they opened upon the two, Ellet immediately ordered full steam ahead, while shots thudded in the water around the two vessels.[29]

For a time, it appeared as if they would make it; then shots began to hit home. One ball hit the *Lancaster*, passed through, severed a steam drum and filled the spaces below with scalding steam. Another shot passed through aft of the bow, opening up a large leak; another took away the wheel. The ram, now obviously doomed, was abandoned by Ellet and his crew, after they had first set her on fire to keep her out of Rebel hands. Before she could be consumed by the flames, however, she went down by the bow, a victim of excellent Confederate gunnery.

John Ellet and the survivors floated until they were picked up by cutters from the *Switzerland,* which had sustained little or no damage.[31] Although this action did not endear Ellet to Porter, at least now Farragut had another gunboat adapted to patrolling the rivers and its tributaries and a chance for another try up the Red River, whenever the opportunity presented itself.

CHAPTER SEVENTEEN

The Noose Tightens

It would not be difficult to visualize General Grant sitting before a map of the Vicksburg area and contemplating his next moves, in early 1863. His problem was not strength, it was terrain. After pulling his army north he had rejoined Sherman (and McClernand) and the combined Union army, assembled just north of Vicksburg on the west bank of the Mississippi, was now the most formidable force in the department. The Union navy likewise was powerful and growing. But nature had supplied Vicksburg with defenses that would challenge even the strongest of armies, and the Confederates were taking full advantage.

To the north of the city the quagmire known as the Yazoo Delta, 60 miles wide, was simply impassable for ground troops. It was paralleled by a long line of bluffs, rising to heights of from 80 to 100 feet, and, as Sherman had learned, bringing troops in by boat to the foot of these bluffs was no solution. Rolling out eastward was high ground cut through with a plethora of valleys and ridges. And, of course, to the west there was the Mississippi running past and below the entire length of the city. To the south the river bluffs ran all the way down to Port Hudson, a still-unbowed Confederate fortification. Even the DeSoto Peninsula, across the river from the city, was another lowland of marshes and swamps. It was evident that Vicksburg could only be taken from the east.[1] And it would be a job for the navy to get them there.

Remembering the success of the canal that had propelled

Union forces past Island No. 10 the previous year, engineering schemes came to the fore to open up a waterway for transports. Grant approved a similar plan to accomplish the same objective in the DeSoto Peninsula, to run from Young's Point and exiting at a spot below Vicksburg. In that way, enough water would be diverted from the Mississippi, to make a passageway for gunboats and transports to float through, thereby allowing troops to land south of the city. Lincoln himself had navigated the river in his earlier days, and knew its twists and bends, plus its potentialities and its eccentricities, and had approved the plan.[2]

Without delay, 4,000 troops were given picks and shovels. With the help of a dredge and a circular saw on a raft—the type used at the Island No. 10 project—they built a dam on the west bank of the peninsula. Unfortunately, the river decided to rise, wiped out the dam, flooded the unfinished canal, swamped equipment and sent workers fleeing for their lives. Actually, the canal might not have worked anyway, because the Confederates had learned about the project and had positioned heavy guns on the banks opposite the exit point, with the capability of enfilading the entire canal. It was an ambitious plan, but was doomed from the start.

Another attempt at a canal was made at Duckport, 20 miles below Vicksburg, but it too never reached fruition. Then the Yankees noticed a promising spot at Lake Providence in Louisiana, just a bit south of the Arkansas border. The lake had been carved out by the fickle meandering of the Mississippi, and it was deep. If a canal were to be cut into the lake, from the Mississippi, a sizeable amphibious force could be floated through into Bayou Baxter, into the Tensas River, into the Ouachita River, and finally into the Red River—which would allow access to the Mississippi River far below Vicksburg.[3] It would be a roundabout trip of 400 miles, all safe from the Confederates. So Grant put his troops to work on the 80-foot-wide by 5-foot-deep project. Once again, it was a well-meant experiment, but, as with the others, the gap between theory and practice proved too wide to overcome. Next, everyone looked to the Yazoo.

Yazoo Pass, 150 miles north of Vicksburg, just below Helena, Arkansas, feeds into Moon Lake, thence into a 10-mile-long bayou, which feeds the Coldwater River, which feeds the Tallahatchie, which in turn feeds the Yazoo. The bayou was 80 feet wide and 30 feet deep, enough for the large vessels to navigate. In former times, the waterway had been used as a shorter route by steamers plying between Memphis and Vicksburg; however, the Mississippi poured much water into the region, flooding it so that it became necessary to build a levee 100 feet thick by 18 feet high.[4]

Grant saw the opportunity for a flotilla of gunboats, transports and auxiliaries to sweep into the pass, follow the winding route and eventually land somewhere above Haynes Bluff. His troops would overwhelm the strong fortification there and open a direct approach to the Chickasaw Bluffs from the north. It would entail a tortuous route of 700 miles, but it would do the trick. Grant wrote that he expected the expedition to capture all the transports and supply vessels on the Yazoo and its tributaries, and to destroy two gunboats rumored to be building at Yazoo City.[5] This project, however, was compromised by rising water on the Mississippi and all its tributaries, so the effort had to halt.

Then Admiral Porter came up with an idea: Why not set a mine in the levee and blow it open? This was done, on February 2, and the resulting explosion opened a deluge of water into the pass. After three weeks, the area was flooded enough to allow the gunboats to pass through. Assigned to this expedition were the *Chillicothe, Baron DeKalb, Rattler, Marmora, Signal, Romeo, Petrol* and *Fort Rose*, along with the rams *Lyoness* and *Fulton*, a towboat, three barges containing coal, and transports with 6000 troops. Lieutenant-Commander Watson Smith was the commander of the task force. To that date it was to be the largest river expedition of the war.

The vessels floated down the pass, without much incident, but once in the Coldwater they ran into trouble from both nature and a determined enemy. The waterways, particularly the bayous, were lined with sycamore, oak, pecanwood and willow. The branches of many of these trees were so close to the water that they damaged chimneys and pilothouses. Also, thick underwater growth threatened the vessels' paddle wheels.[6]

The real danger came when the Confederates cut down trees,

some of them with a four-foot diameter and a weight of many tons, to block the waterway. The Union boats were forced to halt while crews removed these encumbrances, using rope cables with 500 men to a cable.[7] In some cases, the bends in the Coldwater were so sharp that the boats had to be snaked around them, using cables attached to trees.

The going was rough. In four days, the expedition traveled a distance of only 40 miles. When it reached the Tallahatchie it was easier going; the vessels were placed in single-line formation with the gunboats in the van and transports and support vessels to the rear.

But the Confederates were prepared; they knew this armada was coming and had arranged a reception. Confederate General William W. Loring had established an earthworks at the confluence of the Tallahatchie and Yalobusha rivers named Fort Pemberton. It was an almost impregnable site because it commanded all approaches on the river and was constructed of cotton bales covered with earth and armed with a Whitworth gun of 6.4-inch caliber, three Parrott 30-pounders and an array of 12- and 13-pound field pieces—plus a force of 1,500 troops. In addition, a few sunken hulks, including that of the famous *Star of the West* (now the C.S.S. *St. Philip*), were blocking Smith's way.

The Union commander called his flotilla to a halt in order to study the situation. The fort was situated on an island surrounded by floodwaters, unapproachable by land. Smith hesitated for a few days while deciding what to do. Apparently he was not of the mind to come up and blast away at the fort with his big guns. Instead, he seemed paralyzed with indecision. However, realizing he must soon act, he sent *Chillicothe* and *Baron de Kalb* to shell the installation.

Chillicothe was a 395-ton sidewheeler with a 162-foot length and a 50-foot beam. It had two screws in addition to the side wheels. Her two engines pushed her along at seven knots and she carried two 11-inch smoothbores and a 12-pounder smoothbore. The *Baron de Kalb*, renamed from its original title of *St. Louis*, carried one 10-inch smoothbore, two 8-inch and two 9-inch smoothbores, six 32-pounders and two 30-pounder rifles.

It is strange that Smith failed to send another vessel to supplement these two. The 165-ton *Rattler*, for example, with her two 30-pound rifles and six 24-pound smoothbores, would have been a better choice. Perhaps the illness he was suffering at the time clouded his judgment.

Both Smith and Porter had not reckoned with the fort's commander, William Loring. This Confederate general was from the old school, grizzled and hard. He was a lawyer and legislator at the time the Mexican War broke out, but went on to earn two brevets, though losing an arm at Chapultepec. Later, he became an Indian fighter and, soon after, was sent to Europe to study its armies. When the Civil War broke out, Loring was commissioned a brigadier general; he was transferred to Vicksburg in 1863. In the course of the Civil War he earned the nickname of "Old Blizzards," because, during the exchanges with the Union boats he climbed atop the parapet and waved a sword, shouting, "Give them blizzards, boys!" This was the man who met the *Chillicothe* and *Baron de Kalb* as they approached his fort.

Both gunboats were pounded repeatedly. One hit exploded a 10-inch shell being loaded into a gun, killing two men and wounding 11. The gunboats came back the next day, but the *Chillicothe* suffered heavy damage and had to withdraw; the installation was too formidable. Smith, after some futile hand wringing, decided to withdraw the force back to Yazoo Pass. His operation was a failure, and had cost six men killed and 25 wounded.[8]

It seemed as if the plans for getting around Vicksburg by plodding the back waterways were all doomed to failure. But the indefatigable Porter came up with another idea: entering the Yazoo to Steele's Bayou, then ingressing the Sunflower, which flowed from a considerable distance northward down from the spot where it conjoined with the Yazoo above Haynes Bluff. The troops would land 20 miles above that bastion, assault and take it, turn the right flank of the Vicksburg defense and open a way to the city itself.

On March 15, Grant boarded Porter's flagship, *Black Hawk*, and together they took a trip up the Yazoo into Steele's Bayou. The general was flabbergasted when Porter had the steamer veer off the main channel and float through surrounding lowlands now covered with water. To Grant's further surprise, the channels were much deeper now than they had been before, thanks to heavy rains and the opening of the Yazoo Pass, which, flooded everything in the delta southward.

Grant was satisfied; he dropped back to his headquarters and immediately ordered Sherman to take 10,000 men to board transports and follow Porter's fleet up Steele's Bayou.[9] Porter chose for this sortie the gunboats *Carondelet, Cincinnati, Louisville, Pittsburgh* and *Mound City*, the ram *General Price*, four mortar boats and a towboat with four barges; he was gambling most of his ironclad fleet on this operation, along with a division of troops.

As with other river operations, the gunboats were in the van when the flotilla entered the Yazoo on the 16th and proceeded upstream without opposition. The stream was wide enough to allow easy passage, even for the heavy gunboats. When they entered the smaller stream of Rolling Fork, the going got tougher. The vessels churned over paddlewheel-clogging undergrowth that brushed against the ships, knocking down chimneys and breaking windows on deck levels and pilothouses.

To some the scenery was worth noting, in spite of the grim mission. One of the soldiers aboard reported a combination of sycamore, willow and cypress, festoons of moss hanging down like green icicles from the low branches. The birds, he claimed, sang cheerfully; fish jumped out of the water, and even a flock of chattering parrots flew over the flotilla. At a nearby plantation, some marines went on a foraging expedition and gathered huge numbers of ducks, chickens, geese, bacon, hams, guinea hens and a young bull, for fresh fare.

Crowds of slaves cheered the force on as it sailed. Some even brought fresh eggs for the crews.[10] It was to be the happiest time of the expedition, for soon things got perilous.

Confederate sharpshooters lurked in the underbrush along the river and made it dangerous for crews to come out of the casemates to deal with impediments. Adding to the problems were wildlife of all sorts: raccoons, snakes, cockroaches, mice and lizards driven to the trees by the floodwaters. These dropped on decks as the low branches were encountered. They were swept aside by crewmen armed with brooms.[11]

Slowly, with paddle wheels thrashing, the gunboats moved on, sometimes knocking down trees, using their great weight as huge bulldozers, occasionally flailing the shoreline with cannister and grape against snipers. Then crews would hack away at underbrush or snake big trees out of the way using capstans, all the while trying to dodge musket balls from the pesky Southern gunmen.

When the flotilla approached the Sunflower River, Porter's lookouts spotted a Rebel transport disgorging troops and unloading light artillery on the levee. The troops were estimated to be around 4,000, more than Porter had aboard his vessels, because Sherman's transports had earlier dropped back to clear out Black Bayou and to speed up reinforcements that were on their way.[12] Porter found himself without troop support.

Things grew even more ominous when artillery fire began to descend on his vessels. To the rear of his force, the sound of chopping indicated that the Confederates were trying to block the only exit the fleet had. He therefore wrote a note asking for immediate help and sent it to Sherman by way of a local slave who hid the message in a tobacco pouch.

Sherman acted swiftly. He boarded troops on a steamer and headed upstream at full speed. When obstructions halted the vessel, he disembarked the troops and marched them through canebrakes and water to their destination. At night the men used candles in the muzzles of their muskets to guide them.[13]

In the meantime, Porter attempted duelling with the enemy artillery, but because the levees upon which the Rebels had placed their field pieces were higher than the river level, he was unable to elevate his guns in response. Instead, the big naval guns thundered away at troops in the thick underbrush of the riverbanks. By this time, the situation had reached the point at which the admiral seriously considered scuttling and burning his vessels, rather than have them fall into enemy hands.

Sherman's troops finally came to the rescue. Porter had never been more happy to see blue-clad soldiers, while his sailors lustily cheered them on.[14] The Yankees charged the Rebel troops along both banks, driving them off. The way was now clear for the flotilla to descend the river back to safety. While Sherman's troops routed the enemy woodchoppers down below, and removed the felled trees, Porter unshipped his rudders, and the gunboats laboriously floated and bumped their way downstream toward the Mississippi.

Another expedition had ended in failure. One cannot help wondering what consequences would have ensued if the Confederates had indeed been able to capture Porter's fleet. No doubt the entire naval picture on the Mississippi would have changed drastically.

Grant was now ensconced in his headquarters steamer at Milliken's Bend on the Mississippi while his Army of the Tennessee was billeted along the river for 60 miles, from Young's Point north to Lake Providence. Sherman joined him and some serious conferences took place. The long, flood-dogged winter had passed, waters had begun to recede, and movement by land, long denied by winter, was now possible.

Alternatives were discussed. One was to take the army back to Memphis, and then down to Vicksburg by the route originally planned by Grant until the Holly Springs fiasco hit. But Grant demurred, stating that it would be a "step backward," and that the political climate in the North would forbid it. Indeed, in the east the Army of the Potomac had largely been inactive for months while gearing up for its next great offensive (which would end at Chancellorsville). If Grant were suddenly to conduct what to all eyes would resemble a withdrawal back up the Mississippi, he would probably not retain his command.

The discussion then turned toward an earlier plan, that of moving all three corps a short distance down the Louisiana side of the river, now fairly dry, to a point south of Vicksburg called New Carthage, across from the enemy bastion at Grand Gulf.[15] Porter would then get his warships and transports past Vicksburg to ferry Grant's army across the river. Once south of Vicksburg, but finally on the east bank of the Mississippi, Grant's forces would be isolated, and possibly outnumbered, but they would be in a position to attack. The Louisiana movement was one that Grant had entertained for some weeks, and in view of the failure of all the other schemes, it became time to put it into execution.

The land operation proved to be slow and tedious, in spite of the dryer weather. Flooded areas still existed and, in many cases, roads of logs had to be laid down ahead of the wagon trains. The earlier plans to use canals to connect the intricate network of bayous and streams was abandoned. The army practically inched itself down to its New Carthage objective. It became obvious that more troops and supplies would have to come downriver, under the protection of Porter's gunboats.

North of Grant, preparations were accelerated. Porter issued a general order to his commanders, giving instructions for the dangerous run at night. In the van would be *Benton* with the tug *Ivy* lashed alongside, *Lafayette* with *General Price* alongside, *Louisville, Mound City, Pittsburgh, Carondelet*, three army transports and the side-wheeler *Tuscumbia* astern, in order to keep transports from turning back when they came under fire.

For added protection, each vessel was to have a coal barge lashed alongside, on the starboard side, and each was to have heavy logs and wet baled hay stacked around vital parts. Furthermore, no lights were to be shown, ports would covered until ready to fire, and exhausts were to be shunted into wheelhouses for silence, such as was done on the *Carondelet* during her run past Island No. 10 the year before. Porter ordered each vessel to steam far enough apart to keep from fouling when one was disabled. All guns would be set for 800 yards. If any vessel were to run aground, she must be burned and completely destroyed.[16]

At 7:00 P.M. on April 16, upon signal from the flagship *Benton*, the flotilla got underway, as General Grant and his son watched from a navy tug above the city. The vessels moved silently across the water, each keeping in formation. So far, the enemy failed to spot them, as they made the turn of the river above the city. For a moment it looked as if the fleet would get by most of Vicksburg before being seen, but some Confederate pickets in a skiff spotted the dark shapes, gave the alarm and, at great danger to themselves, rowed across the river to light up bonfires and some houses on the Louisiana side, in spite of the presence of Union troops there. By 11:00 P.M., barrels of pitch, plus houses and bonfires, were ignited, throwing Porter's fleet into silhouette against the opposite side of the river and completely spotlighted it on the

Vicksburg side.

In Vicksburg, a ball had been in progress. The band played on, while officers and their ladies were gliding across the dance floor. Suddenly someone came in and gave the alarm. The affair broke up swiftly, officers dashed off to their commands as the ladies sought out shelter. Many citizens crowded such vantage points as Court House Hill and Sky Harbor Hill. The streets came alive with horse-drawn caissons, hauling field guns to various locations; officers and men, shouting at each other, as the dark shapes of Porter's fleet were sliding by.

The batteries poured out a heavy barrage against the vessels, but Porter's gunners maintained up an equally fierce fire, keeping a lot of Confederate gunners' heads low, minimizing damage to the gunboats. All were hit, but at first with no serious damage. Then a heavy shot hit the transport *Henry Clay*, which staggered under the impact. Eight more direct hits left her a drifting, burning wreck. She floated downriver a few miles then went down; remarkably, all her crew were saved.

The *Lafayette* was next to get hit, nine times, sending her almost aground on the Louisiana side; but she was quickly taken in tow and moved downstream out of danger.[17] Other vessels shuddered under heavy hits, but with no serious damage. One officer described the firing Rebel guns as "lightning flashes."[18] Gunfire from the boats reflected off the buildings on the bluff. Gunsmoke and smoke from fires swirled in huge clouds, obstructing the pilots' visions for a time and through it all was the heavy, rolling thunder of angry guns belching flame and shell.

After almost three hours, it was over. The fleet had run the batteries and had assembled at New Carthage, each vessel being greeted personally by Sherman in a skiff. There was general jubilation in the Union camp, but for the Confederates it was outrage and disappointment, in spite of their sinking one Union vessel and damaging another.

One Confederate soldier reported the gunboat run in his diary: "There was no damage to the lower batteries," he said, "but one gun burst, killing two and wounding six men." He mentioned that the city received much damage.[19]

A few days later, more of Porter's fleet made the run: six

transports with barges floated safely past the Vicksburg guns, losing one transport, *Tygress*, which had been Grant's headquarters for a time. But the rest got through safely.[20] A Union captain was moved to write in his diary: "We were jubilant over the success of our boats which came past Vicksburg last night. Six transports made the attempt, and all passed this side of the river furthest down when one, the *Tygress*, was sunk from leaks from enemy shot."[21]

Once safely below Vicksburg, Porter tallied the damage to his fleet. The *Benton*, having fired over 80 shots, took five hits, the worst of which was a 10-inch roundshot that passed through the casemate plating and shattered the casemate from top to bottom; *Lafayette* received nine shots, the worst being one that passed through the port wheelhouse, luckily not disabling the paddle wheel; *Louisville* was struck four times and suffered little damage; *General Price* had her upper works, "badly cut up," and her wardroom and steerage slightly damaged and the officers' quarters smashed; the *Pittsburgh* received several hits; *Carondelet* was struck nine times, also with little damage. Other vessels were hit, but suffered no serious damage. Porter considered the run worthwhile, in spite of the loss of *Tygress* and the successive damage to other vessels. He congratulated his crews on their daring exploit.[22]

Many of the admiral's men commented not only on the accuracy of the Confederate gunners, but on the projectiles they used. Some were of wrought iron and steel pointed, 14 inches long and 8 inches in diameter; it was these that did the heaviest damage to the boats. His fleet having suffered 74 casualties, plus damage to his vessels, Porter set about repairing his battered ships. He then stood by for further orders from Grant on his future movement, and that move was just around the corner.

Once his army had assembled on the west side of the river at Hard Times, because New Carthage was untenable as a base, Grant laid his plans for the amphibious operation that would land his army on the opposite side, on Mississippi soil, below Vicksburg.[23] It was clear that the batteries at Grand Gulf would need to be silenced, and once again it would be the province of Admiral Porter's fleet. That Rebel fort, commanded by General

John S. Bowen, had 13 guns, including a 100-pound rifle and two eight-inch rifles. Its strength depended on two batteries: one atop the bluff; the other on the shore line; they were placed a quarter of a mile apart, completely commanding the river approaches.

On April 29, 1863 at 8:00 A.M., the fleet, consisting of *Benton, Louisville, Carondelet, Mound City, Pittsburgh, Tuscumbia* and *Lafayette* moved up to the Confederate works. Upstream of Grand Gulf, 10,000 troops in transports crouched low, awaiting signals for the landings which would surely follow, after the fort was neutralized.

The *Louisville, Carondelet, Mound City* and *Pittsburgh*, in the van, led the attack on the lower batteries, while *Tuscumbia, Benton* and *Lafayette* hammered the upper. The lower batteries were quickly silenced; then the entire gunboat force concentrated on the upper ones. Meanwhile, however, the excellent gunnery skills of the Confederates began to tell: the *Benton* took a hit in the pilothouse, wounding the pilot and disabling the wheel and the huge vessel drifted downstream to lick her wounds.[24]

Thunder rolled along the Mississippi as the fleet not only contended with the amazing precision of enemy gunnery, but with a strong six-knot current producing eddies that could easily spin the vessels around. The *Tuscumbia*, in particular, was whirled about like a top. *Pittsburgh*, coming up to relieve the stricken *Benton*, suffered hits, with 24 casualties, as did the 575-ton ironclad *Tuscumbia*, a vessel designed by Joseph Brown, that proved to be poorly built and unable to stand up to punishment. Porter described her as "a poor ship in a hot engagement."[25]

Soon the fire from the upper batteries slackened. Porter's boats had expended over 1,000 rounds, and had suffered 18 killed and 56 wounded, most of them in *Benton* when a round penetrated the casemate and exploded.

The admiral conferred with Grant about running the transports past the enemy gunners, whose fire he had weakened somewhat. Grant concurred, so at 5:00 P.M., the gunboat flotilla, followed by the transports, ran upstream safely past the batteries under cover of heavy barrages by the gunboats. The engagement lasted over six hours, and managed to silence some of the enemy guns, but others on the river's east side were still operative so

Grant could not cross from New Carthage. Grant had to cross somewhere. But where? A silenced Grand Gulf would have offered the most desirable spot.

At this time, a sympathetic former slave from a nearby plantation was brought to Grant to inform him that there was a tolerable road leading out of a place called Bruinsberg, Mississippi some six miles down from Grand Gulf.[26] The commanding general unloaded his army and, under protection of the gunboats, the transports ferried troops across the river.

Grant covered all angles. He knew that Pemberton's attention would be diverted while the Army of the Tennessee crossed the river and, later, advanced on Vicksburg; he therefore ordered Sherman to make a diversionary movement up the Yazoo, to make a "feint" at Haynes Bluff, at about the time Porter's gunboats were blasting away at the Grand Gulf batteries.

Sherman took ten regiments of his corps, put them on board as many vessels as he could round up at the mouth of the Yazoo and at Lake Providence. These expedition boats would be accompanied by eight gunboats, left above Vicksburg for just such a purpose. The war vessels were *Tyler, Chocktaw, Baron de Kalb, Signal, Romeo, Petrol* and *Black Hawk*, plus three mortar boats and ten transports. While the gunboats peppered away at the upper works at Haines's Bluff, the troops unloaded and made quite a show of activity, fooling the Rebels into thinking another attack was taking place. Fortunately for the Union, Pemberton's attention was diverted.

The Confederate commander found himself on the horns of a dilemma. He had sent a large force to relieve Grand Gulf and, upon hearing of Sherman's "attack" on Haynes Bluff, he recalled the troops and force-marched them to that arena. Sherman reported that the enemy troops had marched 60 miles without rest and were so exhausted, when they approached Haynes Bluff, that many lay alongside the road "completely fagged out."[27]

In addition to the Yazoo "feint," a daring cavalry raid by General Benjamin Henry Grierson diverted much of the Confederate attention away from the Bruinsberg landing. Grierson's cavalry, 1,700 strong, covered 600 miles in 16 days, running from La Grange, Tennessee, east of Memphis, destroying railroad tracks and depots, raiding towns and ammunition depots and ending up at Natchez. It was, according to Grant, "a most brilliant cavalry exploit of the war and will be handed down in history as an example to be imitated."[28]

Having gotten to the east bank of the Mississippi below Vicksburg, Grant now made a momentous decision. He had been instructed by Halleck to await the forces of General Banks that were coming up from Natchez to join in a combined assault on Vicksburg, but when Banks failed to appear, Grant decided to strike out with no supply lines and live off the countryside by foraging. This was an amazing display of military strategy, and, of course, a major gamble for the Union. The audacity of the plan created the possibility that he could be decisively defeated by a sudden combination of Rebel forces, and his entire army would be lost. General Joseph Johnston was in the area, and was rumored to have assembled a large force of troops.

But Grant was an exception to Napoleon's stated preference for generals who were lucky, rather than good. The Union general, as ever, had a flawless sense of his own strength relative to the enemy's, and his risks were always carefully calculated. Grant intended to march inland and cut Vicksburg off at Jackson from rail support and reinforcements. Then he would turn and deal with the last major impediment to Union control of the Mississippi.

CHAPTER EIGHTEEN

Twilight of Vicksburg

G eneral John Clifford Pemberton replaced Earl Van Dorn as commander of Confederate forces at Vicksburg on October 14, 1862. Pemberton, an 1853 graduate of the U.S. Military Academy, was a Pennsylvanian by birth, however he had many friends in the South, and had married a Virginia girl, causing his loyalty to shift to the Confederacy after secession. While Pemberton was not a charismatic individual, he did possess a sort of dogged determination that induced him to dig in his heels, as the vast array of Union military might closed in on his city.

Ulysses S. Grant was now operating to the east of Vicksburg. The Union general had moved swiftly and with precision, following his landing below the town with 17,000 troops. Instead of taking the Bruinsberg road, as expected, he struck north, captured Port Gibson[1] and then accepted the surrender of Grand Gulf, which was hastily evacuated on May 3. Moving inland, he brushed aside resistance at a small town called Raymond, and then marched on Jackson, the Mississippi state capitol.

Joseph Johnston, who was still raising his army, chose not to give battle and retreated to the north. The Union forces overcame resistance led by two Confederate brigadiers, John Gregg and W.H.T. Walker, and this important rail hub, Vicksburg's last connection to the rest of the Confederacy, was abandoned. The Confederate toll so far was 1,000 dead and 650 prisoners, while Union losses were 850 killed and wounded. Now Vicksburg was cut off from land, as securely as it had already been isolated from the river by the gunboats. Grant, steadily receiving reinforcements, now marched against Vicksburg itself.

Pemberton was receiving conflicting orders from his superiors: Johnston told him to abandon the city and bring his considerable army into the field where it could combine with Johnston's own forces and hopefully challenge the Yankees with a major battle. Jefferson Davis, on the other hand, urged him to defend the city at all costs. Rather splitting the difference, Pemberton marched out to fight Grant, but only in the context of a strategic defense of Vicksburg.[2]

The two forces collided at Champion Hill, midway between Jackson and Vicksburg, on May 16. By this time Grant's force had swollen to 29,000 men and Pemberton was able to lead 20,000 from the city's defenses. The Confederate general had hoped that Joseph Johnston would support his move against Grant with an attack in the Union rear, however this was not to be. After an intense, four-hour battle, Pemberton was dislodged and his men streamed back toward Vicksburg. Both sides had suffered over 2,000 casualties in the fighting but in the retreat the Confederates began to show signs of disintegration. Their rear guard was routed at the Black River, losing 1,700 prisoners, however a destroyed bridge prevented the Federals from exploiting the confusion. By May 18, Grant had joined with Sherman and the Union army was outside Vicksburg itself to begin the siege that would last for six weeks.

As for any question of Grant's personal bravery, his troops learned about the kind of man he was at Champion's Hill. During the battle, the general rode up on his big bay horse, dismounted and stood observing, while offering suggestions, completely oblivious to his own danger. The reporting corporal, Samuel H.M. Byers, wrote that his fellow soldiers were concerned lest their commander be killed and the army left without its leader, but they deeply admired his courage.[3]

In a little over two weeks, Grant had landed on Mississippi soil, fought and won five battles, that netted him 100 guns and 12,000 prisoners, at a loss of only 5,000 men. Now he stood before Vicksburg with an army of 70,000—a ring of steel around

Pemberton's soldiers and loyal civilians. He was determined to shell or starve the proud city into submission.

Meanwhile, the Union Navy was also busy. While Grant was moving toward Vicksburg, Admiral Porter had returned to the Yazoo anchorage, where he made contact with and provided provisions and materiel to General Grant. Then, in order to expedite some unfinished business, he took the ironclads *Baron de Kalb* and *Choctaw*, plus the tinclads *Forest Rose, Linden,* and *Petrol* up the Yazoo, which was now open to navigation. There he found Haynes Bluff abandoned, and reported the works to be "very formidable," with 14 guns and an enormous quantity of ammunition cached for a long siege. The encampments there, which he found to be some of the best he had seen, were promptly torched.[4]

The fleet approached Yazoo City and stopped to destroy a chain stretched across the river. Then, moving closer, they sighted the town's navy yard in flames, including three gunboats under construction: the *Mobile, Republic* and an unnamed monster hull 310 feet long with a 70 foot beam. This hull had been designed to have six engines, four side wheels and two screw propellers.

The navy yard itself, which consisted of sawmills and carpenter and blacksmith shops, was burned to the ground. No longer would it build threatening Rebel war vessels. In Yazoo City itself, Federal demolition squads burned a sawmill and a lumberyard. While there, they discovered a hospital with 115 Confederate patients, whom they promptly paroled. The fleet proceeded farther up the river and destroyed seven Confederate steamers.[5]

Later, on July 13, the fleet again steamed up river and, as the gunboats plodded along, the *Baron de Kalb* struck a Singer mine under her bow. Water streamed in and she began to settle by the head. Then a second mine exploded under her stern, sinking the vessel; but her crew was saved. Like her sister *Cairo*, she had fallen victim to the increasingly effective Confederate mine warfare.[6]

After two Union attempts at storming the works were beaten back with heavy casualties, meanwhile, the siege of Vicksburg had gone into high gear. The town's citizens were caught between two giant claws: Grant's army to the rear and Porter's gunboats and mortar schooners to the west on the river. Many of the civilians had fled earlier, but the proud and defiant stayed behind and suffered privations alongside their fighting troops, 30,000 of whom had withdrawn into the city's defensive works.

When shells slammed into the city day after day, many citizens dug caves in the bluffs and hills around the city and lived in them. One diarist, Mary Loughborough, wrote about the rigors and frustrations that she and her neighbors and friends experienced while living in caves and scrounging about for food. "We were terror-stricken," she wrote, "while shell after shell followed each other in quick succession." She maintained she was much in prayer, during the ordeal, to prepare herself for sudden death.[7]

The siege began to take its toll as food became scarce. Pets disappeared and even rats were trapped and eaten. As usual, the poor suffered the most, as prices soared: flour was $1,000 a barrel; molasses $10 per gallon and cornmeal $140 a bushel. Mule meat was common fare, as was a bread made up of ground peas. Cornmeal was nearly non-existent.[8]

Even the fighting soldiers were feeling the pinch. In fact, flannel cartridge bags were in short supply for the 10-inch Columbiads—not a yard of flannel could be had at any store in the city—and men were urged to give up their flannel shirts. Then the ladies heard of the appeal and donated their flannel petticoats. By these means, 500 cartridge bags were procured. Wrote one observer, "Every cartridge bag used by the 10-inch Columbiads in the bombardments was made of flannel petticoats of the women of Vicksburg."[9]

The noose tightened around the port city, as Grant intensified his efforts. Admiral Porter's gunboats became bolder as they closed in and bombarded the town, while Grant's gunners shelled it from the east. Unfortunately, Porter's audacity was about to cause another Union gunboat to be lost.

On May 27, the ironclad *Cincinnati* was ordered to run down to Vicksburg and destroy a masked Confederate battery on Fort Hill which was menacing a planned move by Sherman. The gunboat approached the shore on the north end of the river to get into position for shelling. Emma Balfour, a Vicksburg citizen, described the ironclad as a "monster compared to five smaller boats that were [there]."[10]

The fickle currents of the river worked against the gunboat; she was forced to round to and use her stern batteries. However, that stern was weakly armored and she became an excellent target for the well-practiced Rebel gunners. A shot passed through the magazine and through the keel, flooding her rapidly. Then the starboard tiller was shot away and, thus disabled, she began to turn uncontrollably while still more 8- and 10-inch shots penetrated her casemate and wrecked her insides.

The commander of the stricken vessel, Lieutenant George M. Bache, ordered her moved upstream at three knots, keeping close to the shore. The ill-fated ironclad was in a sinking condition, so she was run aground. A hawser was run out and made fast to a tree; however, the hawser failed to secure properly and it gave way, allowing the gunboat to slide into three fathoms of water with just her jackstaff protruding above water. Many of the crew managed to scramble to safety. There were 40 casualties, most of which were caused by drowning.

In Vicksburg, there was tumultuous cheering and waving of flags and handkerchiefs by the ladies, as the *Cincinnati* slid under the waves.[11] It was a short-lived euphoria, however, because even as Grant was receiving additional reinforcements in troops and guns, word arrived that Joseph Johnston was in no position to come to Pemberton's aid. If he had tried, Grant would have overwhelmed him with superior forces.

Finally, the sorrowful situation within Vicksburg forced Pemberton's hand. Faced with a starving army and populace, and no hope of rescue—or even assistance—he asked Grant for terms. The two men met on July 3, and on July 4, 1863, the great campaign for Vicksburg was over. The surrender of the Confederate army of 30,000 was the largest in history to that time. Interesting, too, was Grant's comment after the war that the 60,000 Rebel small-arms captured at Vicksburg were of better quality than those the Union troops were using. Grant recommended that his men trade in their old modified flintlocks for the Rebel guns, which were the latest European design, brought through the blockade.

As expected, the news of the fall of Vicksburg was electric for the North and devastating to the South. Of course, General Grant gave Admiral Porter and the Union Mississippi River Fleet much credit for the final great victory.[12] As commerce began to move freely up and down the river once again, Lincoln proclaimed: "The Father of Waters rolled unvexed to the sea."

The historians Hermann Hattoway and Archer Jones have maintained that it was not the loss of the Mississippi River that cut off the Confederacy from vital sources of food, men and materiel, because the loss of New Orleans the year before had already logistically separated the two parts of the South.[13] But the fact of the matter is that until the fall of Vicksburg, no such split had definitively occurred. The Mississippi and its tributaries—the Yazoo, the Arkansas, the White Rivers and others—continued to be conduits for Southern war resources up until the point the Mississippi was irrevocably seized. And, in fact, there was one more job to be performed by the Union gunboats in order for this network to be secured.

CHAPTER NINETEEN

Sequel on Red River

After the surrender of Vicksburg and the subsequent capitulation of the forces at Port Hudson, Grant cast his eyes on another military objective: Mobile, Alabama. With his huge, victorious army, he could have overwhelmed the Confederate garrison there, and by so doing, would have relieved the pressure on Union armies fighting to the east against Lee's powerful forces and thwart any further Rebel moves in the Mississippi.

But the Mobile campaign was not meant to be. Chief of Staff Halleck, who still had clout in the government, opted for an operation against Texas via a thrust up the Red River during the spring of 1864. The antics of the French in their occupation of Mexico City were threatening the Lone Star State, which was considered to be of more vital interest than Mobile. It was common knowledge that Napoleon III was in sympathy with the Southern cause, and his attempts to make Maximillian of Austria the Emperor of Mexico, further increasing French prestige, was a matter of concern in Washington. Unable to invoke the Monroe Doctrine because of the war, the administration decided to prevent any possible French encroachments in Texas. Such encroachments would have been helpful to the Confederacy in its war efforts.

In addition, any Union incursions into Louisiana and Texas would surely terminate Confederate resistance in Louisiana, and hopefully mobilize the silent Union sympathizers in Texas, according to Halleck's way of thinking.[1]

General Nathaniel Banks' army, enlarged by 10,000 of Sherman's troops, moved across the Mississippi in March of 1864, for the planned expedition up the Red River to Shreveport and beyond to Texas, supported by Porter's gunboats. It was to be an operation to warm Banks' ambitious, politically motivated heart.

Grant expressed his disapproval of the plan, but he was powerless to do anything about it because it had the backing of the Lincoln administration. Grant could not countermand the order, but he would do his best to limit its length.

From a strategic standpoint, the Red River was a good highway for such an operation.[2] Actually, it was the last avenue open to the Union in this theater. An attempted Union landing from the Gulf, at what was then Sabine City, Texas, in September of 1863 had been repulsed by a small Confederate garrison. However, a second attempt, against Brownsville, near the Mexican border, using 3,500 men and the warships *Monongehela, Owasco* and *Virginia* in order to gain access to the Rio Grande, was successful and it secured the eastern coast of Texas.

The Red River, so-called, because of the red sediment it carried, touched four states during its meandering course, and had a drainage basin covering 90,000 square miles. It was then a major river highway, as it still is today

Rising in northern Texas, near Amarillo, the river forms a boundary between Oklahoma and Texas, then it courses through southwestern Arkansas and into Louisiana, where it bisects the state and finally empties into the Mississippi above Baton Rouge- a course of 1300 miles. Normally the river would have been wide and deep enough for large vessels to ply, but in this spring of 1864 was exceptionally dry, and the shallowness of the river was a matter of concern to Porter and his officers.

The Federal high command was also well aware of the commerce that moved down the Red into the Confederate war effort. Almost two million bales of cotton were stored along the stream; cotton and wool cloth for Confederate uniforms were woven near Shreveport, and that city was host to foundries, shops and munition, plants that supplied the Southern armies. Halleck had observed that the occupation of Shreveport would be comparable to the occupation of Chattanooga.[3]

To support the 20,000 troops Banks had assembled in March, Porter gathered 19 war vessels from his fleet, including the ironclads *Eastport, Benton, LaFayette, Choctaw, Chillicothe, Ozark, Louisville, Carondelet, Pittsburg, Mound City, Osage* and *Neosho*, accompanied by the shallow-draft gunboats *Ouachita, Lexington, Fort Hindman, Cricket, Gazelle, Juliet* and the flagship *Black Hawk*, plus transports and supply vessels. This was perhaps the most powerful flotilla so far assembled by the crusty admiral for an expedition.

Porter's and Grant's concern was that the usual spring rise had not occurred and that the splendid flotilla would have to navigate unusually shallow waters.

The land operation called for Banks' 17,000 troops to move up to Bayou Teche, from the south, and meanwhile, join Sherman's 10,000 troops moving up the river. General Steele, in Little Rock, would march down and join them with his 15,000 troops.

On March 12, the armada churned upstream, halted at Simmesport to unload troops for an assault on Fort De Russy, which had been captured by Union forces in May 1863 and then later abandoned. The fort was now in the process of being resurrected by the Confederates. The half-completed site was easily taken and removed as a potential obstacle to river approaches. Next, the river-borne, amphibious force moved up and occupied Alexandria, on March 24, and prepared for an assault on Shreveport. On the 29th, the armada of gunboats, transports and supply train once again moved upriver, with the *Osage* in the van, to support land operations against Shreveport. Along the way, all in the fleet observed tons of cotton being torched by the Confederates, and the air became so filled with smoke that "the sun was almost obscured."[4] The way was slow going, because sharpshooters and masked field pieces became a serious menace.

On April 7, Porter, in his flagship *Cricket* in the van of a task force, moved upstream with 20 transports of troops to reinforce Banks' land forces. These troops were disembarked at Springfield Landing, their objective being to aid Banks in his investment of Shreveport. But at this point, Porter learned of Banks' defeat at and retreat from Pleasant Hill west of him, and decided that the fleet should return to the Mississippi. The low water level, plus the obvious failure of Banks to capture Shreveport, intensified his skepticism of the whole operation.

The troubles for the fleet began. As it turned and descended the river, the vessels became prime targets for sharpshooters and Rebel masked artillery positions on the high bluffs on either side. Captain Selfridge and his crew of the 500-ton, 180-foot long river monitor *Osage*, found the going difficult because of shallow water and the sharp turns in the river. A transport was lashed alongside to aid the *Osage*. The gunboat ran aground and, during the time it took to refloat her, she and the transport came under heavy fire from Confederate gunners. The angry ironclad responded, however, with cannister and grape, scattering and routing the enemy.[5]

The fleet finally reached the hamlet of Grand Ecore on the 15th. Then tragedy struck. The 570-ton ironclad *Eastport* struck a mine, eight miles downriver, and promptly sank. Porter called up two pump boats from Alexandria, and soon the gunboat was refloated. Then, at 40 miles downriver, she ran aground again. This time there was no saving her, so Porter reluctantly decided to destroy the *Eastport*. Her guns were unshipped and a ton and a half of gunpowder was distributed around her vitals. She was then blown up, almost killing her skipper, who was getting away in a cutter as huge pieces of her casemate bracketed his boat.

Flagship *Cricket* was riddled with minie balls and shots from a masked battery on the bluff. Hit 38 times, she suffered 12 dead and 19 wounded. One of the pump boats, the *Champion 3*, took a hit in her boiler, scalding to death a number of crew members, plus a contingent of slaves recruited from nearby plantations.

But this was only the beginning of problems for Porter and Banks. By now the river was down to three feet in some places and many of the heavier gunboats with seven-foot drafts could possibly be stranded or, worse, the entire gunboat flotilla would be in danger of being captured by the enemy. At the falls above Alexandria, the fleet came to a halt because it could not pass the double rapids; here the river was only six feet deep.

About this time, Lieutenant Colonel Joseph Bailey, Chief of Engineers for the 19th Army Corps, entered the scene. A lumberman in earlier years, and familiar with rivers and rapids, he proposed a solution: dam the river above the rapids, by constructing a series of wing dams, using large trees weighted down with rocks in some spots, cribs filled with boulders and bricks at other spots. Between the wing dams, and to connect them across the river, he sunk four navy coal barges.

Porter agreed to the plan, and work commenced immediately, using all available troops. By April 8, the project was completed and the water rose to five feet.[6] Porter then sent three lighter craft over the falls. When the pressure pushed aside the sunken barges, making a passage 66 feet wide, he ordered the *Lexington* over, followed by *Osage, Neosho* and *Fort Hindman*—a parade accompanied by hearty cheers from everyone.

Six heavy gunboats and two tugs were still stranded above the falls, but Bailey, undaunted, set about constructing another series of wing dams so constructed as to funnel the current through one channel. The water was raised to six feet, making it possible for the remainder of the gunboats to slide over the falls to safety during the nights of the 12th and 13th of April, with the help of heavy hawsers run to the shore and manned by the troops.

The Red River flotilla reentered the Mississippi on April 21, and Commander Selfridge was moved to write that the expedition was "one of the most humiliating and disastrous that had to be recorded during the war."[7] Seven vessels were lost, and for naught. The incident would cause much derision and many recriminations.

As was expected, an uproar was heard in Washington and Richmond. When the fall out settled, generals on both sides were removed from their commands, including the inept General Banks, who became the subject of a congressional investigation.

The frightening aspect about the expedition is that the Union came very close to losing a good portion of its gunboat fleet. And this was not through any fault of Porter's; the sagacious admiral was opposed to the expedition from the first, but, being a good sailor, he followed orders from his superiors and did his best to do his duty and to preserve the fleet. That was accomplished, thanks to an army engineer named Bailey.

On the plus side, the Red River was of no more use to the

Confederacy; all riverborne commerce was finished on the stream and the rich farm and plantation produce, plus manufactured products from Shreveport plants, were denied to the Southern war effort.

In the final analysis, it meant that the river war was fundamentally over for all intents and purposes. Ironically, in spite of the fact that Porter's entire gunboat fleet was involved, the end did not come in a clap of thunder, as heard frequently along the mighty Mississippi during the past two years, but rather it came with a whimper. However, Union control of the Father of Waters was now unchallenged from Cairo to the Gulf, and Federal steamboats and warships were free to traverse the waters, upstream and down, in no danger from the Confederates. The great goal had been achieved.

CHAPTER TWENTY

A Glance Backwards

Today it is commonly agreed that the Union's achievement of ultimate victory in the epic struggle for the Mississippi River, coupled with its victory at Gettysburg, produced two turning points of the war.[1] For the South, the Trans-Mississippi region was an artery that ran through the left sagittal plane of the body of the Confederacy. Although not a vital artery, it did supply Southern troops with food, materiel and manpower from the rich farms, plantations and factories of the states of Arkansas, Louisiana and Texas, Missouri having been lost to the Confederacy early on in the war. And even though the loss of supply from these states was were not a fatal blow at first, they would eventually affect the eastern campaigns in that shortages of foodstuffs and manpower pools would sap a great deal of strength from the Southern fighting machine at its most critical time.

The naval aspect of the Mississippi-based campaigns suggests that gunboat actions were harbingers of things to come. These war craft not only sounded the death knell for the wooden warship, but had an important effect on future ship designs. One immediately thinks of modern warships, but a more interesting sidebar is the riverine craft of the Vietnam conflict, which were designed with the Eads ironclads in mind and served much the same purpose in the Mekong Delta waterways—but without the heavy ordnance of their predecessors.

The Eads ironclads were unique in naval history. As children of their age, they were ideally suited for the tasks they were built to perform. Heavily armored and armed, their shallow drafts enabled them to operate in rivers, tributaries and bayous of the great river, with their big guns and limited troop-carrying capacities, attacking forts or landing troops for special tasks. In addition they could act as a protective screen for large amphibious assaults. In fact, they foreshadowed the specially designed war vessels in the navies of the world: destroyers, gunboats, destroyer escorts and, in one sense, light cruisers.

The big question concerning these unique fighting vessels, whether or not it was in mind when they were designed, was their efficacy against forts. This was a matter of deep concern to navy men.

The first real test came at Fort Henry on the Tennessee River, when the gunboats—timidly at first—moved up and shelled it, in preparation for a land assault. And, although the fort's response was weak, it later caused severe damage to one of the gunboats. The fort surrendered, but not so much from the bombardment as from the withdrawal of troops to Fort Donelson; another factor was that the flooding river inundated Henry's lower battery.

Fort Donelson was on the other hand, a grim story. The gunboats approached too close to the fort and received exceedingly heavy damage from plunging fire upon their vulnerable spots. At first the fort got the upper hand, but its defenders were finally subdued by a combination land and river assault. Once again, as later at Vicksburg, the Confederate gun batteries were too high on the bluffs for the gunboats to elevate their guns to them, and once again the ironclads took a fearful beating.

In spite of these shortcomings one must remember that the spectacular run past the Island No. 10 batteries by the *Carondelet* spelled doom for that bastion plus a number of wildcat batteries below New Madrid. The *Carondelet*, joined later by the *Pittsburgh*, acted as escort for General Pope's troops to cross the river and capture the island. It was a shining hour for the ironclads.

In close-quarter combat, the gunboats gave a glowing account of themselves. At Plum Point and again at Memphis, they proved their mettle with their big guns, inflicting horrific damage on enemy vessels.

In all fairness, it should be pointed out that a great deal of damage done to the Confederate fleet at Memphis was actually accomplished by the energetic Colonel Ellet's rams. These vessels, proved their worth by ramming and sinking many of the opponent's vessels. Soon both sides of the conflict took a closer look at the ram concept. The Confederates worked feverishly on building and commissioning rams to counter the growing Union fleet All along, however, it was to be an uphill battle for the Rebels, because shortages of skilled manpower, materiel and facilities constantly dogged the Southern efforts. The Confederates, in terms of naval matters, were reluctantly forced into a defensive posture, except for one brilliant, history-making sortie: that of the C.S.S. *Arkansas*.

The short career of the *Arkansas* also serves to illustrate the Confederate government's problems in 1862 in fashioning a navy to match that of the Union. At Memphis, the shortage of workers and materiel prevented the South from even attempting to complete two ironclads at the same time, despite the approach of Union forces from upriver. Consequently, one partially completed vessel was destroyed on the stocks while the other, the *Arkansas*, was towed up the Yazoo River for completion under the most stringent of circumstances. There an inept naval commander allowed the ironclad ram to fall into a state of neglect, full of junk, and in no way seaworthy. It took an enraged populace to finally get things going. Even after the hulk was towed downriver to the makeshift navy yard at Yazoo City, the work was still shoddy; the engines, for example, were never designed to push such a heavy vessel. It was finally General Beauregard, who took command of the Army of Mississippi, who insisted on completing the *Arkansas*, badly constructed or not.[2]

The *Arkansas* sortie, though brave and, as some have said, foolhardy, was an act of desperation. The river level was dropping and the decision was made to move the ponderous ram, otherwise she would have been stranded and of no use to anyone. Captain Brown performed remarkably against the combined Union fleet, although finally could only provide a taste of what might have been, had the Confederacy been able to build more ironclad vessels.

However, much of Brown's spectacular success against the Federal fleet was due to the fact that his enemy was asleep on the watch, with its steam down to conserve fuel. Curiously, Lieutenant Phelps, who commanded the *Benton*, later informed his flag officer that Admiral Farragut had learned about the approach of the enemy ram from a deserter the night before, although nothing was said to the fleet's commanders and no preparations were made.[3] Farragut should have been more prepared for the much anticipated sortie by the Confederate ram down the Yazoo, and alerted the entire fleet, instead of just several vessels—even if one of them was the legendary *Carondelet*.

In any case, the *Arkansas* affair illustrates the fact that the American fighting man, regardless of his loyalties, can perform admirably when the chips are down and when the odds are greatest against him. Brown could not have done more, taking on the entire Union fleet and leaving them with egg on their collective faces. His gunners gave a limited but good account of their superb skills.

Another strategic value of the ironclad gunboats lay in their ability to clear rivers of enemy craft, convoy troops to their destinations and support them with firepower, such as Grant's immense amphibious landings at Bruinsburg, under protection of Porter's guns, for his march on Vicksburg. This event foreshadowed the great pre-invasion bombardments of World War II in the Pacific and in Normandy. In essence, the gunboats were floating artillery batteries which, in short order, could fight surface engagements, blast forts into submission and cover amphibious operations with bombardment.

This water-borne artillery took a fraction of the time it would take an army to move by land, especially in those regions where there were few roads, no railroads and, for the most part, frequent floodings. This was true in the spring of 1863 in the Yazoo Delta expeditions and again in the White and Red River campaigns. Although these expeditions were not always successful, they did point out the strategic advantages of water-borne armies.

The ironclad gunboats, ram vessels aside, were responsible for pushing the U.S. Navy into the future. If anything, they sounded the death knell for the venerable old wooden ships-of-the-line, rendering them obsolete, as they also did for the steam frigates, such as Farragut's grand old *Hartford* and her class.

The Confederates had the distinction of launching the first versions of what was to become the mine in sea warfare. Those early devices, using such mundane objects as demijohns and barrels, were responsible for sinking or damaging 43 Union vessels, including the famous *Cairo*. They were a far cry from today's sophisticated devices that are fired electronically or acoustically, but perhaps they were successful beyond even their creator's expectations.

In addition to a technology that produced the ironclad gunboat and the Dahlgren gun, the Union Navy in the Mississippi Theater enjoyed a unified command, after those early, confused days of control under the army; and thus they reaped the victories. The Confederate Navy never did enjoy that same advantage in technology or command. Frequent squabbles between army and navy personnel resulted in an almost paralyzed state of affairs. Perhaps a reason for this lay in the attitudes of the Confederate officers. Most navy officers were graduates of the same classes as those of the Union and were of the same mold and it did not take long before they came to realize that their boats were no match for their enemy's. They even cultivated a sense of awe toward the Union Navy and its powerful ironclad fleet. They doubtless became demoralized in the South's futile attempt to match its success.[4]

One cannot discount the importance of the fall of Vicksburg and the subsequent opening of the Mississippi. Grant wrote that the "capture of Vicksburg, with its garrison and ordnance stores, and the successful battles fought in reaching them, gave a new spirit to the loyal people of the North . . . the Mississippi was entirely in the possession of the National troops."[5] Bruce Catton has observed that the surrender fatally handicapped the Confederacy. "The way was now open," he wrote, "for Grant or any other general there to start moving east from the river."[6]

Jefferson Davis downplayed the victory with a terse understatement to the effect that the loss of Vicksburg and Port Hudson was "the surrender of the Mississippi to the enemy."[7] General Marshall-Cornwall was perhaps more informative when he maintained that "Vicksburg was the turning point of the war" and that "the Confederacy had received a mortal blow, although its agony was to continue for 20 months longer."[8]

In the final analysis, there is little doubt that, to millions of Americans, the climax of the Civil War occurred on the afternoon of July 3, 1863. It was both a glorious and tragic sight to behold when, at the apex of the greatest battle of the war, 15,000 Confederate soldiers, in three long lines, crossed the field toward Cemetery Ridge near Gettysburg, into a storm of unrelenting Union fire. When the smoke cleared to reveal thousands of Rebel bodies strewn across the field, and the Federal flags still flying from the ridge, the enormous fact hit home that Robert E. Lee and the Army of Northern Virginia had finally been decisively defeated in battle.

But another, far less dramatic, event was taking place that same afternoon. At three o'clock on July 3rd, two men named Pemberton and Grant sat by themselves on a hillside just outside the Confederate works at Vicksburg, Mississippi. The two men had known each other before the war and greeted each other cordially, if not warmly. The subject of their conversation was surrender. Grant (and who can blame him?) suggested "unconditional surrender." Pemberton flatly refused. Grant said, "Very well."

Instead Pemberton suggested that his men, some 30,000 strong, stack their arms in view of the Federal troops and then be paroled to go back to their homes. Officers would be allowed to keep their sidearms. This idea was accepted by the Union general, and the two men shook hands.

If the Union line had broken on Cemetery Ridge, it would take a number of leaps of the imagination to translate that event into an ultimate victory for the Confederacy in the war. However when Vicksburg, and thus the Mississippi River, fell irrevocably to the Union, the fate of the nascent nation was sealed. Though the Vicksburg surrender itself took place on the Fourth of July, the arrangement was concluded on the third. This was the day that the North won the Civil War.

Chapter Notes

ABBREVIATIONS

ORA *The War of the Rebellion: A Compilation of the Official Records of the Union and Confederate Armies*, 128 vols. (Washington, DC: Government Printing Office, 1880–1901).

ORN *Official Records of the Union and Confederate Navies in the War of the Rebellion*, 303 vols. (Washington, DC: Government Printing Office, 1894–1922).

B&L *Battles and Leaders of the Civil War, Being for the Most Part Contributions By Union & Confederate Officers*, 4 vols. (Edison, NJ: Castle Books, 1956 edition).

CWNC *Civil War Naval Chronology, 1861–1865*, 6 vols. (Washington, DC: Naval History Division, 1971 edition).

DAFS *Dictionary of American Fighting Ships*, 8 vols. (Washington, DC: Naval History Division, 1959–1981).

WCWN *Warships of the Civil War Navies* by Paul Silverstone (Annapolis: Naval Institute Press, 1989).

CWD *The Civil War Dictionary* (New York: Vintage Press, 1987).

INTRODUCTION

1. For the Union-estimated strength of the South Carolinian batteries surrounding Fort Sumter, see ORA, Series 1, Vol.1, pp. 130, 161, 172 and 193.
2. Letters and reports on the unhappy *Star of the West* incident may be found in ORA, Series 1, Vol.1, pp. 9–10, 134–40. See also B&L, Vol.1. It's amazing that so little attention has been paid to this incident. It has always been assumed that the first shots fired in anger in the Civil War were those at Fort Sumter. As these publications concur, those first shots were fired at the lonely *Star of the West*.
3. Abner Doubleday, "From Moultrie to Sumter," B&L, pp.40–49; ORA, Series 1, Vol.1, p.3.
4. ORA, Series 1, Vol.1, pp.9–10 in which Colonel Woods remarked that they "remained groping in the dark until nearly day."
5. ORA, Series 1, Vol.1, p.253. It may seem curious that this politician in the service of the U.S. Government at the time was never tried for treason. In fact, few if any Southern sympathizers in Union service were tried.
6. Unhappily, the *Brooklyn* was never sent in. The formidable, 2,532-ton, screw sloop with her 21 guns, one of which was a 10-inch smoothbore, would have knocked out the southern batteries—-that is, if their crews dared fire on her.
7. Swanberg, W.A., *First Blood: The Story of Fort Sumter,* (New York: Charles

Scribner's Sons, 1957), p.148, for Anderson's reaction to the *Star of the West's* retreat. See also B&L, p.611.

Chapter 1: UNPREPARED ON THE WATER

1. E.B. Potter & Chester W. Nimitz, *Sea Power, a Naval History,* (NJ: Prentice-Hall, Inc., 1960), pp.250–51, and Howard P. Nash, Jr., *A Naval History of the Civil War,* (New York: A.S. Barnes & Co., 1972), pp. 15–16.
2. Ibid, p.247.
3. Ralph Volney Harlow, *The United States: From Wilderness to World Power*(New York: Henry Holt & Co., 1949), pp.337–38.
4. For a detailed treatise on the Norfolk Navy Yard Fiasco, see John Taylor Wood, "The First Fights of the Ironclads," B&L, Vol.1, pp.692–716.
5. Excellent biographies of Welles can be found in John Niven's *Gideon Welles: Lincoln's Secretary of the Navy,* (New York: Oxford University Press, 1972); Richard West, Jr., *Gideon Welles, Lincoln's Navy Department,* (Indianapolis, Bobbs-Merrill, 1943). Also there is a reissue of *Diary of Gideon Welles,* (Boston, Houghton-Mifflin Co., 1911).
6. Based on many sources. Among the best works on Civil War ordnance are: Warren Ripley, *Artillery and Ammunition of the Civil War* (New York: Van Nostrand, 1970) and Eugene Confield, *Notes on the Naval Ordnance of the Civil War* (Richmond: Byrd, 1960).
7. On Mallory, the student is advised to consult Joseph T. Dirkin, *Stephen B. Mallory: Confederate Navy Chief* (Chapel Hill: University of North Carolina Press, 1954), *Who Was Who in the Civil War* (New York: Facts on File Publications, 1988) and *The Dictionary of American Biography*, 22 vols. (New York: Scribners, 1928–1932), Vol.1, pp.224–25.
8. Silverstone, WCWN, far and away the most authentic and comprehensive account of both Confederate and Union warships of all kinds. Incidentally, it contains the only available picture and description of the *Star of the West.* See also CWD, p.560.
9. Potter & Nimitz, *Sea Power,* p. 247.
10. CWNC, part 1, p. 26.

Chapter 2: BIRTH PANGS OF IRONCLADS

1. For a reconstruction of wartime *Carondelet,* I'm indebted to Ni Ni Harris, *History of Carondelet* (St. Louis, Published by Southern Commercial Bank, 1991), pp.25–26. The map of Carondelet and the route of the Iron Mountain Railroad was traced from *Colton's Geographic Establishment General Maps,* (New York: Colton's Geographical Establishment, 1896), Missouri Historical Society.
2. For biographical material on Eads, see: *Dictionary of American Biography,* Vol. 1, pp.587–89; *Webster's American Military Biographies,* Charles van Dorn, Ed., (Mass.: G & C Merriam Company, Publishers, 1978), and *Who Was Who in the Civil War,* p. 198; CWD, p.254. Some of Ead's writings are compiled in *Addresses and Papers of James B. Eads,* Estille McHenry, Ed., (1984). Copies of this work are rare.
3. There is a lack of information on this elusive figure. One source available is: *Who Was Who in the Civil War,* p. 515.
4. The best biography on Foote is James Mason Hoppin, *Life of Andrew Hull*

Foote, Rear Admiral, U.S. Navy, (New York: Harper, 1974). For condensed versions, see *Dictionary of American Biography,* Vol.6, pp. 499–500; CWD, p. 287.

5. Descriptions of Ead's gunboats have been culled from many sources. Four are outstanding: DAFS., WCWN, H. Allen Gosnell, *Guns on the Western Waters* (Baton Rouge: Louisiana State University Press, 1949), pp.16–19. And from Ead's own perspective, see B&L, pp.338–42.

6. B&L, pp.341–42.

7. Graphic information on life aboard Civil War warships can be found in Philip Catcher's *The Civil War Source Book* (New York: Facts on File, 1992). And for one in particular, see Myron J. Smith, Jr., *The Gunboat Carondelet, 1861–1865* (Ma/Ah Publishing, Eisenhower Hall, Manhattan, Kansas, 1982). On uniforms, consult Philip Haythornthwait's *Uniforms of the Civil War, 1860–1865* (N.Y., MacMillan Publishing Co., 1975), and Francis A. Lord & Arthur Wise, *Uniforms of the Civil War* (New York: Thomas Yoseloff, 1970).

8. *Daily Missourian Republican,* St. Louis, March 31, 1862, Vol.XA - No.7, in the Missouri Historical Society.

9. William M. Fowler, *Under Two Flags: The American Navy in the Civil War,* pp.140–41; and William N. Still, *Iron Afloat: The Story of the Confederate Ironclads* (Tennessee: Vanderbuilt University Press, 1971).

Chapter 3: THE BLOSSOMING OF LITTLE EGYPT

1. Excellent accounts of the importance of Kentucky to both sides can be found in Colonel R.M. Kelly's *Holding Kentucky for the Union,* in B&L, pp.372–93. Also, John G. Nicolay, *The Outbreak of the Rebellion* (New York: Charles Scribner's Sons, reprint by Archive Society, 1992). Nicolay was Lincoln's private secretary.

2. John Fiske, *The Mississippi Valley in the Civil War* (Boston, Houghton, Mifflin and Company, The Riverside Press, 1900) pp.52–53.

3. Bruce Catton, *This Hallowed Ground* (New York: Pocket Books, 1956) p.44.

4. Fiske, *The Mississippi Valley in the Civil War,* pp. 10–11. There has been some controversy over this incident. However, Fiske, who was a contemporary of the real Mrs. Alexander, related having been shown the bombazine gown and veil by Mrs. Alexander herself. Fiske also maintained that the capture of Camp Jackson was the first really aggressive blow at Secession that was struck anywhere within the United States.

5. "St. Louis, a Fond Look Back," (Published by the First National Bank of St. Louis on the Occasion of its One Hundredth Anniversary, 1956). The full article gives a graphic, detailed look at the Camp Jackson incident, from a bystander's perspective. Sherman was indirectly involved in the incident and was almost wounded, as related in Fletcher Johnson's Life of Wm. Tecumseh Sherman, (N.Y. Edgewood Publishing Co., 1891) pp.81–83. This old, venerable work has been long outdated and out of circulation, but the author is privileged to have a copy in his possession.

6. "Recollections of Foote and the Gunboats, Captain James B. Eads, B&L, pp.338-339.

7. *Yates to Trumbull,* Journal of the Illinois State Historical Society, (Springfield: Illinois State Historical Society, Vol.2, No.3, 1966)

8. Victor Hicken, *Illinois in the Civil War* (Urbana: University of Illinois Press, 1966), p.15.

9. William Pitkin, "When Cairo Was Saved," Journal of the Illinois Historical

Society, (Springfield: Illinois State Historical Society, Vol. LI, No.3 1966),
p.302.

10. New York Times, June 18, 1861.

11. Anthony Trollope, *North America* (New York: St. Martin's Press, 1986)
pp.97–103.

12. Paul M. Angle, *A Pictorial History of the Civil War* (Garden City: Doubleday
& Company, Inc., 1967) p.40.

13. William Onstot to his wife, Sept. 11, 1861, Onstot Letter Collection,
1861–1863, Illinois State Historical Society.

14. James B. Eads, "Recollections of Foote and the Gunboats," B&L, pp.340–41.

15. For a reconstruction of Cairo, the author is indebted to the Cairo Public
Library and its voluminous newspaper files, including invaluable copies of
the Cairo Evening Citizen and The Cairo City Gazette and to the Cairo
Chamber of Commerce for a surprising wealth of information, obtained
while visiting there. See also, Pitkin, "How Cairo was Saved," Journal of the
Illinois State Historical Society, Vol. LI, No.3, pp.284-306. For James Ead's
own impressions of the strategic importance of Cairo, see ORN, Series 1,
vol.22, pp. 278–79. For an excellent book on both historical and modern
Cairo, see Herman R. Lanz's *Cairo: a Community in Search of itself* (Carbondale: Southern Illinois Press, 1972).

16. For an excellent biography on Polk, consult Joseph Howard Park's *General
Leonidas Polk, C.S.A.: The Fighting Bishop* (Baton Rouge: Louisiana State
University Press, 1962. There are excellent biographies in *Who Was Who in
the Civil War*, and Fiske, *The Mississippi Valley in the Civil War* and CWD.

17. The best biography on Halleck is Stephen A. Ambrose, *Halleck, Lincoln's
Chief of Staff* (Baton Rouge: Lousiana State University Press, 1962).

Chapter 4: PRELIMINARY CLASH AT FORT HENRY

1. Walter Rawls, ed., *Great Civil War Heroes and their Battles* (New York:
Abbeville Press, 1985); CWD, p.440.

2. Captain Jesse Taylor, "The Defense of Fort Henry," in B&L, pp. 368–73.

3. Ibid, p.368.

4. M.F. Force, *From Fort Henry to Corinth* (New York: Charles Scribner's Sons,
1881–1883, Reprint by Archive Society, 1992) p.27–28.

5. Trollope, *North America*, p.102.

6. In regard to the general's penchant for dressing in fatigues (he was to later
order a dress uniform from New York), an interesting story is told by Illinois
Governor Richard Ogelesby, while he was a colonel in Grant's army. The
governor relates that he was in command of all forces in Cairo up to
September 4, 1861, at which time two gentlemen walked into his headquarters in the St. Charles Hotel. One was a Captain Clark B. Lagow; the other a
"dirty and unshaven individual in well-worn civilian clothes." Ogelesby dismissed the "civilian," thinking him to be a refugee. Lagow introduced the
"refugee" as General Ulysses S. Grant. And, as Ogelesby looked on in amaze-
ment, Grant sat down, took pen and paper and wrote an order relieving
Ogelsby from his duties and returning him to his regiment. "Which," the governor wrote, "was a pretty strong indication that the gentleman I was
addressing was anything but a refugee."—-Ogelsby to Donaldson, Ogelesby
Papers, Illinois State Historical Society.

7. Ulysses S.Grant, *Personal Memoirs of U.S. Grant* (New York: Charles L.

Webster & Co., 1894), pp.169–70. Grant's constant disappointment with Halleck shows through in this autobiography.

8. CWNC, Part 2, p.16
9. Ibid, p.16
10. Quoted in General Sir James Marshall-Cornwall's *Grant as Military Commander* (New York: Van Nostrand Reinhold Company, 1970). This work is one of the finest books on Grant the author has ever seen. It is authoritative and well-written, from a British military man's perspective.
11. CWNC, Part 2, p.17
12. Henry Walke, "The Gunboats at Belmont & Fort Henry," B&L, p.362. This work is by far and away the best and most authoritative account of the assault on Fort Henry, from a naval standpoint.
13. Catton, *This Hallowed Ground*, pp. 114–15
14. Jesse Taylor, "The Defense of Fort Henry," B&L, p.369.
15. Ibid, p.369.
16. Welles to Foote, Feb.13, 1862, Missouri State Historical Society.
17. Flag officer Foote, Special Order No.3, Feb.2, 1862, S. Ledyard Phelps Letterbook, Oct.'61 to Feb.'62, Missouri State Historical Society.
18. CWNC, Part 2, p.20.
19. Of this often-related incident of Grant's having cut the telegraph wires to prevent an expected negative answer from Halleck, there is no record. It must have been predicated on Grant's known contempt for Halleck's famous indecisiveness.

Chapter 5: STRIKING BACK AT ANACONDA

1. CWCN, Vol. 1, p.18.
2. Jefferson Davis, *Rise and Fall of the Confederate Government*, 2 vols. (New York, NY: Thomas Yoseloff, 1958) Vol.1, p.194.
3. CWNC, Vol.1, p. 40.
4. Davis, *Rise and Fall of the Confederate Government*, Vol.2, p.46.
5. Ibid, p.46.
6. Still, *Iron Afloat*, p.46.
7. Information and specifications on Confederate war vessels have come from many sources. The principle source and, in my estimation, the most complete and authoritative., is Silverstone's WCWN. Other sources are: DAFS and Virgil Carrington Jones' *The Civil War at Sea* (New York: Holt & Rinehart, 1961), B&L and Still's *Iron Afloat*, among others.
8. Davis, *Rise and Fall of the Confederate Government*, Vol.2, p.40.
9. CWCN. Silverstone not only presents technical information on Confederate torpedo boats, but he publishes rare photos of their early submarines.
10. James Russell Soley, "The Union and Confederate Navies" B&L, p.631

Chapter 6: GENERAL BUCKNER'S BITTER LEGACY

1. CWNC, Vol.2, pp.15–16
2. Cornwall, *Grant as Military Commander*, pp.56–57
3. Many interesting facts about the *Carondelet* and her crew and activities on board are based on the aforementioned manuscript by Myron J. Smith, *The U.S. Gunboat Carondelet, 1861–1865*. Also available in the Manuscript Division of the Library of Congress is "An Anonymous Journal on Board the

Steamboat Carondelet, Captain Henry Walke Commanding, 1862–1863."
4. Ibid.
5. Ibid.
6. Grant, *Memoirs*, p.177.
7. WCWN, p.151.
8. Walke, B&L, Vol. 1, p.430; also, F. Van Wyke Mason, *Blue Hurricane* (New York: Cardinal Edition, Pocket Books, 1956), p.296.
9. Walke, B&L, Vol.1, pp.430–31. Also, Force, *From Fort Henry to Corinth*, p. 34. In addition to the Columbiads and the 32-pounders, the fort contained one 8-inch howitzer, two 9-pounders and one rifled gun.
10. Walke, B&L, Vol.1, p.431; Smith, *The U.S. Gunboat Carondelet, 1861–1865*, p.82.
11. ORN, Series 1, Vol.22, pp.585-595.
12. Walke, B&L, Vol. 1, p.431.
13. Grant, *Memoirs*, p.178.
14. A full account of the battle can be found in ORN, Series 1, Vol.22, and Walke's own account in Henry Walke, "Naval Scenes and Reminiscences of the Civil War in the United States, on the Southern and Western Waters, During the Years 1861, 1862 and 1863" (New York: F.R. ed, 1877).
15. Maj. Selden Spencer, *Journal*, p.6.
16. Henry Foote, "Flag Officer's Report to Welles," Feb. 15, 1862, in Report to the Secretary of the Navy in Relation To Armored Vessels (Washington, DC: Government Printing Office,1864) p.359.
17. Ibid, pp. 359–60.
18. ORN, Series 1, Vol.22, pp. 595–96.
19. Spencer, *Journal*, p.7.
20. Ulysses S., Grant, *Personal Memoirs of U.S. Grant, Selected Letters 1839–1865* (New York: Literary Classics of the United States, 1990). This is a new and updated edition of Grant's work. Hereafter, it will be referred to in this book.
21. Spencer, *Journal*, p.205.
22. Ibid, p. 206.
23. Bruce Catton, *Grant Moves South* (Boston: Little Brown and Company, 1960) pp.174–76.
24. Jonathan Blair to Sally Blair, Feb. 20, 1862, Blair Letters, Missouri Historical Society.
25. Catton, *Grant Moves South*, p.174.
26. Walke, "The Western Flotilla," B&L, p.436.
27. ORN, Series 1, Vol. 22, p.625.
28. Abraham Lincoln, *Speeches and Writings, 1859–1866* (New York: The Library of America, Inc., 1989), p.36.
29. John Edward Young, "An Illinois Farmer during the Civil War. Extracts from the Journal of John Edward Young, 1859–1866" from Journal of Illinois State Historical Society, Vol.26 (April-January 1933–1934), p.33.
30. CWCN, Part 2, p.21.
31. Catton, *Reflections on the Civil War*, p.106.
32. Sandburg, *Abraham Lincoln: The War Years, 1861–1864*: p.153.
33. Marshall-Cornwall, *Grant as Military Commander*, p.64.
34. CWCN, Part 2, p.21.
35. Grant, *Memoirs*, p.214
36. Davis, *Rise and Fall of the Confederate Government*, Vol.2, p.21.
37. Fiske, *Mississippi Valley in the Civil War*, p.57.

Chapter 7: CALM BEFORE THE STORM

1. Grant, *Memoirs*, p.215.
2. Marshall-Cornwall, *Grant as Military Commander*, p.66.
3. Walke, "The Western Flotilla at Fort Donelson, Island Number Ten, Fort Pillow and Memphis," B&L, Vol. 1, pp.438–39.
4. Ibid, p.438.
5. CWNC, Part 2, pp.26–27.
6. Ibid, p.27.
7. Walke, B&L, p.439.
8. CWNC, Part 2, p.32.
9. B&L, pp.692–750. For detailed information on the Monitor-Merrimack battle, consult William C. Davis, *Duel Between the Ironclads* (New York: Doubleday, 1975); A.A. Hoehling, *Damn the Torpedoes! Naval Incidences of the Civil War* (N. Carolina, John F. Blair, Publisher, 1989) and Still's *Iron Afloat: The Story of the Confederate Ironclads*.
10. Grant, *Memoirs*, p.214.

Chapter 8: GENESIS OF ISLAND HOPPING

1. Walke, "Western Flotilla," B&L, p.439. Later, *Pittsburgh* was sent back for boiler repairs.
2. ORN, Series 1, Vol.22, P.701.
3. Fowler, *Under Two Flags*, p.152.
4. Walke, "Western Flotilla," B&L, Vol.1, pp.439–440.
5. Ibid, p.439.
6. Colonel Bissell relates his own account of the work on the canal in "Sawing out the Channel Above Island No.10," B&L, Vol.1, pp.460-462. In an interesting sidebar to the article, Major General Schuyler challenges Col. Bissell's claim to be the originator of the canal plan. He cites General Pope's report to General Halleck on the project. Fiske, in *The Misssissippi Valley in the Civil War*, agrees with Shuyler's claim, footnote on p.106.
7. Howard P. Nash, Jr., *A Naval History of the Civil War* (New York: A.S. Barnes and Company, 1972) p.99.
8. Force, *From Fort Henry to Corinth*, pp.82–83.
9. Fiske, *The Mississippi Valley in the Civil War*, p.104.
10. Covered in Walke's own *Reminiscences*; Myron Smith, *The Gunboat Carondelet*, pp. 89–97. The latter work, a privately printed source, quotes in detail the run as seen through the eyes of a reporter from the St. Louis Democrat who was on board.
11. W.D.S. Cook to Colonel Thomas Jordan, ORA, Series 1, Vol.8, p.175.
12. Onset to Onset, Onset Letter Collection, 1861–1863, Missouri State Historical Society.
13. Walke, "Island No. 10," *Reminiscences*, pp.175–99; Force, *From Fort Henry to Corinth*, p.90
14. Grant, *Memoirs*, p.233.
15. H.L. Patterson to M. Brayman, March 7, 1862, John Brayman Papers, Illinois State Historical Society.
16. Davis, *Rise and Fall of the Confederate Government*, p.68.
17. Carl Sandburg, *Abraham Lincoln*, 4 vols. (New York: Harcourt, Brace and Company, 1939) Vol.3, pp.478–79.

Chapter 9: ASSAULT ON CRESCENT CITY

1. Herbert Asbury, *The French Quarter* (New York: Pocket Books, 1966) pp.75–76.
2. Fiske, *The Mississippi Valley in the Civil War*, p.112.
3. Nash, *A Naval History of the Civil War*, p.122.
4. Ibid, p.123
5. Shelby Foote, *The Civil War*, pp. 355–56; ORN, Series 1, Vol.16, pp.712–14.
6. David Porter, "The Opening of the Lower Mississippi," B&L, Vol.2, p.30.
7. Porter, "Opening of the Lower Mississippi," B&L, vol.2, p.25; Wm. M. Fowler III, *Under Two Flags* and Bruce Catton, *Terrible Swift Sword*, p.248. Porter gives his own account of the campaign plan and appears to acknowledge credit for it.
8. *Who Was Who in the Civil War*, p.212; CWD, p.276. There are excellent books on Farragut, but the best, in the author's opinion, is Alfred Thayer Mahan's *Admiral Farragut* (New York: Haskell House Publishers,Ltd., 1968).
9. Bruce Catton, *This Hallowed Ground*, p. 105.
10. WCWN, pp.22–46; Nash, *A Naval History of the Civil War*, p.127.
11. Bruce Catton, *A Terrible Swift Sword*, p.253. In spite of having 3,000 men at his disposal, Lovell had trouble equipping them. They were raw and untrained and he had few or no officers with which to train them.
12. CWNC, Part 2, p.45.
13. There is a map of the fort in B&L, Vol.2, p.34, that clearly shows the effect of the mortar bombardment. The works looked like a sieve; casemates and outer walls were pulverized, drawbridge and shot furnaces destroyed, and all floating craft in the vicinity were sunk. Still the occupants refused to surender.
14. Fiske, *Mississippi Valley in the Civil War*, pp. 122–23.
15. William T. Meredith, "The Opposing Forces in the Operations at New Orleans, La.," pp.74–76; Bern Anderson, *By Sea and By River*, p.121 and Nash, *A Naval History of the Civil War*, pp.133–134.
16. Nash, *A Naval History of the Civil War*, p.133 and Fiske, *The Mississippi Valley in the Civil War*, p.368.
17. Foote, *The Civil War*, p.366. This is the first such reference to tonnage in shells, as opposed to numbers. It is a tribute to Mr. Foote's acumen.
18. Mahan, *Admiral Farragut*, p.151.
19. John Russel Bartlett, "The Brooklyn at the Passage of the Forts," B&L, Vol.2, p.67; Foote, *The Civil War*, p.368.
20. Mahan, *Farragut*, p.165; ORN, Series 1, Vol.18, p.30
21. Foote, *Civil War*, p. 357.
22. Ibid, p.370.
23. Ibid, p.371.
24. Mahan, *Admiral Farragut*, pp.146–50.
25. Jefferson Davis, *Rise and Fall of the Confederate Government*, pp.215–16..
26. Still, *Iron Afloat*, pp.44–45.
27. Davis, p.216.
28. Archer Jones, *Confederate Stategy From Shiloh To Vicksburg* (Baton Rouge: Louisiana State University Press, 1991) p.120.
29. Stephen E. Woodworth, *Jefferson Davis and his Generals* (Lawrence, KS: University Press of Kansas, 1990) p. 110.
30. Ibid, p.110.

Chapter 10: HARVEST AT PLUM POINT & MEMPHIS

1. Force, *From Fort Henry to Corinth*, p. 181.
2. Jones, *Confederate Strategy*, p.57.
3. Woodworth, *Jefferson Davis and his Generals*, p.105.
4. Kellogg to Porter, ORN, Series 1, Vol.23, p.768.
5. Walke, "Western Flotilla," B&L, Vol.1, P.446.
6. Anderson, *By Sea and River*, p.108; WCWN, p.226.
7. Pope to Foote, ORN, Series 1, Vol.23, p.6.
8. Foote to Welles, ORN, Series 1, Vol.23, p. 5.
9. CWD, pp.224–25.
10. *Who Was Who in the Civil War*, p. 453.
11. WCWN, p.226; *Dictionary of American Warships*, 6 vols.
12. Gregory to Davis, ORN, Series 1, Vol. 23, p.15; Walke, "Western Flotilla," B&L, p.447.
13. Phelps to Foote, ORN, Series 1, Vol.23, p.19.
14. Pennock to Davis, ORN, Series 1, Vol.23, p.20.
15. Albert Trevor, *History of Ancient Civilizations*, 2 vols. (New York: Harcourt Brace and Company, 1936), Vol.1, pp.234–36.
16. *Who Was Who in The Civil War*, p.202; Fowler, Under Two Flags, pp.177–79; Shelby Foote, *The Civil War, a Narrative from Fort Sumter to Perryville* (New York: Random House, 1958), pp.386–87.
17. Fiske, *Warfare Along the Mississippi*; The Letters of Lt.Colonel George E. Currie, Norman E. Clarke, ed., Mount Pleasant, Michigan (Central Michigan University, 1961), pp.39–40. This letterpress book contains a wealth of information about the rams from Currie who was a military commander aboard the *Mingo*, one of Ellet's vessels.
18. Ibid, p.xii. Currie maintained that guns were not placed on the rams, until after the Battle of Memphis.
19. Ibid, p.xii
20. Ibid, p.99. According to Currie, the story of the cow remained with the crew long after other exploits had been forgotten.
21. For photos of the Memphis docks and shipyard, consult *The Guns of '62: The Image of War; 1861–1865*, 6 vols. (Garden City, NY: Doubleday & Company, 1982) Vol.2, pp.298–99. After the capture of Memphis, the shipyard ceased to exist.
22. ORN, Series 1, Vol.23, pp.132–34.
23. The Battle of Memphis is described in ORN, B&L, and by Currie who was an eyewitness, aboard the *Mingo*.
24. There has been some controversy over how *General Price* had her sidewheel sheared off. Some accounts say it was the *Monarch* who rammed her; Alfred Ellet, in B&L, claims it was not so. But he is contradicted by Walke's account which claims that the two Confederate rams hit each other after *Monarch* slid by. Incidentally, Currie doesn't mention it, merely saying that *Monarch*'s blow sent *Price* "reeling off to the other shore." Today, most historians agree with Walke.
25. Walke, "Western Flotilla," B&L, Series 1, Vol.23, pp.452–62.
26. Davis to Park, ORN, Series 1, Vol.23, p.122.
27. Currie, *Warfare Along the Mississippi*, p.50, footnote. An eyewitness, Currie gives a graphic account of the exploits resulting from the raising of the Union flag over the Memphis post office building.

28. The Diary of Captain Ralph Ely of the Eighth Michigan Infantry, Mount Pleasant, Michigan (Central Michigan University Press, 1965) p.55. Ely was on his way to the siege of Vicksburg, and he wrote colorful impressions of cities along the Mississippi, plus some hard-hitting descriptions of the siege itself.
29. Currie, *Warfare Along the Mississippi*, p.35.
30. Davis, *Rise and Fall of the Confederacy*, p.77. Davis gives lip service to the fall of Memphis, as if he were trying to somehow minimize it. Later, he had to admit it was a serious blow to the Confederacy.
31. Alfred Ellet, "Ellet and His Steam Rams at Memphis," B&L, VOl.1, p.454.
32. Gosnell, *Guns on the Western Waters*, p.99.
33. Ibid, p.100.
34. Phelps to Tod, June 7, 1862, S. Ledyard Phelps Letterbook, Missouri State Historical Society.

Chapter 11: EYEING VICKSBURG FROM THE SOUTH

1 Farragut to Welles, ORN, Series 1, Vol. 18, p.8.
2. Palmer to Farragut, ORN, Series 1, Vol.18, p.473.
3. Stephen A. Chaning, et.al., *The Confederate Ordeal: The Southern Home Front* (Alexandria, VA: Time-Life Books, 1984) p.98.
4. Palmer to Farragut, ORN, Series 1, Vol. 18, p.478.
5. Ibid, p.489.
6. Christopher Martin, *Damn the Torpedoes*, p.207.
7. "Davis Glasgow Farragut, First Admiral of the Navy," Published by the National Park Service, U.S. Department of the Interior, courtesy of the U.S.S. Cairo Museum, Vicksburg National Military Park.

Chapter 12: TREACHEROUS WHITE RIVER

1. Hindman to Cooper, ORN, Series 1, Vol.23, p. 198. Hindman explained that he had endeavored to impress Curtis with the fiction that he commanded a much larger force than he really had.
2. Edwin C. Bearss, "The White River Expedition, June 10–July 15, 1862," Arkansas Quarterly, Vol.20 (Winter '61), pp.305-362. This is perhaps one of the most singular descriptions of the White River Campaign, as written by a noted Civil War historian.
3. Strangely, in his letterbook, *Warfare Along The Mississippi*, Currie fails to mention this important assignment. However, considering that many pages were missing, it is possible this was among them.
4. ORN, Series 1, Vol.23, p.692.
5. Ibid, p.165.
6. Ibid, p.198.
7. Ibid, p.166.
8. Ibid, p.166.
9. Ibid, p.166.
10. Davis Report, ORN, Series 1, Vol.23, p.171.
11. Ibid, p.171.
12. Ibid, p.171.
13. Farragut to Welles, ORN, Series 1, Vol.18, p. 588. Farragut's disappointment over the purpose of the run, in which he had some ships damaged, is evident

in his report.
14. Ibid, p.588.
15. Frank Ellis Smith, *The Yazoo River* (New York: Rinehart, 1954).

Chapter 13: CONFEDERATE COUNTERSTROKE

1. Lamar Roberts, "The Terror from Yazoo City," pamphlet published by the Yazoo City Historical Society, Yazoo City, Miss; William Still, Iron Afloat, p.62.
2. Guthrie to Beauregard, ORN, Series 1, Vol.22, p. 838.
3. Still, *Iron Afloat*, p.64.
4. Brown to Ruggles, ORN, Series 1, Vol. 18, p.647.
5. Ibid, p.647.
6. I.N. Brown, "The Confederate Gunboat Arkansas," B&L, Vol.III, pp.572–73; Frank Ellis Smith, *The Yazoo River* (New York: Rinehart & Company, Inc. 1954) p.95. Today, the site of the former Yazoo shipyard is occupied by a lumberyard. The main channel of the river changed its course over the years and the Arkansas site is now on a river-shaped lake called Lake Yazoo which occupies the original river bed of 1862.
7. For archival information about Yazoo City, the Yazoo River and the shipyard, the author is indebted to the the Yazoo City Historical Society & the Yazoo County Convention Bureau, Yazoo City, Mississippi. For a definitive history of Yazoo County, Yazoo City and the Yazoo River, The author highly recommends Harriet de Cell & Jo Anne Pritchard, *Yazoo, It's Legends & Legacies* (Yazoo City, MS: Yazoo Delta Press, 1976).
8. Brown to Ruggles, ORN, Series 1, Vol.22, p.649.
9. Van Dorn to Brown, ORN, Series 1, Vol. 18, p. 650.
10. Lieutenant George Grift quoted in Gosnell, *Guns on the Western Waters*, p. 106.
11. Silverstone, WCWN, Some sources have the vessel with 10 guns, but further research seems to indicate eight. She carried two 64-pounders, instead of four as labeled by other sources. Once again, the author is indebted to the Yazoo Historical Society and the Yazoo City Public Library for much of the details on the *Arkansas* and corrective material on events surrounding the vessel.
12. I. Brown as quoted in Gosnell, *Guns on the Western Waters*.
13. Ibid, p.295.
14. Gwin to Davis, ORN, Series 1, Vol. 19, pp.36-37
15. Gosnell, *Guns on the Western Waters*, p. 110.
16. James Russell Soley, "Naval Operations in the Vicksburg Campaign," B&L, Vol.3, p.556. Walke to Davis, ORN, Series 1, Vol.19, p.41. Walke maintained that the *Arkansas* didn't ram his vessel, as was widely reported. The damage to *Carondelet* was due to gunfire.
17. Gwin to Davis, ORN, Series 1, Vol. 19, p.38.
18. Abstract log of Tyler, ORN, Series 1, Vol. 19, p.39.
19. Extract from Joshua Bishop Papers, ORN, Series 1, Vol. 19, p. 36. Bishop was puzzled by the slow reaction of the Union fleet to the gunfire up the Yazoo. In spite of being close to flagship *Hartford* and Davis's *Benton*, he received no orders to stand out.
20. Roberts, "Terror from Yazoo City," p.4; Still, *Iron Afloat*, p.70; ORN, Series 1, Vol.19, p. 747.

21. Quoted in Gosnell, *Guns on Western Waters*, p.115. The author concurs. In times of combat one does his duty without thinking of himself, but rather at preserving one's ship.
22. Richard Wheeler, *The Siege of Vicksburg* (New York: Harper-Collins, 1978) p.64.
23. Still, *Iron Afloat*, p. 73; Roberts, "The Terror of Yazoo City," p.6.
24. Ibid, Still, p.72; Ibid, Roberts, p.7.
25. Wheeler, *The Siege of Vicksburg*, pp. 66–67.
26. Ibid, p.67.
27. Lieutenant Charles Read quoted in Gosnell, *Guns on the Western Waters*, pp.126–27.
28. Ibid, 129.
29. Still, *Iron Afloat*, pp. 74–75; Gosnell, *Guns on the Western Waters*, pp. 130–31; Wheeler, *Siege of Vicksburg*, pp.65–67.
30. Pope to Foote, ORN, Series 1, Vol. 23, p.6.

Chapter 14: FAULTY ENGINES, INFERNAL MACHINES

1. Still, *Iron Afloat*, p.75; Woodworth, *Jefferson Davis and His Generals*, p.117
2. CWD, p.82; Woodworth, *Jefferson Davis and His Generals*, p.120. For a good biography on Breckenridge, see Frank H. Heck's *Proud Kentuckian: John C. Breckenridge, 1821-1875* (Lexington, KY: University Press of Kentucky, 1976).
3. B&L, Vol. 3, p.579.
4. Still, *Iron Afloat*, p.76; B&L, Vol.3, p.579.
5. Stevens, "The Confederate Gunboat Arkansas," B&L, Vol.3, p. 579; ORN, Series 1, Vol.19, p.120; Roberts, "The Terror From Yazoo City," p. 7.
6. Davis, *Rise and Fall of the Confederate Government*, Vol.2, p.244.
7. Ibid, p.123.
8. Letter of Commander Phelps to Flag Officer Davis, August 23, 1862. S. Ledyard Phelps Letterbook, Missouri State Historical Society Archives.
9. Ibid, p.4.
10. Currie, *Warfare Along the Mississippi*, pp.59–62. Lieutenant-Colonel Currie became a member of the brigade and recorded many events surrounding its existence.
11. Ibid, p.59.
12. WCWN, p.221; DAFS, Vol.1, p.
13. Milton F. Perry, *Infernal Machines: The Story of Confederate Submarine and Mine Warfare* (Baton Rouge: Louisina University Press, 1965), p.64. This remarkable work is one of its kind, and is a most important book on Confederate underwater warfare.
14. WCWN, p.221; Perry, *Infernal Machines*, pp.105–08.
15. CWD, p.520; Perry, *Infernal Machines*, pp.8–9.
16. Perry, *Infernal Machines*, pp.10–11.
17. Isaac Brown, "Confederate Torpedos in the Yazoo," B&L Vol.3, p.580.
18. Davis, *Rise and Fall of the Confederate Government*, Vol.2, p.206.

Chapter 15: VIVE LA CAIRO!

1. ORN, Series I, Vol. 22, p.494.
2 The author is indebted to the staff of the Vicksburg Military Park for information on the *Cairo*, its history, its resurrection and installation at the park,

plus voluminous archival materials. Among the latest books available on the Pheonix gunboat is Edwin C. Bearss' excellent *Hardluck Ironclad, The Sinking and Salvage of the Cairo*, Revised Edition (Baton Rouge: Louisiana State University Press, 1980).

3. DAFS, Vol.1; WCWN, p.151; *The U.S.S. Cairo: The Story of the Civil War Gunboat* (Washington, DC: National Park Service, U.S. Department of the Interior, 1971) pp.14–18.

4. *U.S.S. Cairo Engine and Boilers* (Vicksburg: The American Society of Mechanical Engineers Publication, 1990), p.6, Courtesy of Vicksburg Military Park Cairo Exhibit Archives.

5. Based on David F. Rigg's "Sailors of the U.S.S. Cairo: Anatomy of a Gunboat Crew," *Civil War History*, Vol. XXVIII, No.3, Kent State University Press. 1982. pp.268–73.

6. Based on William Still, "The Common Sailor," Part One, "Yankee Bluejackets," Civil War Times Illustrated, February, 1985.

7. William T. Sherman, *Memoirs of General W.T. Sherman* (New York: Literary Classics of the United States, 1990), pp.310–11.

8. James Russell Soley, "Naval Operations in the Civil War," B&L, Vol.3, p.559

9. ORN, Sies 1, Vol. 23, pp. 546–47.

10. George R.Yost Diary, January,1862–March,1863, transcript from microfilm, Illinois State Historical Society, Springfield, Illinois. Yost joined the *Cairo* at Cairo, Illinois, in February of 1862. He kept a journal for 11 months thereafter, giving vivid first-hand accounts of the gunboat's movements, life aboard, and her ill-fated voyage up the Yazoo River.

11. Getty to Walke, ORN, Series 1, Vol. 23, p.553.

12. Sutherland to Walke, ORN, Series 1, Vol.23, p.550.

13. Ibid, p.554.

14. Yost Diary, p.63.

15. Selfridge Report, ORN, Series 1, Vol.23, p.550. Unfortunately for them, but fortunately for us, the crew could save only a small part of personal effects. When the *Cairo* was raised, she contained a treasure chest of personal effects, such as plates, cups, silverware, boots, toothbrushes, photos of loved ones and many more items that shed light on the life of riverine sailors, during this period of the war.

16. Yost Diary, p.63.

17. Bearrs, *Hardluck Ironclad*, p.100; Yost Diary, p.63.

18. Selfridge Report, ORN, Series 1, Vol. 23, p.550; Bearss, *Hardluck Ironclad*, p.100; B&L, Vol.3, p.559.

19. Porter Report, ORN, Series 1, Vol. 23, p.544.

20. The mine, or torpedo, was a new device to the old salt naval officers that commanded ocean-going ships. As far as they were concerned, no mines were ever sown in open waters, but in bays, rivers and inlets only. An example of a salt water commander's contempt for them was the admonition for "Damn the torpedos! Full speed ahead!" by Admiral Farragut in Mobile Bay, August, 1864.

21. Bearss, *Hardluck Ironclad*, p.103.

22. Admiral Porter to General Sherman, ORN, Series 1, Vol.23. p.577

23. Report of Colonel Ellet, ORN, Series I, vol. 23, pp. 593–94.

Chapter 16: GUNBOATS COME TO GRIPS

1. CWD, p.477. Some sources question Stephen B. Lee's relationship with the Lees of Virginia. This book, which has long been recognized as an authoritative source, claims he is not; other sources claim the opposite. The whole subject is worth a study by someone.
2. Sherman, *Memoirs*, p.311. The sad part of this scenario lies in the fact that at Millikan's Bend he paused to send a brigade to destroy the Vicksburg & Shreveport Rairoad, thus allowing Confederate General Martin Luther Smith's force at Chickasaw Bluffs to be reinforced. Unkown to Sherman, the passage of his amphibious armada had already been telegraphed to Smith, through a newly established telegraphic network along the river.
3. *Harper's Pictorial History of the Civil War* (New York: Harper Brothers, Reprint Edition, 1980) p.445. Contrary to its title, this monumental work contains more textual matter than illustrative, and is crammed with information.
4. Jerry Korn, *The Civil War on the Mississippi*, pp.66–67.
5. Marshal-Cornwall, Grant as Military Commander, p.103.
6. Quoted in Korn, Civil War on the Mississippi, pp.66–67.
7. E.B. Long & Barbara Long, *The Civil War Day by Day, an Almanac, 1861–1865* (Garden City: Doubleday & Co., 1971) p.301; CWD, p.447.
8. *Harper's Pictorial History of the Civil War*, p.447.
9. Sherman, *Memoirs*, pp. 320–21; ORN, Series 1, Vol. 23, p.166.
10. Thomas L. Sneed, "The Conquest of Arkansas," B&L, Vol.3, pp.452-453.
11. Ibid, p.453; *Harper's Pictorial History of the Civil War*, p.449; CWD, p.24. For the fleet, the *Rattler* suffered hits, as did the *DeKalb*. As a whole, little damage was done to the fleet.
12. Long & Long, *Civil War Day by Day*, p.318.
13. Maurice Melton, "From Vicksburg to Port Hudson: Porter's River Campaign," Harper's Weekly, February 28, 1863, Vol.12, No.10, Courtesy Cairo Exhibit Archives, Vicksburg Military Park.
14. WCWN, p.155; *Harper's Pictorial History of the Civil War*, footnote, p.450.
15. Kelso to Surget, ORN, Series 1, Vol.24, p.364. Captain John Kelso, C.S.A.,was in command of Fort Taylor at Gordon"s Landing. He maintains that the *Queen* had struck her colors, but there is no other evidence of this. Considering the beating she had taken—steam and smoke filling the compartments and with the pilothouse smashed and chimneys hit—it is improbable that anyone thought of striking colors. He admitted that only 13 of the 31 shots fired at the Union ram hit home, attesting to poor gunnery.
16. Brand to Pemberton, ORN, Series 1, Vol. 24, p.364.
17. Nash, *A Naval History of the Civil War*, p.167; Brand report, ORN, Series 1, Vol.32, p.363.
18. Report of Major Brent, ORN, Series 1, Vol.24, p.364.
19. Lieutenant-Colonel Brand Report, ORN, Series 1, Vol. 24, p.363.
20. Ibid, p.35; *Harper's History of the Civil War*, p.451; Soley, "Naval Operations in the Civil War," B&L, Vol.3, 565.
21. Stevenson to Pemberton, ORN, Series 1, Vol, 24, pp.369-70. When the Confederates gingerly approached the dummy, they saw the hoax. They were angered to see a flag containing skull and crossbones on the jackstaff, and large letters on the wheelhouses: "Deluded People, Cave In."
22. Ibid, p.35; *Harper's History of the Civil War*, p.451; Soley, "Naval Operations

in the Civil War," B&L, Vol.3, 565.
23. Nash, *A Naval History of the Civil War*, p.170; ORN, Series 1, Vol. 24, p.669.
24. Potter & Nimitz, "The Mississippi River Campaign," *Sea Power: A Naval History*, p.304.
25. Nash, *Naval History of the Civil War*, p.172.
26. ORN, Series 1, Vol.24, p.24.
27. Ellet to Ellet, ORN, Series 1, Vol.24, p.478.
28. Ibid, p.479.

Chapter 17: THE NOOSE TIGHTENS

1. Grant, *Memoirs*, pp.295–97.
2. Ibid, p.297.
3. Grant to McPherson, *The Papers of U.S. Grant*, John Y. Simon, ed., 9 vols. (Carbondale, IL: Southern Illinois University Press), vol.7, pp.284–85; Grant, *Memoirs*, p.298.
4. Fiske, *The Mississippi Valley in the Civil War*, p.217.
5. Grant to Kelton, Grant, *The Papers of U.S. Grant*, vol.7, 286; Wilson Report, ORN, Series 1, Vol. 24, p.371.
6. Smith Report, ORN, Series 1, vol.24, p.243 f.
7. Korn, *Civil War on the Mississippi*, p.76.
8. Grant, *Memoirs*, p.300; Wilson to Grant, Grant, *The Papers of U.S. Grant*, pp.435–37.
9. Ibid, p.301; Korn, *Civil War on the Mississippi*, p.80
10. Daniel Kemp, "Gunboat War at Vicksburg," *Civil War Chronicles*, Courtesy of Cairo Exhibit archives, Vicksburg Military Park.
11. Korn, *Civil War on the Mississippi*, pp.81–82. In addition to this natural menace—-some of the snakes were poisonous—-the chimneys had to be lowered to keep them from being permanently ripped off. This effort, as one would expect, substantially lowered boiler pressures, but the slow cruising speeds more than made up for that deficiency.
12. Grant, *Memoirs*, p.302; Soley, "Naval Operations in the Mississippi," B&L, vol.3, pp.563–64.
13. Sherman, *Memoirs*, p.332; Grant, *Memoirs*, p.302.
14. Ibid, p.334
15. Grant, *Memoirs*, p.304.
16. Porter, General Orders, ORN, Series 1, Vol.24, p.554.
17. Walke to Porter,ORN, Series 1, Vol.24, p.557.
18. General Maurey, quoted in Wheeler, *The Siege of Vicksburg*, p.108.
19. Dairy of John T. Apler, Confederate Soldier, Missouri State Historical Society Archives, St, Louis.
20. Sherman, *Memoirs*, p.306.
21. "With Grant at Vicksburg," From the *Civil War Diary of Charles E. Wilcox*, ed. by Edgar l. Erickson, The Journal of the Illinois State Historical Society, January, 1938, Vol.30, No.4.
22. Reports to Porter, ORN, Series 1, vol. 24, pp.552–61.
23. Grant, *Memoirs*, p.317.
24. Porter's Report, ORN, Series 1, vol.24. Porter's frustration shows through in his report, but he managed to keep an upbeat attitude, in spite of it all.
25. Ibid, p.611.
26. Grant, *Memoirs*, p.318.

27. Sherman, *Memoirs*, p.345.
28. CWD, p.360; Grant to Lincoln, *The Papers of U.S. Grant*, pp.301–02.

Chapter 18: TWILIGHT OF VICKSBURG

1. Fiske, *The Mississippi Valley in the CIvil War*, pp.237–40; Grant, *Memoirs,* Chapter 35. An excellent day-by-day account of Grant's battle at Port Gibson can be found in the pamphlet, "Port Gibson, A Battlefield Guide," by Terrance Winschel, published by the Jackson Civil War Roundtable, and is available at the Vicksburg Military Park, or at the Roundtable in Jackson. Another very informative pamphlet is "The Vicksburg Campaign Siege," by Edwin C. Bearss, also available at the Military Park, and is published by the Mississippi Department of Archives & History. These works are valuable for their day-by-day accounts.
2. For more information on Pemberton, see *John C. Pemberton: Defender of Vicksburg* (Chapel Hill: The University. of North Carolina Press, 1942).
3. Wheeler, *Siege of Vicksburg*, pp.150–51.
4. *Harper's Pictorial History of the Civil War*, p.446.
5. Ibid, p.467; *The Battle for Yazoo, 1862–1864,* Yazoo City, Mississippi, published by the Yazoo Chamber of Commerce. Courtesy, Yazoo Historical Society and the Yazoo Public Library.
6. Perry, *Infernal Machines*, p.45.
7. Gordon A. Cotton, *Vicksburg: Southern Stories of the Siege* (Vicksburg, MS: privately published, 1988), p.19. This book is a compilation of experiences recorded by many citizens living under the siege. Some entries present incidences of poignancy, gruesomeness, stark terror and tenacity. Mr. Cotton is the Director, Old Court House Museum in Vicksburg.
8. R.A. Halley, *A Rebel Newspaper's Story: Being a Narrative of the War History of the Memphis Appeal,* reprint, American Historical Magazine, April, 1903. Missouri Historical Society.
9. Ibid, p.28; *Harper's Pictorial History of the Civil War*, p.475.
10. Quoted in Cotton, *Vicksburg: Southern Stories of the Siege*, p.29.
11. Wheeler, *Siege of Vicksburg,* pp.189–90; Korn, *War on the Mississippi*, p.139.
12. Grant, *Memoirs*, p.385.
13. Hattaway & Jones, *How the North Won: A Military History of the Civil War,* pp.419–21.

Chapter 19: SEQUEL ON RED RIVER

1. Grant, *Memoirs*, p.484.
2. Shelby Foote, *The Civil War Narrative: Red River to Appomattox* (New York: Random House, 1974), p.27.
3. Selfridge, "The Navy in the Red River," B&L, Vol.4, p.362. Selfridge, who formerly commanded the star-crossed *Cairo*, and who commanded the *Osage* on this expedition, was liberal in his admiration for Porter, calling him a "courageous and able commander."
4. Ibid, p.363
5. Ibid, p.364; Foote, *Civil War: A Narrative*, p.78; CWD, pp.687–88.
6. Richard Irwin, "The Red River Campaign," B&L, vol.4, pp.358-359; Foote, *The Civil War: A Narrative*, p.78; CWD, p.688.
7. Selfridge, "The Navy in the Red River," B&L, p.366.

Chapter 20: A GLANCE BACKWARD

1. Fiske, *The Mississippi Valley in the Civil War*, p.247.
2. Still, *Iron Afloat*, p.63.
3. Phelps Report, ORN, Series I, Vol.19, p.56. Phelps gives a very graphic account of the battle with the *Arkansas* in his report
4. Anderson, *Naval History of the Civil War*, pp. 301–02.
5. Grant, *Memoirs*, p.348. Grant reveals that no sooner had Vicksburg fallen than his thoughts turned toward taking his huge army and assaulting Mobile.
6. Catton, *Reflections on the Civil War*, p.105.
7. Davis, *Rise and Fall of the Confederate Government*, p.425.
8. Marshall-Cornwall, *Grant as Military Commander*, p.117.

Bibliography

Government Sources:

Civil War Chronology (1861–1865), 6 vols. Washington, D.C.: Naval History Division, U.S. Government Printing Office.

Dictionary of American Fighting Ships (1859–1981) 8 vols. Washington, D.C.: Naval History Division, U.S. Government Printing Office.

Message and Documents: Message of the President of the U.S., Accompanying Documents at the 2nd Session of the 38th Congress. (1864) Washington, D.C.: U.S. Navy Department, U.S. Government Printing Office.

Official Records of the Union and Confederate Navies in the War of the Rebellion (1894–1922) 31 vols. Washington, D.C.: U.S. Government Printing Office.

The 8th Census of the U.S. (1860) Washington, D.C.: U.S. Government Printing Office.

Report of the Secretary of the Navy in Relation to Armed Vessels (1864) Washington, D.C.: U.S. Government Printing Office.

War of the Rebellion: Official Records of the Union and Confederate Armies (1880–1901) 128 vols. Washington, D.C.: U.S. Government Printing Office.

Journals:

Arkansas Quarterly
Journal of the Illinois State Historical Society.
Missouri State Historical Society Journal.

Newspapers:

Cairo City Gazette
Cairo Evening Citizen
Chicago Tribune
New York Times

BOOKS:

Ambrose, Stephen A. (1962) *Halleck, Lincoln's Chief of Staff.* Baton Rouge: Louisiana State University Press.

Anderson, Bern. (1962) *By Sea and By River: The Naval History of the Civil War.* New York: Alfred Knopf.

Angle, Paul M. (1967) *A Pictorial History of the Civil War.* New York: Doubleday & Co., Inc.

Asbury, Herbert, (1966) *The French Quarter.* New York: Pocket Books.

Beach, Edward L. (1986) *United States Navy: 200 Years.* New York: Henry Holt and Company.

Bearss, Edward C. (1980) *Hardluck Ironclad: The Sinking and Salvage of the Cairo.* Baton Rouge: Louisiana State University Press.

Battles and Leaders of the Civil War. (1956) 4 vols. New York: Thomas Yoseloff.

Battles and Leaders of the Civil War. (1956) Ed. Bradford, ed. Single Edition. New York: Appleton-Century-Crofts.

Boatner, Mark, M. (1988) *The Civil War Dictionary.* New York: Vintage Books.

Catton, Bruce. (1960) *Grant Moves South.* Boston: Little Brown and Company.

———. (1969) *Grant Takes Command.* Boston: Little Brown and Company.

———. (1988) *Reflections on the Civil War.* New York: Barkley Books. (Cont'd)

———. (1963) *Terrible Swift Sword.* Garden City: Doubleday and Company, Inc.

———. (1967) *This Hallowed Ground.* New York: Pocket Books.

Command at Sea, 4th Edition. (1982) Annapolis: Naval Institute Press.

Confederate Military History. (1980) 12 vols. Reprint. Harrisburg: Pennsylvania Archive Society.

Congden, Don. (1967) *Combat in the Civil War.* New York: Delacorte Press.

Cotton, Gordon A. (1988) *Vicksburg: The Southern Stories of the Siege.* Vicksburg: Privately printed.

Currie, George E. (1961) *Warfare Along the Mississippi: The Letters of Lt. George E. Currie.* Letterbook. Norman E. Clark, ed. Mount Pleasant: Central Michigan University.

Davis, Jefferson (1958) *The Rise and Fall of the Confederate Government,* 2 vols. New York: Joseph Yoseloff.

Dillahunty, Albert. (1956) *Shiloh National Military Park.* Washington: National Park Service Historical Handbook Series.

Dirkin, Joseph D. (1954) *Stephen Mallory: Confederate Navy Chief.* Chapel Hill: University of South Carolina Press.

deCell, Harriet & Jo Anne Pritchard. (1976) *Yazoo: Its Legends and Legacies.* Yazoo City: Yazoo Delta Press.

Eisenschiml, Otto. (1958) *Why the Civil War?* Richard B. Morris, ed. New York: Bobbs-Merrill Company, Inc.

Encyclopedia of American History. (1976) Richard B. Morris, ed. New York: Harper & Row Publishers.

Fiske, John. (1900) *The Mississippi Valley in the Civil War.* New York: Houghton, Mifflin & Company.

Foote, Shelby. (1959) *The Civil War, a Narrative: Fort Sumter to Perryville.* New York: Random House.

Force, M.F. (1992) *From Fort Henry to Corinth.* New York: Charles Scribner's Sons.

Fowler, William N., Jr. *Under Two Flags The American Navy in the Civil War.* New York: Avon Books.

Glatthaar, Joseph T. (1994) *Partners in Command: The Relationships Between Leaders of the Civil War.* New York: The Free press.

Gosnell, H. Allen (1994) *Guns on the Western Waters.* Baton Rouge: Louisiana State University press.

Grant, U.S. (1990) *Personal Memoirs of U.S. Grant.* New York: Library of America.

———. (1979) *Papers of U.S. Grant.* Carbondale: Southern Illinois University Press.

Great Civil War Heroes and Their Battles. (1991) Walter Rawls, ed. Baton Rouge: Louisiana State University Press.

The Guns of '62, The Images of War: 1861-1865. (1982) 6 vols. William C. Davis, ed. New York: Doubleday & Company, Inc.

Harlow, Ralph Volney (1949) *The United States: From Wilderness to World Power.* New York: Henry Holt & Co.

Harper's Pictorial History of the Civil War. (1980) New York: Harper Brothers.

Hattaway, Herman & Archer Jones. (1983) *How the North Won: A Military History of the Civil War.* Urbana: University of Illinois Press.

Haid, Larry. (1966) *River City: A Hometown Remembrance of Cairo, Illinois.* New York: Exposition Press.

Haythornthwaite, Philip. (1975) *Uniforms of the Civil War.* New York: Macmillan Publishing Co.

Hicken, Victor. (1966) *Illinois in the Civil War.* Chicago: University of Illinois Press.

Hoehling, A.A. (1989) *Damn the Torpedoes! Naval Incidents in the Civil War.* North Carolina: John F. Blair, Publisher.

Holbrook, Stewart H. (1972) *The Story of American Railroads*. New York: Bonanza Books.

Howarth, Stephan. (1991) *To Shining Sea: A History of the United States Navy 1775–1991*. New York: Random House.

Jones Archer. (1991) *Confederate Strategy from Shiloh to Vicksburg*. Baton Rouge: Louisiana State University Press.

Jones, Vergel Carrington. (1961) *The Civil War at Sea*. 3 vols. New York: Holt*Rinehart*Winston.

Josephy, Alvin M. (1991) *The Civil War in the West*. New York: Alfred Knopf.

Lanz, Herman R. (1972) *Cairo: A Community in Search of Itself*. Carbondale: Illinois University Press.

Lincoln, Abraham. (1974) *Speeches and Writings*, 2 vols. New York: Library of America.

Lockie, Robert. (1990) *None Died in Vain, The Saga of the Civil War*. New York: Harper Collins.

Long, E.B. & Barbara Long. (1971) *The Civil War Day by Day, an Almanac*. New York: Doubleday & Company, Inc.

Lord, Francis & Arthur Wise. (1970) *Uniforms of the Civil War*. New York: Thomas Yoseloff.

Marshall-Cornwall, James. (1970) *Grant as Military Commander*. New York: Van Norstrand Reinhold Company.

Mitchell, Joseph B. (1955) *Decisive Battles of the Civil War*. Connecticut: Fawcett Publications, Inc.

Martin, Christopher. (1970) *Damn the Torpedoes: The Story of America's First Admiral:, David Glasgow Farragut*. New York: Abelard Schuman.

Musicant, Ivan. (1995) *Divided Waters: The Naval History of the Civil War*. New York: HarperCollins Publishers.

Nash, Howard P., Jr. (1972) *A Naval History of the Civil War*. New York: A.S. Barnes and Company.

Nevin, David. (1983) *The Civil War: the Road to Shiloh*. New York: Time-Life Books.

Nevins, Allan. (1959) *The War for the Union: The Improvised War 1861–1862*. New York: Charles Scribner's Sons.

Nicolay, John G. (1992) *The Outbreak of Rebellion*. Reprint, New York: Charles Scribner's Sons.

Nivin, John. (1973) *Gideon Welles, Lincoln's Secretary of War*. New York: Oxford University Press.

Noel, John, Jr. (1988) *Naval Terms Dictionary*. 5th ed. Annapolis: Naval Institute Press.

Park, Joseph Howard. (1962) *General Leonidas Polk, C.S.A., the Fighting Bishop*. Baton Rouge: Louisiana State University Press.

Perry, Milton F. (1961) *Infernal Machines: The Story of Confederate Submarines and Mine Warfare*. Baton Rouge: Louisiana State University Press.

Porter, Horace. (1897) *Campaigning With Grant*. New York: The Century Co.

Pratt, Fletcher. (1956) *A Short History of the Civil War*. New York: Pocket Books, Inc.

Robertson, James, Jr. (1963) *The Civil War*. Washington: U.S. Government Printing Office.

Sanburg, Carl. (1954) *Abraham Lincoln: The War Years 1861–1864*. New York: Dell Publishing Co.

Sea Power, A Naval History. (1960) E.B. Potter & Chester A. Nimitz, ed. New Jersey: Prentice-Hall, Inc.

Sherman, W.T. (1990) *Memoirs*, 2 vols. Reprint. New York: The Library of America.

Sifakis, Stewart. (1988) *Who Was Who in The Civil War*. New York: Facts on File, Inc.

Silverstone, Paul H. (1989) *Warships of the Civil War Navies*. Annapolis: Naval Institute Press.

Smith, Frank Ellis. (1954) *The Yazoo River*. New York: Rinehart & Company, Inc.

Stern, Van Dorn, Phillip. *Soldier Life in the Union and Confederate Armies*. Connecticut: Fawcett Publications, Inc.

Still, William N. (1971) *Iron Afloat: The Story of the Confederate Ironclads*. Tennessee: Vanderbuilt University Press.

Swanberg, W.A. (1957) *First Blood, The Story of the Fort Sumter*. New York: Charles Scribner's Sons.

Trevor, Albert A. (1936) *History of Ancient Civilization*. 2 vols. New York: Harcort, Brace and Company.

War on the Mississippi. (1985) Jerry Corn, ed. Alexandria, Va: Time-Life Books.

Ward, Geoffrey C. (1990) *The Civil War: An Illustrated History*. New York: Alfred A. Knopf.

Webster's American Military Biographies. (1978) Massachusetts: G. & C. Merriam Co.

West, Richard S., Jr. *Mr. Lincoln's Navy*. New York: Longmans, Green & Company.

Wheeler, Richard. (1978) *The Siege of Vicksburg*. New York: Harper Perennial.

Woodworth, Stephen. (1990) *Jefferson Davis and His Generals*. Lawrence: University of Kansas Press.

Index